My Unforgettable Season
1970

My Unforgettable Season

1970

Red Holzman
and Leonard Lewin

TOR ®

A TOM DOHERTY ASSOCIATES BOOK
NEW YORK

MY UNFORGETTABLE SEASON—1970

Copyright © 1993 by William Holzman

This book is printed on acid-free paper.

A Tor Book
Published by Tom Doherty Associates, Inc.
175 Fifth Avenue
New York, N.Y. 10010

Tor® is a registered trademark of Tom Doherty Associates, Inc.

Library of Congress Cataloging-in-Publication Data

Holzman, Red.
    My unforgettable season—1970 / Red Holzman with Leonard Lewin.
        p.   cm.
    "A Tom Doherty Associates book."
    ISBN 0-312-85453-6
    1. New York Knickerbockers (Basketball team)—History.
    2. Holzman, Red.   I. Lewin, Leonard.   II. Title.
GV885.52.N4H9   1993
796.323′64′097471—dc20   92-44107
                                                              CIP

First edition: March 1993

Printed in the United States of America

0 9 8 7 6 5 4 3 2 1

*To one of the greatest groups of players
and people ever put together
—the 1969–70 NBA Championship Knicks*

Acknowledgments

Whenever you author a book, there are so many people to thank. A lot goes into it, especially since the subject matter covers so many years of my life. It's been a long, long road for me in basketball, and places and faces start to fade as you get older. But there are some special people who had an influence on *My Unforgettable Season* in one way or another, so bear with me while I go through the lineup.

First but foremost were the members of the 1969–70 championship team to whom I would like to say—quoting my good friend Yogi Berra on a night he was honored—''Thanks for making this night necessary.'' In other words, without Captain Willis Reed, Dave DeBusschere, now-Senator Bill Bradley, Walt Frazier, Dick Barnett, Cazzie Russell, Dave Stallworth, Mike Riordan, Nate Bowman, Bill Hosket, Donnie May and John Warren, this book wouldn't have been necessary.

They were the leading characters of the Knicks' first championship and one of the most exciting seasons in NBA history. It couldn't have been done without Eddie Donovan, our General Manager, who left in mid-season to handle expansion—Buffalo's entry into the league; Danny Whelan, our beloved trainer who was the mother hen of the team; and Frankie Blauschild, whose sense of

7

humor and ability to handle the fullcourt press made things a lot smoother for me. Not to forget Gwen Bloomfield, the secretary behind our success, Jimmy Wergeles and the whole management crew at the time.

What would we have accomplished without TV voice Bob Wolf, whose rendition of our record nineteenth-straight victory against the Royals in Cleveland has become legendary, or Marv Albert, who was young then as he "yessed" Knick fans into a delirium and is still doing it as good, old Marv Albert.

How can I overlook Andrew (Fuzzy) Levane, who has been connected to me like my hip bone is to my leg bone. We have been an entry throughout a parallel pro basketball career for all these years and we are still with the Knicks. We have seen many changes together that now include Dave Checketts, Ernie Grunfeld, Pat Riley and John Cirillo, who not only are creating their own chapter on the Knicks, but have been so helpful to me and this book of memories. And what can I say about George Kalinsky, the Garden photographer who has been recording me and the Knicks in pictures all these years?

I owe a lot to my CCNY coach Nat Holman, and my first pro basketball coach Les Harrison, both of whom are in the Hall of Fame. Besides them, Bernie Sarachek, who molded me as a teenage player. There's been a special personal NBA relationship through the years with Cotton Fitzsimmons. And then there was Feets Broudy, the Garden's legendary timekeeper who lived and died basketball.

Ira Berkow of the *New York Times* has been helpful as has Dick Klayman of the *New York Post*, among a group of media people too numerous to name. On a more personal note, there has been the loyalty and patience of my wife, Selma, my daughter, Gail, and her husband, Charley Papelian, my brother, Jules, and my sister-in-law, Roz Puretz. Also, Phoebe Lewin, who constantly discussed game strategy on the phone with my wife throughout the years, and her mother, Minnie Schuster, whose knitted muffler was my good luck charm in *My Unforgettable Season.*

I'd like to thank Manny Azenburg and Bob Wallach. Also, agents Arthur and Richie Pine, who really made this book possible by selling it to Tor Books. And last but not least, to all the wonderful Knick fans who have never forgotten what the 1969–70 team achieved. They came along for the ride and are still there.

Foreword

Building a championship team takes hard work, dedication and sacrifice; essentially, a commitment to excellence by each individual. The 1969–70 New York Knickerbockers, coached by a very special man in Red Holzman, had those ingredients for success.

They were a team made special, made unique, by playing the game at its highest level. They were unselfish, each member of the team playing his role as orchestrated by Red Holzman.

As a player who competed against them, you could truly see five men playing as one. Certainly, they had the talent; but they combined those skills with incredible basketball fundamentals and a savvy and intelligence that may not have been seen since then.

Red created an environment in which some of the game's greatest players could really flourish. Willis Reed. Bill Bradley. Walt Frazier. Dave DeBusschere. All Hall-of-Famers. Add to the mix Dick Barnett, Cazzie Russell, Dave Stallworth and Mike Riordan. They all had tremendous respect for Red Holzman. They trusted Red because he was very sincere and equally competent.

Great coaches have the ability to make a team succeed because of their knowledge of the game and leadership. Red was unparalleled in each of these areas. You cannot coach a player who does not want to be coached. Players will play for you and allow you to coach them if they can rely on you.

Part of the psyche of a true champion—which each of those Knicks were—is to never be satisfied, either as a player or a coach, until you achieve the ultimate goal. It is quite clear that those Knickerbockers pursued that highest level of excellence and would not be satisfied until they had passed into legend.

What follows now is an account of a great team that banded together under a great coach to become World Champions. The 1969–70 Knicks were a team that brought New York to its feet in applause, a team that will never be forgotten.

Pat Riley
Head Coach
New York Knickerbockers

My Unforgettable Season
1970

1

It wasn't too long ago. I had arranged for Bill Bradley, Dave DeBusschere and Danny Whelan, the former trainer of the Knicks, to meet me at Madison Square Garden.

The purpose was a good old bull session about the 1969–70 NBA championship season. Time does strange things to memories. We needed a refresher course on that long journey into the history books of the game. So I called a special session to review what had happened in that special season 22 years earlier.

I decided it would be smart to refresh myself on that unforgettable season. DeBusschere, Bradley and Whelan were only three important contributors to our slice of sports history. Others were the captain and leader, Willis Reed, Walt Frazier, Dick Barnett, Cazzie Russell, Dave Stallworth, Mike Riordan, Nate Bowman, Donnie May, Bill Hosket and John Warren.

Only Bowman is gone. His role as part of the Minutemen, which is what the bench players were called, has not been forgotten. Neither has what happened to that team in that season.

Believe it or not, people still come up and say: "Thank you." Imagine that. My immediate reaction is to answer: "Thank you for what?" After all, 1969–70 was only one basketball season in a lifetime of basketball seasons. I've had so many, sometimes it seems they should all look alike to me.

When you think about it, with all ego aside, what that Knick team did in that one season was something special. My basketball life span has been spread over fifty-five years now and the Holzman Odyssey has been filled with laughs, ups and downs, firings, fulfillment and memories.

So the calls went out to DeBusschere, Bradley and Whelan. The meeting, of course, depended mostly on Senator Bradley's busy schedule.

DeBusschere, Whelan and I still live in the New York area. Dave is in real estate; Whelan does some physical education work in an East Side school, and I spend most of my time trying to improve my tennis, as well as acting as consultant for the Knicks.

Bradley had a few more important priorities. One day he would be on C-SPAN participating in some congressional hearing and sometimes even chairing it. Another day he might be out in the Northwest for a speech in Washington or down in Florida pursuing the successful political career we had all predicted for him.

It was finally arranged and here we were—DeBusschere, Whelan and I—sitting and waiting for Bill at the Garden. Suddenly there was a message. Bradley had called and he would be late. It was a combination of routine New York traffic jam and his own frenetic schedule.

He walked in a few minutes later. He apologized. I couldn't resist smiling and thinking back nearly a quarter of a century. History was repeating itself right before my eyes. I flashed back to the time I replaced Dick McGuire as the coach of the Knicks. It was my very first day on the job. I had called a team meeting for 10 that Monday morning before our first practice.

I am no great speechmaker. I never was and never will be. In fact, ask DeBusschere if you ever get the chance. He will laugh and say he remembers that my pregame motivational talk always was: ''This is a big game''—except for those times when I really got excited and expanded it to: ''This is a really big game.'' I obviously borrowed that from Ed Sullivan.

I was in the dressing room bright and early that first day. Well, early, anyway. I had all my ad-libs ready. They had nothing to do with Dick McGuire and what he had or hadn't done. I was adopting the obvious strategy for any coach stepping into a losing situation.

It was this: If the previous coach was too soft, then be tough. If he was too tough, then be soft. That's for starters, of course. If McGuire had been tough, I would've begun with Teddy Roosevelt's theory: Speak softly but carry a big stick. Since McGuire was a nice guy who was soft on the players, I became an instant tough guy.

So it was that on December 28, 1967, my first day on the job, I watched some of the Knicks reporting late. They just wandered in like chattering college kids having fun. Among them was Bradley, the young man from Princeton and Oxford.

> *"If you guys make my life miserable, I'm going to make your life miserable."*
>
> —*Red Holzman*

My job was to turn the Knicks into a professional team in every respect. The material already was there but it needed direction and some serious work-and-game ethic. They were all young and talented players but undisciplined at their stage. I had to harness their power.

I picked the stragglers off one at a time. I was standing near the door as they strolled in. I was clocking them with my trusty $3 pocket watch which became a historical timepiece to the players. Whenever I pulled the watch, the fines game started. I still have that watch somewhere.

Bradley was one of the late arrivers. I told him he was fined. He looked at me with surprise. This had never happened to him before but he paid. So did Butch Komives, Dick Van Arsdale and Walt Bellamy. It cost Van Arsdale, Komives and Bellamy more because they arrived later.

I remember it as though it was yesterday and I don't have the best memory in the world. Most things that have happened, I have to look up. That incident I remember very well.

We were still in the old Garden on 49th and 50th streets at 8th Avenue. The new Garden hadn't as yet been finished at its present site over the Pennsylvania Railroad Station near 34th Street and 8th.

Bradley had strolled nice and easy across the court toward the dressing room. It was an Ivy League crawl. He felt comfortable because a Garden clock had indicated it was a minute before 10. No rush even if he was a few minutes past the deadline. That's what he thought.

Down the street from the Garden, Komives and Van Arsdale had left their hotel and decided to stop first for breakfast. Van Arsdale thought our team meeting was at 10 but Komives insisted it was 10:30. So they went to a coffee shop.

Meanwhile, Bellamy got out of bed in his hotel room a few blocks from the Garden. He took his time dressing and then strolled along 8th Avenue to the Garden. He walked across the court and opened the dressing-room door.

They all walked into fines. I had never had a system of fines before as a coach but I had to think fast. There was no way I was going to let my first day on the job get off like that. It was no time for a show of weakness.

Actually, it was a spur-of-the-moment thing that jolted the players. I had no intention of being a soft touch. I delivered my instant message. The players had provided the opportunity. I was able to establish a sense of team responsibility right away—a very important beginning. They knew me very well as the scout for the Knicks but not as the coach and boss.

The guilty ones all copped a plea. ''The clock outside said a minute to ten but the clock in the dressing room said two minutes after ten,'' was Bradley's alibi. ''Give Danny five dollars,'' I told him.

''I told Komives the meeting was at ten,'' moaned Van Arsdale. ''I went in for an English muffin and coffee and the damn breakfast cost me ten sixty-five.'' They were each hit $10. The extra 65 cents Van Arsdale spoke of was what an English muffin and coffee cost in those days. How times have changed.

It also cost Bellamy $10 for being 10 minutes late. My instant reaction turned out to be a stroke of genius. It was the foundation for the togetherness that built Bradley, Willis Reed and all the Knicks into a smooth machine. It also introduced a fining system that became a fun thing on the team. I had simply hit on an important way to handle the players.

I was thinking of all that when Bradley arrived late for our recent meeting. It was 25 years later and I was tempted to say: "Give Danny five dollars," but controlled myself.

How would it look? Bradley is now the distinguished U.S. senator from New Jersey and it would have been disrespectful of me. Besides, he might still be President someday, and why jeopardize our future plush jobs?—the ones we plan to get if and when Bradley makes it to the most powerful position in the country.

I remember how Dick Barnett always reminded Bill that all he wanted was to be Secretary of the Treasury. Barnett always wanted to be close to the money. As for me and Whelan, we constantly reminded Bill that we also wanted to be part of his handpicked cabinet in important roles.

I would take the Atlantic Ocean area and the boardwalk not far from my Cedarhurst home where I still reside. Whelan wanted the Pacific Ocean around San Francisco where he used to live. We'd each file on-the-beach reports at our discretion, at a reasonable salary to be negotiated—with all franking privileges and other perks, of course.

Bradley owes us that much. He can't forget how the players and I always treated him with respect. We called him Mr. President from the time he was a raw rookie. It was to Bradley's credit that he studiously ignored all of us without hurting our feelings.

I certainly couldn't ignore him when I decided to take a look back at what our 1969–70 team had accomplished. It was only one season in the 46-year history of the team—but what a season.

Yes, the Knicks won another championship three seasons later with fundamentally the same players. It's strange how people sometimes forget we won twice. What they seem to best remember is the fifth game of the 1969–70 championship when Reed got hurt. And the seventh game when he limped onto the floor and proceeded to inspire the team to overcome Wilt Chamberlain, Jerry West and Elgin Baylor for the title.

There was also the 18-game winning streak that not only was a record but is inscribed on the championship ring everyone wears—

that and so much more that went into the greatest and most exciting season the Knicks have ever known.

All New York was a part of that magic moment and still is after all these years. Though we went on to win another championship in 1972–73, no one makes a fuss about that one. It's almost as though it never happened, though it was fundamentally a repeat for the same players.

Actually, I believe that with a little luck, we might've won four straight championships during that stretch. I know a lot of the players feel the same way—that we really were a dynasty that would have had more than two titles if not for critical injuries to Reed and DeBusschere at the wrong time. Come to think of it—when do any significant injuries come at the right time?

Only the Minneapolis Lakers and Boston Celtics have produced major dynasties. George Mikan and the 1948 Lakers were the first dominant team when the National League merger created the NBA. They won five times in their six seasons.

I was with the Rochester team that interrupted the Lakers' streak after they had won twice in their first two seasons. It was then we beat the Knicks in seven games and kept them from winning their first title until I became the coach.

The Bill Russell era of the Boston Celtics is the granddaddy of all dynasties, with due respect to the New York Yankees. They won an unbelievable 11 titles in 13 years during the Russell regime. I'm planning to hang around until someone does better—or until David Stern, the enterprising NBA commissioner, puts a franchise on the moon.

The Knicks "dynasty" stands next in my opinion. We didn't win four straight when we had the chance but I have no doubt we were the dominant team those years. Reed, Bradley, DeBusschere and Walt Frazier all were voted into the Hall of Fame from the 1969–70 team alone. And Earl Monroe followed them as a Hall-of-Famer once we got him from the Baltimore Bullets and we won again in 1972–73.

It's hard for even me to believe the impact the Knicks had on people—that they still have, so many years later. You would think they'd ask Senator Bradley about the economy or when he is going to run for President.

"They come up and say thank you," he said. "They are still thanking the Knicks for something that happened so long ago."

I take my Knick basketball now as a spectator and consultant. I still marvel at the recognition that team receives. People see me and recall things as though they had just happened.

I guess it's because they like the type of basketball we played. It was New York–style, and most had grown up playing it in the schoolyards around the city. It was team ball that featured passing, defense and intelligence.

The 1972–73 championship team played the same with fundamentally the same players. We changed six parts but didn't miss a beat with Jerry Lucas, Earl Monroe, Dean Meminger, Harthorne Wingo, Henry Bibby and the return of Phil Jackson. They replaced Cazzie Russell, Mike Riordan, Dave Stallworth, Bill Hosket, Donnie May and John Warren.

That '72–73 team was also outstanding. It played the same thinking man's basketball but didn't have the privilege of winning the Knicks' first title. The additions fit beautifully and New York loved them, though not quite as fanatically as the '69–70 team.

They recite all the drama of that final 1969–70 series with the Los Angeles Lakers that brought the Knicks their first championship ever. How Reed was hurt in the fifth game. How we still came from far behind and won despite the awesome power of Wilt Chamberlain, Jerry West and Elgin Baylor.

Those three Lakers are all Hall-of-Famers now and probably the greatest trio of players one team has ever had in the same lineup. Yet, with DeBusschere, only 6'6", and Dave Stallworth at 6'7" playing Chamberlain at times, we won the game that kept us alive.

I sometimes wonder what would have happened to NBA history if we had lost. Where would the 1969–70 Knicks be if the Lakers had won that fifth game and gone home leading 3–2 with Reed not able to play the sixth game? Where would all the books be that have been written about that special season? Including this one, of course.

That's how close we came to not happening that season. So much would have been different. There probably wouldn't have been a seventh game—therefore, no sign of possibly the most dramatic moment in NBA history. That's when a crippled Reed dragged himself onto the court amid the frenzy of 19,000 Garden fans to become a legendary hero forever.

It was a season that didn't just happen. Getting to that final game with the Lakers brought a lot of people together from a lot of different directions. It's hard to explain all the strange bounces that seem to take place at the right time. It just happens, and it happened to us.

I was a fairly good student when I played basketball at City College in New York, but I never majored in chemistry. Yet that was an important ingredient in the making of those special Knicks. If they want to give me an A for Knicks chemistry, I'll take it.

It didn't develop overnight, though. In fact, the Knicks had failed to establish all the things it takes to win a championship since they had started in 1946. They had come close many times but never made it. I knew from experience. As I've said, I was there as a 30-year-old with the Rochester Royals when they beat the Knicks in the 1950–51 NBA final.

It is ironic how things turn out in life. They are simply unpredictable, nor can I explain why I, of all people, was designated to coach the Knicks to their first championship in the first place. All I know is I was there. It was a roundabout, long journey for me but a quicker one for the players.

I can explain how all the 1969–70 players got to the Knicks because I scouted all of them. That's another story that has no real rhyme or reason except for one common denominator in my pro basketball life. Andrew (Fuzzy) Levane is his name.

Levane has had the most influence on my destiny—that is, other than my wife, Selma, who has been at my side the longest and sometimes is suspected of being the real coaching brains in the family. I was a fairly good college basketball player in my time but Fuzzy was responsible for every pro basketball job I ever had.

Few people know this, but I almost became an original Knick. Those were the days when New York college basketball was huge.

Ned Irish, who was a sportswriter on the *World Telegram*, had introduced intersectional basketball to Madison Square Garden in 1934 and it zoomed right away.

Every game became a sellout. New York University, Long Island University, St. John's and CCNY were the key New York teams. All the players who appeared in the Garden became the source of supply for a new professional league. It was inaugurated in 1946 as the Basketball Association of America and the Knicks stocked up on local players.

It was smart business for two reasons: (1) New York–style basketball was tops in those days and (2) it was a natural showcase for the most publicized college players of the time. Those were hard-sell days for pro basketball. The college game had the fever. The pros were struggling to establish and it wasn't easy.

For example, the Knicks were the richest team in the league because they represented the wealth of Madison Square Garden. They had the only traveling media and the only traveling trainer because they were the only team that could afford one.

In fact, some teams didn't have any trainer, and the Knicks' trainer would also service the home team on the road. Those were the conditions when Neil Cohalan, the first Knick coach, took the team to Cleveland for the first playoffs.

That was at the end of the 1946–47 season when the Garden college basketball was at its peak. An open date in the schedule enabled New York writers to get away from their college assignments to cover the first and only playoff game of the series in Cleveland.

There was a load of them—too many to be handled by the Cleveland Rebels, as they were called before they eventually folded. There weren't enough credentials left for the New York press, so the Knicks had to actually buy some tickets.

It's important to know that's how the new pro basketball league conducted its financial business in its first season. Salaries were around $5,000 and below for 48 games. That's when I was approached by the Knicks to play for them. It was the first strange turn in the crazy trip that eventually landed me in New York many years later.

I already had a job at the time with the Rochester Royals. They were in the National League that had been formed before the BAA forerunner to the NBA. I had some classic sports teammates on that team. Otto Graham, the Hall of Fame quarterback who had played basketball at Northwestern. Del Rice, the St. Louis Cardinals catcher who had played basketball in high school. Chuck (The Rifleman) Connors, the first baseman who had played basketball at Seton Hall. And good old Fuzzy Levane of St. John's.

Levane had gotten me the job with the Royals when I got out of the service. Les Harrison was the owner and he had told Fuzzy he would like to get a Jewish ballplayer. So Fuzzy recommended me. It turned out to be funny at the start.

I sat on the bench and hardly played. Harrison, who also was the coach, needed a ballhandler and shooting guard badly. So Fuzzy stepped out, again. He convinced Harrison that, while he had signed me because I was Jewish, I could also play.

I appreciated the opportunity because I needed the money. It was only $400 a month but I was married. Besides, when I wasn't playing for the Royals, I was moonlighting with a team in Troy, New York, and a few other places.

I was getting around $75 a game with Troy. Thus, when Cohalan came to me and offered me a job for $8,000 to $9,000 with the Knicks, I turned it down. That was a lot of money at the time—more than most NBA teams were planning to pay their players because the Garden had more money to throw around.

It was tempting, but I was young and loyal in those days. I felt obligated to Harrison for what he'd already done for me, though the money wasn't that great. I couldn't just walk out on him.

Besides, I've always been smart or lucky in business. I even still have some of the Eastman Kodak stock I obtained during my playing days in Rochester. Also, when it came time to re-sign with Harrison, he boosted me to $12,000. I felt wealthy.

Harrison was generous with me, once he discovered I could play. He persuaded me to give up my outside ball by raising my pay enough to cover what I'd been making with other teams. I eventually became the highest-paid player in the league, though the others didn't know it.

Things like that were secretive in those days. There were no agents or Players Association to share such information as today. Besides, when you consider the millions they throw around these days, who'd be interested in inside information on the salaries they doled out in the pioneer days?

My journey to the Knicks resumed when I was dropped by Rochester in 1953 and immediately got a call from Levane. Who else? He was then coaching the Milwaukee Hawks. That produced another of those unpredictable turns in my life.

I probably was destined to become part of the glory days of the Knicks but never realized it. How else do you explain Levane's firing 22–35 games into his second coaching season and my being hired as his replacement and what happened later?

I remember how badly I felt about Fuzzy. He's always been a happy-go-lucky guy and he told me not to worry about my getting his job. It still was very difficult because I owed him so much. He was gone and I was there. Not for long, relatively speaking, but it was nice while it lasted.

I had the pleasure and unique experience of being Bob Pettit's first coach. I like to think I did something to help him make the Hall of Fame. Our relationship didn't last to long.

I had been able to handle all the moves that take place in the insecure world of basketball. But when I was fired by Ben Kerner in 1957 it was the end of the world.

I was out of basketball for the first time in 35 years. I had my wife, Selma, and daughter, Gail, to support. I was on a dead-end street. That's when I made up my mind never to coach again.

Too insecure. Besides, who'd ever hire me? So I took a job selling insurance. It wasn't much and I really didn't like it. I was part of an unofficial team of Levane and Ralph Branca, the Brooklyn Dodger pitcher, that worked with Cy Block.

Block was another Brooklyn guy who made it to the 1945 World

Series with the Chicago Cubs as a third baseman. He made it big in the insurance business and we'd open doors for him.

I did some additional work for Arthur Brown. He owned Freight Forwarding and also the New Jersey Americans, the original ABA franchise that became the Nets. He was also into harness racing, where he had some outstanding horses.

I would go out and solicit freight business for him. I did a decent job for him, though I didn't like what I was doing. Then I got the offer from the Knicks to scout and I wanted to do both. Brown wanted me to stay but didn't want to pay any money.

I also worked for Gimbel's at the time, selling food plans. They'd sell you a refrigerator and deliver food to you. I wasn't a good salesman but I made a few dollars. If I had to ask someone to buy something, I couldn't do it. I was terrible at insurance. I was terrible at all that stuff.

I enjoyed and knew basketball best. I really missed basketball. Guess what? I got another call from Levane. This time he had just been named coach of the Knicks for 1958. He had been scouting but moved up when Vince Boryla decided to quit coaching and concentrate on his other job as general manager.

I didn't know Boryla that well but Fuzzy talked to him about me. I got the job for less money than I had been making. It didn't come as easy as it sounds despite the Fuzzy connection. For some reason, I wasn't one of Ned Irish's favorite people, and he was the boss of the Knicks at the time.

I don't know why he felt that way. I can only assume it might have been related to my rejecting the original Knicks' offer—or, possibly, the fact that I was an important factor the season the Royals beat his team out of the 1950–51 NBA title in seven games.

This much I know because I was told. Irish apparently wanted someone else for the scouting job. Boryla made the ultimate decision and he picked me. I couldn't have been more grateful. He didn't realize how badly I wanted and needed that job.

My salary was only $2,500 because it was a part-time job. But I was back doing what I liked and getting paid for it. Also, I was in the Knicks' organization, which put me in position to be there when they needed a coach nine years later.

I guess that's when I came up with another of my favorite expressions: Never worry about things you can't control. There are certain things in your life that you can't control but that control you. That's how I was there to become the coach of the 1969–70 championship Knicks.

Otherwise, I might still be selling insurance. Needless to say, Boryla and I became good friends. I used to travel with him on scouting assignments. We both loved handball and we'd find a place to play wherever we went. There was always a health club where we'd play and he'd win most of the time.

Those were the days when the Knicks were trying to recapture their lost glory. They made the playoffs nine times during their early years and had only two coaches: Neil Cohalan the first season and Joe Lapchick the next nine.

They made the finals twice under Lapchick; losing to Rochester in seven games and then to the Minneapolis Lakers 4–3 in 1952. I wasn't there but I remember the Lakers series for one thing. It involved Al McGuire, a part-time player with the Knicks then who made the Hall of Fame on his coaching not long ago.

It was one of the weirdest things that ever happened in the playoffs—certainly in a championship series. It happened in the first game, which was played in the Twin City of St. Paul because of floods in Minneapolis.

That was strange in itself and makes a good trivia question. Then during the heat of a game the Mikan Lakers won 83–79 in overtime, Al McGuire drove the lane for a shot.

Yes, as Marv Albert, the former Knicks ballboy, would say today. The running shot went in and McGuire was fouled—a three-point situation until the referees awarded Allie two shots.

How could McGuire get two foul shots if the shot went in? The problem was neither of the two refs saw it go in. They both were watching the foul.

McGuire went crazy. Lapchick went crazy. He also appealed to Pat Kennedy, who was then the chief of NBA officials, as well as commissioner Maurice Podoloff. They both refused to overrule the refs, though they had seen what had happened.

To this day, those Knicks believe they might have won their first title if not for the missing basket. McGuire made both foul shots but lost a point that meant so much when the teams wound up tied at the end of regulation.

The Knicks figured they would have won the series opener if not for the error by the referees. They would have won their first title 4–2 when they took the sixth game 76–68.

Unfortunately, the record book says the Lakers won a seventh game 82–65 at home. So the Knicks had to wait another 18 years before the 1969–70 team managed to give Madison Square Garden its first NBA championship.

That explains why New York exploded when it finally happened. So much blood, sweat and tears went into it from so many people who made it close through the years.

People like Al McGuire were left with only memories of what might have been. In his case, he can tell his grandchildren of the missing basket. Or how Bob Cousy kept him in the league for three years.

Allie had always ridden the shirttail of his brother Dick—at St. John's and with the Knicks. Dick was the older and quiet one—a brilliant passer in college and the pros. Allie was the extrovert with an aggressive game that earned him the nickname Allie Cat at St. John's.

Lapchick used him to annoy Cousy when the Knicks played the Celtics. One Sunday afternoon in Boston, the Knicks had lost as usual and were cooling off when local writer Clif Keane walked in.

Keane was a notorious Cousy fan in an area that was very late in recognizing the Cooz's unusual talent. Al spotted Keane and immediately hopped onto the trainer's table. He proceeded to mock the way his brother Dick played Cousy all the time.

"You don't know how to play Cousy," Al shouted. "I know how to play him. I own Bob Cousy." It was hysterically funny because everyone in the dressing room knew it was a put-on.

Al played Cousy only one way. He'd come in, distract Cooz by roughing him up and foul out in about five minutes. The Boston writer took it seriously, though. He saved the story for the Knicks' return to the Boston Garden. The Celtics won. Al fouled out quickly but he prolonged his career beyond his ability with ''I own Bob Cousy.''

The Knicks didn't miss a playoff until 1955–56, when they lost to Syracuse in a regular season tiebreaker. They got back in two seasons later and were knocked out again by the Nats, who eventually switched their franchise and became the Philadelphia Warriors.

That was the start of the worst playoffs span in team history. The Knicks went eight years without making it. I was out there searching for the players who were good enough to bring it all back.

It took me through many cities and coaches before the Knicks rediscovered the formula. Levane lasted as the coach until one night in Boston in the 1959–60 season.

Fuzzy had taken over a team that had gone 35–37 under Boryla and had missed the playoffs for the second time in a row. Levane did a great job with a 40–32 turnaround. He became one of those what-have-you-done-lately victims when the Knicks got off 8–19 the next season.

Fuzzy had no idea what was about to happen to him. He took the team to Providence for a Friday game with the Celtics and the Knicks lost. They met again the next night in the Boston Garden.

It really was a mismatch on paper and on the court. Bill Russell already had arrived in Boston. He had just led the Celtics to the 1957–58 championship, the first of many.

Everyone now knows how Russell revolutionized the game. He made defense a magic word. He was Star Wars in action. He was the shield that destroyed the ballistic missiles the NBA sharpshooters fired.

It is significant that the Celtics never won a championship until Russell showed up. Let's put it this way: Bill Sharman and Cousy never won a championship until Russell became a Celtic. They were the heartbeat of the team that was only a Russell away from winning it all.

Russell was the missing link. He put the Celtics over the top—just the way DeBusschere did for me with the Knicks. Of course, Russell had the greater impact on the game itself.

He wound up in Boston and not in St. Louis—or in New York, where they had been searching so long for a franchise center and a championship.

That could have happened if not for the inexplicable tricks of fate. Hindsight is always 20–20. You know: "If I knew then what I know now," I would have saved all the baseball cards and collectibles. I could have owned my own team by now.

There have been many stories as to how Russell got to the Celtics—also as to why Lester Harrison, my shrewd boss during my Rochester days and a good judge of talent, didn't use the first pick to draft him. I even heard that Harrison and Irish had discussed a deal for the first pick that year.

That Harrison-Irish scenario has been handed down for years. It suggests that Harrison discussed a deal with Irish that involved the Royals' first pick the year Russell was eligible.

Rochester had finished with the worst record. The St. Louis Hawks were to draft next, followed by the Minneapolis Lakers, Syracuse and New York. There were only eight teams at the time.

Rochester finished 31–41 and St. Louis 33–39. The Lakers picked third, though winding up tied with the Royals, and took Jim Paxson—yes, the father of John and Jim, Jr.

Irish had the ultimate say in those days. He was the decision maker. The Knicks had two seven-foot centers—Ray Felix and Walter Dukes, in that playing order.

Dukes was the most expendable and he was the one Harrison wanted. Les was having serious trouble in Rochester. The game was outgrowing the city where I had played. Basically, the arena was too small in a league that was beginning to expand to larger buildings.

In order to survive, Harrison went to Irish and offered a deal. Les needed a gate attraction. As the story went, Harrison informed Irish he would deal the rights to his first pick for Dukes, who was from Rochester but had played his college ball at Seton Hall. Les also needed money and is supposed to have also asked Irish to throw in $100,000.

That was before the franchise began its cross-country trip as the Cincinnati Royals, Kansas City Kings and finally Sacramento Kings. Teams were struggling to survive and $100,000 was a lot of money in those days. Not for the Garden, though.

Actually, when the St. Louis Bombers—a league original— folded after the 1950 season, Irish offered $100,000 for the franchise. He was only interested in Easy Ed Macauley, the skinny St. Louis University center.

Irish had fallen in love with Macauley when the Billikens beat Adolph Schayes and an outstanding NYU team for the National Invitation Tournament title in the Garden. New York fans also adopted Macauley despite what he had done to one of their favorite teams.

Macauley became instant excitement. Irish saw him as a means to an end. The infant pro basketball league was still crawling in New York. The colleges were the hot item, selling out every night.

Irish gave them the most dates in the 18,000-seat Garden. Consequently, the Knicks played most of their home games in the 2,000-to-3,000-seat Armory on Lexington Avenue at 26th Street. In fact, none of their home games in the 1952 championship series with Minneapolis were at the Garden.

They played only seven games at the mecca of basketball in their first season. Irish gave them more dates after the 1951 scandal damaged the college game but it didn't help right away. From 1961 to 1965, the Knicks were playing over 30 games in the Garden yet averaged only 8,000 to 9,000.

The Knicks were a hard sell for a long time. That is why Irish was ready to buy all the Bombers just to put Macauley in a New York uniform. Macauley was such a hot item that a youngster named Bill Bradley learned some of his basketball at an Easy Ed camp in the St. Louis area.

Irish failed. Ironically, there was a dispersal draft that sent Macauley to the Celtics. That's where he was when he became the key player in the deal for Russell.

That's the crazy way basketball can bounce and generally does. It certainly did for me in the years I was involved, a matter of 57 years—so far.

Getting back to Irish and Harrison, the story had Harrison ready to make Russell or anyone Irish desired the first pick of the 1956 draft. Irish actually wasn't interested in Russell. That despite Russell's having come to the Garden with K. C. Jones to win it big for San Francisco University.

The Knicks wound up with Ron Shavlik, a 6'8" center from North Carolina State. He played seven minutes in seven games in his rookie season. He finished his career with one minute a game.

Harrison decided to make Sihugo Green the number one NBA pick. That put Ben Kerner of the Hawks in position to trade the draft rights to Russell to solve his more immediate problems. The Hawks weren't drawing, either. They needed some shock treatment at the gate after moving from Milwaukee to a better sports market—one that had baseball and pro football teams.

Kerner was a hard worker. He did everything but sell tickets—in fact, he did that at times. He was the sole owner and, therefore, responsible for the money and the team's right to survive. He'd be in the office until 10 or 11 at night.

He also needed players who could draw and win. He couldn't afford to wait and see what might happen with a draft choice—especially someone like Russell, who didn't have overwhelming credentials at the time, or someone like Wilt Chamberlain when he first came into the league.

The St. Louis Hawks had serious problems at center, which was the lifeline of any pro team then. They had my old Rochester teammate Jack Coleman and seven-foot Chuck Share. Neither was a household word in St. Louis. On the other hand, Macauley was from St. Louis and was considered one of the top centers in the pros.

Kerner was anxious to surround Bob Pettit with better players. So one day, Kerner said: "Let's go. We're going to Boston. We're going to make a deal with Walter Brown."

Brown was another original owner who was a hockey man and lived long enough to see the egg turn into a golden goose. Kerner went to Brown's office and the deal was made. Kerner got the players he wanted.

Macauley was the central figure for the Hawks. Kerner also received two players from a powerful Kentucky University team. Those were the Adolph Rupp days and he always had one of the top teams in the country. Also, the top players.

Cliff Hagan and Lou Tsiropoulos were the other players in the deal. To appreciate how highly-rated Kentucky U. players were, Red Auerbach drafted three of them off the same team in 1953.

Frank Ramsey, who was to be the NBA's first celebrated Sixth Man, was the Celtics' top pick. Hagan was Number Three and Tsiropoulos Number Seven. The Hawks proceeded to win five consecutive Western Conference titles from 1957 to '61.

Besides, Kerner saw the 1958–59 team of Pettit, Macauley and Hagan beat the Celtics for the Hawks' only NBA title. It's true that Russell was hurt in the series but St. Louis won. So Kerner's addition of Macauley and Hagan was right for him.

Macauley and Hagan also played themselves into the Hall of Fame. Besides, what other players do you know came close to playing Tarzan in the TV series? Hagan did.

Cliff was a bullish six-five who played the pivot in those days. That was his strength. It was that strength and his Tarzan build that attracted producer Sy Weintraub, who had just obtained the TV rights to the renowed movie series.

Hagan could have had the deal if he hadn't decided to hang on a little longer in basketball. I guess he wasn't ready to swing through the trees and start learning how to say: "Me Tarzan, you Jane."

It looked like a great deal for the Hawks then. They were acquiring three proven players in the pros for the draft rights to a rookie center hardly anyone really knew or realized how good he was to become. As they say in French: *C'est la guerre.*

That's the way the world turns. Where it stops, nobody knows *until* it stops. My world was full of turns and stops. No one escapes in pro basketball. Time and everything eventually catches up with you.

Fuzzy discovered that once more the night after the defeat in Providence by Russell and the Celtics. He didn't see anything significant when Irish suddenly showed up the next night at the Hotel Kenmore in Boston for the second Celtics game.

In fact, after the Knicks lost, again, Irish indicated he would meet Fuzzy and the media later. They were going to the Polynesian Room in the Somerset Hotel a block or so away from the Kenmore.

There was a midnight curfew on liquor because of Boston's strict Sunday law. So they ordered a few shots of Irish's favorite vodka and placed them at the end of the table where he would be sitting.

Irish never showed. He was back at the hotel hiring Carl Braun to become player-coach immediately. Fuzzy was gone and I remained as scout to see other coaches come and go.

Eddie Donovan was next. He came in from a successful coaching career at St. Bonaventure, where he featured the press. But his most significant contribution to the Knicks and their first championship came when he became general manager.

Meanwhile, it was Harry Gallatin's turn next. Harry the Horse, as he was called, was part of the Knicks' era when they were making the playoffs all the time. He was a workhorse under the boards and his rebounding eventually got him into the Hall of Fame.

Those were the days when the Knicks' most heated rivalry was with Syracuse. The Nationals or Nats played in a relatively small gym. There were guy wires attached to each backboard to keep them in place.

One night, however, a smart kid working for the Nats found a way to help his favorite team beat the Knicks. At a crucial part of the playoff, the basket suddenly started shaking while the Knicks were shooting fouls.

Lapchick was coaching and he called time. He complained. The referees pointed to the exhaust blowers in the ceiling. They said that was what was making the basket shake. "Why the hell isn't it shaking at the other end when they shoot fouls?" asked Lapchick.

The ballboy was responsible. He had placed his foot on the upright and simply pushed when a foul shot was taken. Lapchick could only convince the officials to remove the kid but could not get a substitute throw. The basket stopped shaking, though.

Another Knick game in Syracuse produced a really weird incident. Gallatin drove to the basket and went sliding headfirst toward a floor mat at the baseline. Pete Rose never did it better.

Gallatin's head disappeared. It was frightening at first. There was this headless body stretched out on the floor. It looked like his head had been crushed until they removed the mat.

Harry survived that to eventually come back to the Knicks as coach. It coincided with Donovan's moving up to general manager and probably the most important milestone in the history of the Knicks—one that eventually led to winning the first championship.

It was then that the power of decision changed hands. Irish decided to yield the control he had maintained since the first year of the Knicks. That gave Donovan more authority. It also increased my responsibilities as scout as well as my input.

Irish retained the right to know. He still had the final decision but he let us handle the 1964 draft with no interference. Accident or not, it turned out to be an outstanding draft that laid the foundation for the Knicks' greatest years.

Gallatin inherited it. We got Willis Reed, Bad News Barnes, Butch Komives and Emmette Bryant out of it. We were on our way but we didn't know it at the time. It was the start of meaningful draft picks that led to the 1969–70 championship.

I will go into that later. Gallatin took over in midstream and finished the 1964–65 season 19–23. I knew he wasn't long for the world when I dropped into his first training camp the next season.

It was in Fairfield, Connecticut. We used the college gym and stayed at a motel with the greatest food. I don't consider myself a gourmet but I like food. This motel served an outstanding buffet, all the food you could eat for one price.

That's pretty dangerous when you have a load of big athletes to feed. Generally, most players in those days were junk-food eaters. But when they saw the buffet display, I think they ate that place into bankruptcy.

Besides, the team was paying for the food in training camp. When the season's on today, the players get $54 per diem on the road and most of them exist on it. When I started it was $5 a day and they expected us to live on that.

Anyway, it was Gallatin's first training camp and he preferred to be alone. There were no three, four or five assistants as there are today. In fact, when I became head coach of the Knicks, I had no assistants until I hired Dick Barnett when he retired as a player.

One coach was the routine in the NBA until the Lakers decided to give Jerry West the job when he quit playing. They immediately gave him two assistants while he was learning on the job. Now they even have guys who handle the films, an offensive coach, a defensive coach, a scouting coach, a conditioning coach.

I was all of that rolled into one when I coached. So was Gallatin when he opened training and introduced his new ideas to the team. One of those ideas was the strangest conditioning program I've ever seen—then or now.

I had dropped in as a spectator only. I was curious to see Gallatin operate. Besides, we had just gone through this great draft and Gallatin had Reed, Barnes and the others in his camp for the first time.

Irish had the same curiosity. He also drove up from New York and almost dropped at what he saw. Reed remembers it to this day despite all the far more significant things he experienced in his Knick years.

"Harry had us running up and down the stairs in the gym," recalled Willis. "There was nothing strange about that. But when I ran up the stairs I had Bad News on my back. And when he ran down, he had me on his back."

I was in shock. Irish was in shock. Here we had just struck gold with players we thought would bring the Knicks to life. And there was Barnes, who had been our top draft pick, carrying the 240-pound Reed on his back. Worse than that, Willis was hauling the 235-pound Barnes up the stairs.

Weird to say the least. I suspected right then that Gallatin wouldn't be around too long unless he got off too well to be removed.

When the Knicks got off 6–15 at the start of 1965–66, Gallatin's

Knicks coaching saga ended. That's when Red Holzman's coaching saga moved one step closer to reality.

I didn't know it at the time and I didn't care, anyway. I had no intention of coaching again. I was perfectly satisfied with scouting. I had gotten it down to a system that seemed to be working.

Now that I have the luxury of looking back, I see that it began working very well in 1964. I've already said that but it's worth a deeper look at what occurred. It was the Knicks' first major move toward the making of the championship team.

We were stagnant at the time. There was anguish in the Garden because we had been watching the world go by. Our organizational meetings placed the emphasis where everyone in sports must place it—on talent.

No one has yet found a way to win without it. The Knicks situation was more serious because the Garden had all the resources and everyone expected New York to win. What complicated it even more was that Irish was, in effect, the Father of Big-Time Basketball and he was driven by that success.

He took the college game out of the small arenas. He created the National Invitation Tournament, which elevated it to another level. The pioneer owners of the BAA couldn't have had a league without him and the Garden.

I don't know if the BAA was his concept but it was organized by hockey people looking to add more dates to their arenas. That's how Maurice Podoloff became the first commissioner. He and his brother operated the New Haven Arena in Connecticut.

Irish's fingerprints were all over basketball. He also had originated the National Invitation Tournament, which was such an instant success. Now, of course, the NCAA has sped away from the NIT. And the NCAA not only has passed the NIT, but has tried its best to bury it.

It's important to know all of this in order to understand the special pressure for winning with the Knicks. No matter how much money the Garden spent, no matter how many good players it acquired, they just couldn't win a championship.

Philadelphia won the first one, the original Baltimore Bullets won before they folded, the Minneapolis Lakers won, the St. Louis

Hawks won, the Rochester Royals won and Boston came along to win almost every time during the Bill Russell era.

Never a championship ring for the Knicks. Never even a brass ring for the Garden. Once in a while the merry-go-round spun away a Knick to another team for a ring. Carl Braun, Willie Naulls and Emmette Bryant all earned one when they went to the Celtics.

Otherwise, the years piled up. So did the frustration in the Garden, where the search for the Holy Grail went on for 24 years. Coaches came and went. So did players, scouts, general managers and even top management.

I survived, I guess, because I was inconspicuous. A scout can go on the road and hide—until someone suddenly decides to take a look at him. Since no one pointed the finger of blame at me, I have to assume I was doing a good job.

I was still there when the philosophy changed and Donovan was handed the full authority to draft. Management stepped back and relied on the team of Donovan and Holzman.

It had its immediate rewards in the 1964 draft and from then until we finally won a title. It was a nine-team league then and we had just finished last with 21–59. That should shed some light on why upper management decided to step aside and let someone assume the draft authority and blame.

There were other changes going on. The Nats were abandoning Syracuse and moving to Philadelphia to become the 76ers. They were filling the void that existed when Eddie Gottlieb, the original owner-coach, sold the Philadelphia Warriors to Frank Mieuli in San Francisco.

The Syracuse-to-Philadelphia switch had some historical ramifications. That's when Wilt Chamberlain returned to the city that had drafted him. He was traded by the Warriors.

It's normal to wonder how a man of Chamberlain's ability could be expendable. Well, at the 1963 draft, the one in which the Knicks made Heyman the first pick, San Francisco chose next and took Nate Thurmond.

Gottlieb was managing director and was in charge of the draft. People thought he was crazy when he took the 6'11" Thurmond. He had the 7'1" Chamberlain, who was playing 48 minutes every game, so why waste a high pick on a big man?

"You never pass on a big man who can play," he said. "Besides, if you have two, you can always trade one." Gottlieb was a shrewd individual who had gotten his education promoting Negro League and other baseball games.

He had a computer mind that the NBA used to make up all the team schedules after he left management. Now they do it by computer. Anyway, Gottlieb was right as usual.

The one to go was not Thurmond but Chamberlain. By then, Thurmond had established himself as the second-best defensive center in the league. No one played Russell better.

The Warriors had to clear some playing time for Thurmond and there was only one way. Chamberlain had to go. He was shocked and so was everyone in the league. It was like the Yankees trading Babe Ruth.

Chamberlain's first reaction was surprise, of course. Then he looked around the league for a place where he'd like to play. It was a hurried look. Not much time elapsed between the time the Warriors put him on the market and a deal was made.

He did all he could to get the Knicks interested. I don't know what really went on. It was not my job to know. Wilt did solicit help from some New York newspapermen.

The deal was announced at the All-Star game in Stan Musial's St. Louis restaurant. Chamberlain won his first championship in Philadelphia and his second when he went to the Lakers.

We already had Reed and Barnes in place, so that might have influenced the Garden's decision on Chamberlain at the time. In fact, Reed made the All-Star game that season, so we knew we were on the right track.

Reed was another example of the luck it takes to win a championship. We never should have gotten him. He went on the second round. Everyone, including the Knicks, passed on him the first time around.

We, at least, can now better justify what we did. At the same time,

I can't imagine what would have happened if someone else had taken Reed. Not that he wasn't high on our draft list that year.

It should be well known by now that we couldn't separate Reed, Barnes and Lucious Jackson. They were the three best centers coming out by far. We spent so much time studying films of their games, I wished I was getting paid by the hour.

> *"No one who played in the NBA ever had a bigger heart than Willis Reed. He gave you all he had, all the time, and not only demanded your respect, but earned it."*
>
> *—Walt Frazier*

Actually, we borrowed the films because in those days they weren't passed around freely. You had to have dealt with the schools and used your personal contacts.

It was a triple dead heat. Too close to call, not just for us but for many NBA people—for example, Jim Karvellas. He's been broadcasting NBA games for 30 years, including the Knicks.

He was in Baltimore when we were considering Jackson, Barnes and Reed. "The Knicks were starting to rebuild their club," he recalled.

Karvellas rated Barnes way ahead of Reed and Jackson. His reasoning was simple. Bad News had the better credentials.

"Bad News was the big name because he had played on the team that had beaten Pat Riley's Kentucky team—Texas Western," Karvellas recollected. "He got recognition because, in those days, there was one game a week on TV. Luke came from Pan-American and no one ever heard of Pan-American. Reed came from Grambling and that school was known for football players."

Bad News had played on national TV. The world of basketball had seen his team upset Rupp's Runts, which was Pat Riley's college team. It was a big story.

All of that influenced us to lean toward Barnes. He was more athletic than Jackson and Reed. He had the bounce and the speed. Reed was mentally and competitively tough.

So was Jackson. Besides, he had been picked for the Olympic

team. That was a big plus in his column and I must admit we were impressed like all the others.

Donovan and I finally gave a slight edge to Barnes. If someone had picked him before our turn, we would've taken Jackson. We were as wrong as everyone on Reed but at least we wound up with him. You can't win them all but we won this one in a review of history.

First, the Sixers solved part of our dilemma by taking Jackson ahead of us. We were prepared for that, though it was a surprise in view of our rating Barnes the No. 1 center. Anyway, everything always looks so much clearer from a distance of more than a quarter of a century.

Take the 1984 draft, for example. Portland picked first and took Sam Bowie. That gave the Chicago Bulls the opportunity to take Michael Jordan. It looks silly now. But then the Trailblazers needed a seven-foot center with Bowie's credentials at Kentucky University. They needed Bowie more than the Jordan of that time.

Mistakes are inevitable in any draft, but you only know if they're mistakes later. Reed is the perfect example. After we decided to take Barnes, the rest of the teams had a shot at Reed but passed.

They had their own reasons. The Celtics, picking last on the first round as champions, took Mel Counts. I still remember Red Auerbach saying: "Just imagine. A seven-foot forward."

I can now say: Just imagine where the Knicks would have been without Reed. Or Barnes, for that matter. We picked first on the second round and got Willis. Later, we used Barnes to get Walt Bellamy and used him to get DeBusschere.

Smart, lucky or both. Take your pick. What was important is that we sat and barely breathed as one team after another didn't take Reed. We didn't know how Willis felt about all this until long after he joined the team.

He was upset, of course. He figured he was a first-rounder. He also probably assumed the Knicks were high on him because I had gone to Grambling many times to scout him. If I didn't know any better, I'd say that he was motivated by the way so many teams snubbed him.

Not that Reed had to be motivated. One of the things I saw in him in the first place was his competitive meanness. He's basically a peaceful man but there is a side of him that would kill to win.

I was told many times when I visited Grambling that the football coach wanted him to play football. They had Buck Buchanan and a lot of other monsters down there but the basketball coach wouldn't give Reed up.

Reed was pleasant and docile but it was disastrous when he got mad. I always marveled at how he managed to control himself in a game that was getting more physical all the time.

I was a small guy who came from the era of finesse. I always questioned why the league, and therefore the referees, seemed to legislate against finesse.

I guess it was our hockey mentality that came from the original group of hockey owners who also owned us. The game kept getting more physical and still is. That puzzles me.

Basketball players are the best athletes in the world. They are not only getting bigger every year, they are fast and as agile as ballet dancers. It seems to me the finesse of these exceptional athletes should be accentuated.

I realize that the public interest in the pros is at a peak. Commissioner David Stern has done a remarkable job of merchandising—so much so that the other sports would hire him faster than you can say $10 million, the bonus the commissioner was given when he signed his latest contract.

The league seems to prefer a contact sport which eliminates much of the finesse. It also is responsible for many more fights than the old days. Come to think of it, one of the best fights I ever saw involved Reed.

It happened one night in the Garden when I was still a scout. Knick fans most likely will remember it, though it was almost 30 years ago. Neither Muhammad Ali nor Rocky Marciano put on better shows.

It was Reed against almost the whole Los Angeles Lakers team. Rudy LaRusso, a big forward who had gone from a Brooklyn high school to Dartmouth, was the instigator.

For some reason, LaRusso took a swing at Reed after they had been in a rebound scramble. Rudy must have misunderstood Willis's placidity. What a mistake. Reed decked LaRusso, then started swinging at every Laker who made a move at him.

Reed cleared the floor quicker than Laker fans leave the Forum in their rush to beat the drive-home traffic. Darrall Imhoff, a 1960 Knicks first-round draft pick, was flattened. John Block wound up with a broken nose.

As Drew Pearson, a news columnist and radio commentator, used to say: ''It was a prediction of things to come''—a bit redundant but accurate where Reed was concerned. A few years later, as we all know, he made a big impact on the Lakers once more.

2

We were on our way. Reed, as things turned out, was the force that triggered the Knicks. My job wasn't done. I was beating the bushes for all the talent we could find. There were a lot of missing pieces.

Barnes helped us solve one of them. That's what we thought when we went after Walt Bellamy—again, I might say. The Knicks had been chasing him since he was drafted by the Chicago Packers.

Chicago re-entered the league in 1961 as part of expansion. The Chicago Stags were one of the original teams. They left their imprint on NBA history in a unique player disposal when they folded in 1950.

It was decided at the time to help New York, Boston and Philadelphia with a special dispersal lottery. The names of three players were put in a hat. They were Max Zaslofsky, Andy Phillip and a rookie out of Holy Cross named Bob Cousy.

Zaslofsky was the hot item because he had been the Zephyrs' top scorer every season. Phillip was next because he had been the second-best scorer and had led the team in assists. Then came Cousy, who had been a Tri-Cities top draft pick but never played there.

Chicago had traded for Cousy but he never played there, either, because the team folded. Irish and the Knicks got what they wanted when they picked first and landed Zaslofsky. Philadelphia was satisfied when it drew Phillip.

Boston got stuck with Cousy, whom it had ignored in the 1950 draft and really didn't want. As unusual as it seems now, he was actually with three different teams before he played a game—an NBA record?

So much for history and the guessing game that goes on in every draft. You scout but, except in some unusual cases, you really never know until they play the NBA game. It's a lot easier rolling the dice in Atlantic City or Las Vegas.

Bellamy was a perfect example. The Knicks needed a center desperately and Irish intended to use their first pick to get him. However, it was an expansion year and the owners decided to give the Zephyrs the first choice. They wanted to help the new franchise get off fast by giving it the best player in the draft.

Can you imagine a concession such as that now with investors spending over $50 million for a franchise? Chicago didn't even benefit from the league benevolence, which Irish interpreted as typically anti–New York.

"Beat New York" was as popular then as it is now. I'm not a psychologist so I won't go into the intricacies of that. The fact is, it was the Garden or Irish against the tide in those desperate days for the league.

Irish would enter most decision meetings with the other owners saying: "I guess it will be 9–1 again." To his credit, he made a joke of it and so did everyone else.

Bellamy lasted only two seasons in Chicago. The franchise moved to Baltimore as the Bullets with new ownership. It was the second crack for the Bullets, who had come into the league in its second season and lasted seven years.

They folded 13 games into the 1954–55 season. One of the players was Al McGuire. The boss was Clair Bee, who had tried to get me to play for him at Long Island University. It's a small world, after all. It was the last pro stop for Bee and McGuire before the Hall of Fame in Springfield, Massachusetts.

The Knicks finally got Bellamy for Barnes and two other Knicks who had been extreme Garden favorites: Johnny Green and Johnny Egan. Plus cash. No, not Johnny Cash.

Barnes was the key man for the Bullets. So was Paul Seymour, as

far as the Knicks were concerned. He was the Baltimore coach then
and I assume he had some input with the trade. Coaches generally
do. If they don't, they should.

I realize it can depend on just how strong a coach is in an
organization. Sometimes an owner will spring his own surprise on a
coach and general manager. It happened to me when I returned to
coaching the Knicks after I was re-hired in 1977.

It was in December of 1979 when Sonny Werblin informed me
we had traded Bob McAdoo to the Celtics. Sonny was running
Madison Square Garden at the time for Gulf + Western. He had
come over from the Meadowlands Sports Complex in New Jersey,
which he had helped build.

We had talked about improving the team and McAdoo's name
was included. He had the big name and still was productive. He was
only 28 but the Knicks were rebuilding and needed some new, fresh
parts.

McAdoo had the greatest trade value. That was the situation when
the Celtics came to the Garden one night. They had two owners at
the time: John Y. Brown and Harry Mangurian.

John Y. was best known as the Kentucky Fried Chicken man as
well as for having married former Miss America Phyllis George. He
later became governor of Kentucky. Mangurian was a well-known
horse owner and still is.

Werblin invited Brown to the Garden's VIP room after the game.
They had a few drinks. They talked. When their little social session
was over, Sonny had traded McAdoo to the Celtics for three
first-round picks.

Boston had loaded up on first-rounders that season and Brown
couldn't resist getting McAdoo's shooting talent. Werblin had made
a good deal in his first crack at it. We used the picks to get Bill
Cartwright, Sly Williams and Larry Demic.

They were three serviceable players but not exceptional. Cartwright was the best of them and the Knicks eventually used him to
acquire Charles Oakley's rebounding from the Bulls. I wasn't there
then but I've been associated with the Knicks long enough to know
how they operate.

Of course, when I was the Knicks' general manager and coach, I talked to myself. I always kept the brass informed, though. After all, they were paying me.

Seymour was in a similar position with the Bullets when the Knicks went after Bellamy. He had a say as the coach in the deal that brought Bells to New York and appeared to give the team a franchise center.

History has a way of repeating itself. I didn't invent that but it sure applies to what happened. Seymour also was the coach when we traded Bellamy to Detroit for Dave DeBusschere. That took care of a nagging problem in New York.

Barnes turned out to be the Knick the Bullets wanted because he was young in the league and still had a reputation. Bellamy was a true center who had some flaws. But he gave the Knicks some good years before we used him to get DeBusschere.

There were some obvious risks involved when we made the deal for Bellamy. It pushed Reed back to big forward. We considered that but Bellamy looked like our missing link at the time.

We had just had a second straight successful draft in 1965. We had two picks in the first round. So did San Francisco. We had finished last in our division and the Celtics were killing everyone.

So the league contrived a special type of draft to help the weak become more competitive. We got Bradley and Dave Stallworth that way. Plus Dick Van Arsdale as a 15th pick. San Francisco wound up taking Rick Barry, who became a Hall-of-Famer, and Fred Hetzel, a center out of Davidson.

Those were the days of the territorial draft. The league allowed a team to claim the rights to any college player within 75 miles of its franchise. It stemmed from the pioneer days when the league needed local big names to stimulate interest.

That's how the Knicks got Bradley after a fight. He had played at Princeton and Philadelphia insisted he also was inside its territory. That situation brought me an instant flashback about Wilt Chamberlain.

I thought back to the time Philadelphia got the draft rights to Chamberlain. He had grown very tall at Overbrook High in

Philadelphia but picked Kansas U. over hundreds of college offers. He was in such demand that the Celtics attempted to get him to play for a college in their territory so they could draft him.

Eddie Gottlieb had too much influence. He talked the owners into what turned out to be a one-shot high school territorial gimmick. They agreed to allow the Warriors to protect Wilt no matter where he went to college.

Chamberlain quit Kansas after his junior year. He went to the Harlem Globetrotters for a year. He couldn't be drafted right away because of the rule that his class had to be graduated for him to be eligible.

So he sat out a year with the Globetrotters. I remember the press conference that Abe Saperstein staged for Wilt's signing. It was at Toots Shor's, the popular sports hangout in New York.

Saperstein was a super-showman who had an instinct for publicity. He had Wilt pose with a huge bag of silver dollars. Abe knew that picture was sure to make the papers. It did.

Wilt toured with the Globetrotters before Gottlieb signed him. The Chamberlain era was on and he had an immediate impact when players read what he was going to get paid.

It was reported to be between $50,000 and $75,000, with an attendance clause that could make it $100,000. That created a small revolution. It was 1959–60 and Bill Russell already was two seasons into his historic presence.

I had just joined the Knicks as a scout and Wilt's money was unreal. I think Bob Cousy's $25,000 was tops. The players couldn't understand how Gottlieb could pay a raw rookie so much—even someone with Chamberlain's acknowledged gate appeal.

I understood the players and didn't understand them. I had been involved in the money game from the day I became a professional player. I had no agent, so I had to wriggle my way through all the negotiations.

It was clear to me that the players were missing the point when they complained about what Chamberlain was going to make. They should have been grateful that he raised the standards. He moved them into the upper brackets without their realizing it.

We see how salaries pyramid today. They no longer are based purely on performance, though that's the principal ingredient. Now when one player gets to a $2-to-3-million level, the others want to renegotiate. They want the equivalent or better.

We won the Battle of the Turnpike and got Bradley but not right away. He had a prior commitment to his education at Oxford. We had him but we didn't have him because he never really intended to play pro basketball. That's what he said.

The Knicks heard that but they drafted him anyway. He was worth the gamble because we felt he had all the other ingredients we needed. Bradley was the excitement generated from his classic NIT battle with Cazzie Russell plus the Ivy League image.

I had seen enough that night in the Garden when Princeton and Michigan met in the semifinals of the Holiday Festival during Christmas. It was strictly Bradley vs. Russell, and what a show they put on.

It was one of the greatest ever seen at the Garden. Princeton and Bradley had it won until he fouled out late in the game. Cazzie then took over and Michigan went on to win not only that game but also the championship.

Bradley was a near-unanimous MVP choice by the writers. He missed a clean sweep only by the vote of another Michigan man who had covered the tournament. Bradley was so sensational, he ran away with the award, though Princeton didn't make the final.

I had seen Bradley play in tournaments. I had watched him in his sophomore and junior years. You could see he was a ballplayer and a first-round pick. That wasn't a tough decision.

The Holiday Festival game with Cazzie made it easier. I never realized then that I would be coaching them both. Bradley was a great scorer, unselfish, a good passer, very smart about the game. He had all the good qualities. He was my type of basketball player and we couldn't pass on him.

When I think back, what a strange situation that was. There I was sitting in the Garden watching Bradley and Russell playing a sensational game with no idea how much they would contribute to the history of the Knicks. I didn't realize then that I was ever going to coach the Knicks, let alone have these two who were to play such important roles on the team—in my life, too.

A couple of years later, Bradley vs. Russell resumed—this time as teammates. They went at it head to head for the same starting position. I was in the middle of that one. I had to make a decision that had a distinct impact on our winning the championship.

I was still a scout when I watched that Holiday Festival game. Dick McGuire was coaching the Knicks then. Everyone in the organization was impressed with what Bradley had just done.

He had the basketball intelligence and skills that fit the team we were trying to build. He was a thinking man's player. He was a throwback to the game I played when everyone was smaller—when no one played the game over the rims.

> *"Bradley the rookie looked like he'd been a pro for a dozen years."*
>
> *—Red Holzman*

We were determined to make Bradley our first pick. We were guaranteed to get him that way because of the territorial rule. It was a bonus pick, in effect, so what did we have to lose?

That was the last year of the territorial rule because the league had outgrown it by then. We had to sweat out Bradley despite our determination to take him. We had to go on without him while hoping he would change his mind.

For two years, we really didn't know what he was thinking at Oxford. He studiously neglected to respond to any inquiry. He preferred to continue his education and prepare for a life without basketball.

He eventually explained it this way: "I was determined when I left the United States in 1965 that I was finished with basketball, or more appropriately, I was finished with the public acclaim that surrounded the game."

He loved the game but there were fringe aspects he couldn't tolerate. There was too deep an intrusion into his privacy. The media hype was distorting his expectations and his life to the extent that he was even thinking of discarding a career in politics.

We didn't know what was happening across the ocean. We were locked into moving the Knicks toward their first championship. We never even knew Bradley had undergone a sudden change of mind.

One day he simply went to the Oxford gym to shoot around for the first time in two years. All by himself. It all came back: the touch of the basketball. The fun and thrill of the game. The things every player misses when he leaves or is forced to leave.

Bradley wasn't forced to leave. He realized, as we all do, that he missed the basketball life after all. "Three weeks later I signed a contract with the New York Knicks," he later remembered.

By then, the Knicks were on the move. They were heading for the championship as we kept strengthening the team with every draft. Russell was next. We had seen enough of him during his NIT matchup with Bradley to confirm our intention.

Cazzie became our first draft pick in 1966. He didn't come easy, however. His agent was Art Morse, a Chicago attorney who had also promoted DePaul games in Chicago Stadium. He had just made a significant breakthrough by getting Jim Grabowski major money for a rookie from the Chicago Bears.

We were next for the Morse code. He wanted major money from the Knicks for Cazzie. That caused a problem. Reed was the best player and he was being paid $25,000 a year, as I recall. Morse wanted $100,000 a year for his client.

He managed to sell it to Irish. How, I don't know. It had to do with some tax-dollar idea Morse concocted. Cazzie also staged a workout with the White Sox to give him more leverage. It had absolutely nothing to do with the deal that opened the big-money door wide for future NBA rookies.

Bradley was the first beneficiary. He was offered more than Cazzie as an additional lure in the deal negotiated for Bradley by Larry Fleisher, the head of the Players Association.

The Knicks signed Bradley for $125,000 a year. That's how a Knick writer pinned "Dollar Bill" on him right away. It was an instant natural nickname he will carry to the Presidency someday—I think, anyway.

We were now coming very close to becoming a championship

team. We almost had the full complement of players who were to manage it. We were only two people away—DeBusschere and Holzman. Every essential player had come to the Knicks through the draft except Dick Barnett.

We had already drafted Walt Frazier in 1967, much to his surprise. "Clyde" had impressed me every time I scouted him, and I couldn't believe the other teams let us get him. He really impressed me when he led Southern Illinois to the NIT championship in his junior year. He distributed the ball in the first half and his team fell behind. He took over the scoring when it was urgent and his team won.

That was quality leadership. It was obvious to everyone from agents to other teams. Clyde looks back at it today and laughs. He is now a part of the Knicks' broadcasting team and still a celebrity in New York. That's what the wonder season of 1969–70 did for him and all the Knicks.

He loved to tell the story of how he came to the Knicks. "The funny part is, I heard from the Bullets, the Chicago Bulls and Seattle," he said. "The Knicks never talked to me after I was MVP in the NIT. This was all before the draft.

"The Bullets were talking about twelve thousand dollars, the Bulls around fifteen thousand and Seattle twenty thousand, I think. My agent asked what about a signing bonus and he was told the bonus was in the offer. I think Seattle offered me a bonus but it was so long ago."

The agent is a story by himself. Lloyd Zimmerman really wasn't an official agent. Frazier had redshirted one season so he had another year of eligibility if he chose. He was eligible for the draft because his class was being graduated that year.

There was no such thing as hardship, as there is today, where a player can leave school at any time and be drafted. Frazier hadn't as yet decided to pass on his senior year of eligibility. He would have been banned by the NCAA if he had signed with an agent.

What he needed was someone to handle all the inquiries from NBA teams. Jack Hartman, his college coach, recommended Zimmerman, a local attorney. They knew each other.

Hartman's intention was to ease the pressure of all approaches to his best player. He simply was doing Clyde a favor so that he had a clear head for school and basketball—especially for his final season.

That's exactly the way Frazier saw it at the time. He was curious but not really interested in the draft. "This is what happened," he recalled. "I knew the day of the draft. I went to class. After class, I ran over to the attorney's office. He had a law practice just outside of town."

Well, he didn't exactly run. He didn't drive, either, because he didn't have a car. "Maybe a friend drove me over," he said. "When I got there, the attorney was like me. He was flabber-gasted. He goes: 'The Knicks drafted you.' And I say: 'The Knicks? What do they want with me?' I'm shocked."

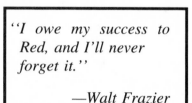

> "*I owe my success to Red, and I'll never forget it.*"
>
> —*Walt Frazier*

He couldn't understand why we took him when we had Cazzie Russell, Bill Bradley coming in, Howard Komives, Emmette Bryant and Freddie Crawford. We knew something he didn't know. He was our future.

Frazier was in Carbondale, Illinois. It was a long way from reality. So he let his imagination run. "I said: 'What do they want with me?' The last thing they needed was more backcourt," he remembered. "I felt bad because I believed they drafted me to trade me."

He would be stepping into an overcrowded backcourt and it didn't make sense to him. It was similar to when the Knicks made Rod Strickland their first pick and he said: "What do they need me for? They already have a point guard in Mark Jackson."

Frazier was disappointed when the Knicks picked him until Eddie Donovan called to open negotiations. "I still hadn't made up my mind I was leaving school," said Clyde. "My attorney was just listening to what the Knicks had to offer."

It became a different situation when he learned the Knicks couldn't trade him. There was a special rule against dealing first-round picks because the NBA was interested in creating some parity. That changed Frazier's mind completely.

He wanted to play in New York because of his NIT experience, "because of the feeling that I felt during the NIT," he recalled. "I never saw people react that way about basketball."

He had no idea what New York City basketball excitement really was like until 1969–70, of course. Meanwhile, this tale was developing of two men: Zimmerman and Hartman.

The coach was telling Frazier to stay in school and the attorney had discovered that his client might be serious about leaving. "Hartman is telling me . . . he's extolling the virtues of staying in school. I would get my degree," Frazier said. "The Olympics were coming up. There were certain things the school would be able to do. We had all our team coming back."

Hartman was envisioning another NIT championship or even the NCAA title. Frazier was envisioning playing in New York. Zimmerman was envisioning an interesting deal for his client. What he didn't envision was Hartman, the innocent bystander with the vested interest who was about to lose his best player.

Hartman pressed Clyde every day for a decision and Frazier told him: "I don't know yet." He was telling the truth. So was Zimmerman because the talks with Donovan were in progress. Nothing had been agreed upon.

"I don't recall exactly when I made my decision," said Frazier. "But I was surprised that, when I did, I was a bigger hero than when I was a college player with the people there. People didn't begrudge my decision."

He finally made up his mind to accept the Knicks' offer because he could no longer concentrate on studying. "I was obsessed by the opportunity to play for the Knicks," he explained. "It never was a dream for me. As a youngster I never even dreamt of being in the NBA. I knew I had professional talent only after the NIT."

It was that Garden exposure that convinced the NBA teams, such as the Knicks, that Frazier had the pro skills to make it. No one realized he would make it as big as he did. He was a hidden asset at

Southern Illinois, where they never had the advantages of major TV coverage.

There are players you just never know about despite all the sophisticated scouting. Scottie Pippen is a fine example. He played in almost total anonymity at the University of Central Arkansas. Only a scout would know that the college was in Conway, Arkansas.

Pippen averaged 23.6 points and 10 rebounds in his final year. Good-looking statistics, but numbers didn't reveal how he played the game—his intelligence, his skills and team attitude.

Chicago obviously saw something special in him. Jerry Krause of the Bulls, picking eighth, made a deal with the SuperSonics, picking fifth, that helped him build Chicago's first championship.

Krause had Seattle gain the rights to Pippen, then drafted seven-foot Olden Polynice for the Sonics. Polynice was a highly regarded hardship case out of All Hallows of the Bronx who had gotten national attention before playing for the highly visible University of Virginia.

I wonder what would have happened if the Bulls hadn't gotten Pippen. I also wonder what would have happened if Frazier hadn't excited the Knicks and New York in the NIT.

Frazier read about everyone else in college but never saw his own name. "My name was strange to everyone other than some scouts," he said. "You know why? Because I played in my freshman year and in my sophomore year I was good. Then I sat out a year. I guess they forgot about me."

The Knicks didn't forget. We just put him aside until the time came to draft. By that big night in the Garden he had convinced us that he had exceptional talent. That championship performance was the clincher.

We saw a lot in Frazier in that NIT. That's why we didn't call him. We didn't want our interest to show. We were picking fifth in 1967. We didn't want to create any unnecessary competition for ourselves.

As things turned out, it was a year for guards. In those days the teams that finished last in the two divisions tossed for the first pick.

Detroit won and chose Jimmy Walker of Providence. Baltimore was next and got Earl Monroe.

A year later, the Bullets lost another coin toss. They were obviously weak in flips. That time it was the San Diego team that beat them to the top pick. The Rockets took Elvin Hayes.

Baltimore was "stuck" again, this time with Wes Unseld. That's the way NBA history goes. The Bullets lost two straight pots and still wound up with a pair of aces: two Hall-of-Famers.

Frazier was so full of joy when the Knicks signed him to play in New York, there was no way he would go back to school. Someone had to tell his coach. After all, Hartman had done Zimmerman a favor by recommending Zimmerman to ostensibly divert the inquiries.

"Zimmerman, the attorney, had to tell him," said Frazier. "Hartman got mad at him. I remember something Hartman said in a paper pertaining to my signing. That he had trusted Zimmerman and look what Zimmerman had done to him."

Frazier doesn't know to this day if they ever signed a peace treaty. He is sure that Hartman never sent the attorney any birthday or anniversary gifts. I knew Hartman for a long time and empathized when we signed Frazier.

I was working for the Knicks as a scout, so my true feelings and loyalty went only in one direction. Frazier was to be the last significant draft. We had been on a strong run from 1964 to 1967. Now we were in position to really challenge everyone for the title.

McGuire was the coach and the Knicks still hadn't settled on the starting lineup of the championship season. There were more experimenting and decisions to come. Most of the key players were in place, though.

We had obtained Dick Barnett from the Los Angeles Lakers in 1965. He was a quality player. We intended to draft him but Syracuse beat us to him in 1959. Syracuse picked just in front of us, otherwise the Knicks would have had him then.

At the time, we were groping. Our backcourt was getting old and we needed an injection of youth. I had scouted Barnett at Tennessee State. I knew he was a good shooter and a fine defensive player.

What we didn't realize was how smart he was. He was one of the smartest guys we ever had. He could play any type of game. He had a great basketball brain and could play the tough guy defensively.

We had Frazier, who made the all-defensive team almost every year. But I'd often give Barnett a lot of the tougher assignments. It depended on who was out there. If there was a guy Frazier could use his fast hands on, okay. If there was a Jerry West and you had to belly up on him, then it would be Barnett.

He was a great team player, even though he looked flamboyant—you know, Fall Back Baby and all that. He had a sharp mind that quickly picked up anything we were going to use.

Barnett also was a sharp dresser. I remember the first time I ever saw him in the Garden. He strolled through the hall leading to the Syracuse dressing room wearing spats, a homburg and a cape. He looked like something out of *Dracula*. I believe he had a great influence on Clyde, who eventually took over the role as the Knicks' best dresser—at least, the most conspicuous with his fur coats and wide-brim hats.

We had to wait for him as he played for the Nats, the Cleveland Pipers of the American Basketball League and then the Lakers. An unknown from Cleveland named George Steinbrenner owned the Pipers.

Barnett had a money problem in Syracuse and bolted to the Pipers in the new league. They were coached by Bill Sharman, the former Celtic who was also to coach the Lakers one day. Steinbrenner also signed Jerry Lucas to a personal services contract but the team folded before he played a game.

To this day Barnett claims the Pipers still owe him money. The statute of limitations has run out, I think. We were lucky time didn't run out on us where Barnett was concerned.

He was one of three players we tried to get in the draft: Barnett, DeBusschere and LaRusso. We failed on all. Two out of three isn't bad, especially when DeBusschere and Barnett became starters on our championship team.

It's ironic that Barnett was involved in two critical decisions early in his Knick years: first when we decided to trade Bob Boozer, a good scoring forward, for him; then when it came time for the 1968 expansion draft.

Phoenix and Milwaukee were coming into the NBA. They had to be stocked and the league allowed teams to protect seven. Reed, Bradley, Bellamy, Frazier, Russell and Phil Jackson were musts.

Jackson had been one of our sneaky picks. He was a gawky guy out of unknown North Dakota State who slipped by everyone until we took him on the second round. He had just given the Knicks solid playing minutes, so we weren't about to expose him.

We knew we'd be losing an important player. It came down to Barnett and Van Arsdale and let me tell you it was tough. Van was an excellent defensive player we used as a 6'5" swingman.

Van Arsdale was a big man in the backcourt with a good outside shot. He had the body for the muscling at small forward. He was a better all-around ballplayer than his identical twin brother, Tom, who went to the Cincinnati Royals in the draft.

They were hard to separate. They had gone through the Little League and school together and they both are now settled in Phoenix. It was so difficult to tell which was which when they were kids that they played games with people. The Little League has a rule that you can only use a pitcher for three innings. Dick was a shortstop and Tom a pitcher. They would make believe they were switching but then wouldn't switch. They would change hats and shirts. Tom would go back to the mound and Dick would go back to short. No one, including their coach, knew the difference. Dick claimed they would even take tests for each other.

Once, Eddie Donovan came close to putting the NBA to the test. He was thinking of having Dick and Tom switch uniforms for a Royals exhibition game with the Knicks. He dropped the idea because he figured the league would get upset if it found out.

Our Van Arsdale always was assigned Rick Barry when the Knicks faced the San Francisco Warriors, who later switched to the Oakland area. It was a fiery matchup, with the aggressive Van Arsdale usually irritating the testy Barry.

It erupted one night during the opening game of a doubleheader in Baltimore. Van played Barry tight and got on his nerves, as usual.

Suddenly they squared off. Rick was about to swing when a fist came from out of nowhere and knocked out a front tooth.

Barry claimed that Bellamy, then with the Knicks, had done it. Everyone knew Bells was a peaceful man. He never became angry enough to fight.

The culprit remained a mystery. Then Willis Reed was seen extracting the missing tooth from a knuckle. He didn't have time to see a dentist.

We hated to do it but Van was the one we exposed to the expansion draft. We felt we had enough insurance in the backcourt and up front. He was taken by Phoenix and still works TV for the Suns.

We kept Barnett and we never regretted it. We kept him because I had a big say in the decision. I had taken over the team by then. The Knicks weren't growing fast enough for Irish and Donovan, so McGuire's regime ended shortly after the 1967–68 season started.

McGuire was a smart basketball man. He had a young team that needed direction. He had to fit in all the new parts in a hurry. It wasn't fast enough for management, though the job was difficult under the circumstances.

They gave him Bradley and Russell as guards when they were to become forwards later. They gave him Bellamy, who played like a superstar when he wanted to. He had a wonderful habit of looking great against Chamberlain and Russell. He had a terrible habit of being so-so against all the others.

Nobody ever found a way to balance him. He was Rookie of the Year as well as MVP in his first All-Star game. Oscar Robertson kept hitting him with long breakaway passes and he'd spike the ball in the basket. It was Joe Montana to Jerry Rice long before their time.

That's why Irish always wanted Bellamy on the Knicks. Bells was an easygoing individual. He just wasn't predictable. For example, there was the time when I was coaching the team and we were leaving Atlanta for New York. Everyone was on board the plane but Bellamy. I think it was the last Atlanta–New York flight of the night. Where was Bells?

"I saw him on the phone in the waiting room. I just passed him as we came aboard the plane," said a writer. We took off without him—by the pilot's clock, though my trusty watch would have dictated the same thing.

We left Bellamy in a phone booth not far from where the passengers had boarded. I fined him the automatic $50 for being late and he also had to pay his own way home. He never blinked.

That was Bells. Always the cool one. His hand never shook when it came to money. He lived well. He spent well. He even offered to underwrite the Knicks during an airline emergency.

McGuire was the coach and the Knicks were on their way to play a game with Chicago in Evansville, Indiana. That's where Jerry Sloan came from and he was the Bulls' best player. NBA business wasn't too good then, so the Bulls scheduled the game to exploit Sloan's excitement in his hometown.

The Knicks left New York in bad weather. They landed in St. Louis and changed for a flight to Lexington, Kentucky, where they hoped to get a connection to Evansville. That's when it really got complicated.

There was one big commercial plane ready to leave for Evansville but there weren't enough seats to take the whole team. Someone spotted a private-plane counter. It was decided to fly at least the starters to Evansville in as many planes as it took.

Bellamy volunteered to solve the problem. "How much is a plane?" he asked the person at the counter. He was told it would be $175. "I'll take one," he said.

He was serious. He would have paid the $175 but the club wouldn't let him. The Knicks hired two of the small planes for the first six players. The remainder of the team and the media managed to get on the commercial plane because of no-shows.

We never had those problems when the NBA was a railroad league. We would pile onto a train, fill a drawing room with sandwiches and play cards all night. I guess that's why players were closer in those days.

Today they fly all over and don't have time to create the relationships we used to have. They are also too busy fulfilling their commercial commitments. I never had a paid speaking engagement or an endorsement in all my playing days.

I was lucky to be getting paid for a game I enjoyed so much. They tip the ballboys more than what we got way back then. There were no chartered MGM-Grand luxury jets like the Lakers, Bulls, Knicks, and other teams use.

It's still a fantasy world to me, though everything's been first-class since I've been with the Knicks. I just can't believe how pro basketball has grown into a major industry since my playing days. Of course, that's almost 50 years ago.

That's why I was amazed when I read that Michael Jordan flew his own plane to and from the All-Star game in Orlando. We had private cars in the old days but we had to stop off at the Green Parrot Inn in Indiana to get them.

We would take the overnight train from Rochester to our games with the Fort Wayne Pistons. We would arrive at this whistle-stop in Indiana at five in the morning. We'd lug our equipment bags through the street and across the tracks to the inn.

We'd knock on the door and a sleepy guy would open up. He'd order the cars while we were having breakfast. The best thing about it was that they had great bacon and eggs. That was our luxury in those days.

What a contrast to when I took over the Knicks and we started to use charters. We'd stock the plane with food and liquid refreshments. We had all the embellishments except menus.

Frankie Blauschild, our traveling secretary, would take home all the leftover miniature drinks. He made sure that it was only two a customer. I think he probably had to build a new wing for what he took home after every charter flight.

I changed a lot of things once I became the coach and had some authority. We struggled through another growing season in 1967–68 before that happened. Bellamy and Reed represented the heart of a team that finished 36–45.

Out of adversity comes luck at times. Everything was going our way but you can't appreciate that when you are losing. By winding up low in the standings once more, we had another good draft—I would say a meaningful one, considering who we got. That's the year we picked third and took Frazier—also Jackson on the next round. Yes, 1967 was a very good year. We had finally stacked the Knicks.

It turned out to be a remarkable stretch of scouting for me. I saw the team developing and it gave me a good feeling. It solidified my job, which was all I desired at the time.

I was determined to remain a scout and not to coach. Donovan had approached me when Gallatin was released but I suggested he give the job to McGuire. I escaped—then. But not for long.

Meanwhile, I watched McGuire trying to put all the new parts together. Bradley finally reported—late, of course.

He was late for his first press conference at Leone's restaurant. He also was late for his first season. He had a legitimate excuse for both. It wasn't Bradley's custom to be irresponsible about anything.

He was serving out a military commitment at the McGuire Air Force Base in New Jersey when he was late for his signing announcement. Uncle Sam had priority. Bradley walked into a media mob that had waited a half hour for him.

They were lucky. We waited over 20 years for him to fill the role that helped the Knicks finally win the title. We also waited until he was ready to play the 29th game into the 1967–68 season.

He sat in the radio booth at the Garden and watched the Knicks beat the Bullets on December 15, 1967. He practiced for the first time two days later. He played his first game on December 9 and it was a mob scene.

Every shot he took, every move he made, sent the sellout crowd wilder. You couldn't believe the dressing-room scene. The media had Bradley pinned against the wall like a Picasso. I squeezed in but was squeezed out right away.

"Unbelievable," said Cazzie Russell. "I expect the CIA in here any minute to rescue the President."

One paper headlined the game this way: "Pistons Top Knicks, Despite Bradley's 8 Points." It was also recorded—for the history that it was—this way: "It was 9:04 p.m., Dec. 9, 1967—exactly two years and seven months (and approximately ten hours) from the time the Knicks had drafted him, knowing he was a Rhodes scholar who would be going to Oxford first.''

Whew. I don't think General MacArthur's peace signing with the Japanese got that treatment. But it explains how Bradley's first game shook sophisticated New York.

I never saw anyone come into the league for the first time and generate such excitement—not even Wilt Chamberlain when he arrived to challenge the Bill Russell era and help carry the NBA to another level.

The Knicks devised a special way to handle all the requests for a Bradley interview. They arranged a press conference the first time he arrived in each city. It reduced the pressures on Bradley. I guess it also prepared him for the press conferences to come after his life in the NBA.

Little did I realize I would be coaching him about three weeks after his first game for the Knicks. It caught up to McGuire by then. He was near the end of a rocky situation with Cazzie Russell and his friends.

It had started the season before. There was no room in the crowded backcourt so McGuire moved Cazzie to forward, where there wasn't much room either.

Cazzie's friends made McGuire's life more miserable than his losing record did. I felt sorry for him.

I felt even sorrier when I took over and ran into a similar problem with Cazzie and Bradley. That one was over starting and not playing time.

It was to be my only really sticky situation. I wasn't thinking of that when the McGuire-Russell matter first hit the papers in New York with this report:

> First it was objective. Then it became sniping. Now the criticism aimed at Dick McGuire has become ruthless.
>
> For example, there was this most recent expertise offered in another paper. The guy who wrote it is unknown to anyone covering the Knicks. Yet he was able to inform his readers that most of the Knick writers have criticized the job McGuire has done with Russell.

In order to get his point across, the writer ran through the players competing with Cazzie for time in the backcourt. That's where Cazzie broke in and that's where McGuire's judgment is being questioned.

The writer's theory described the weakness of Dick Barnett because he was only a shooter. Look how Butch Komives throws the ball away while also being an erratic shooter. And isn't Emmette Bryant too small to play Jerry West, Oscar Robertson and all the other big guards? And how about the way McGuire substitutes?

It went on and on. I know it bothered McGuire but he never said anything. He seldom does—even to this day, when he still has the scouting job he took when we switched assignments on December 28, 1967.

The Knicks were 15–22 after losing a Sunday-afternoon game to the 76ers in the Garden. I was going to be there in my role as a scout.

I was about to leave on a trip to the coast. I drove to the Garden with my wife, Selma, intending to resist. I wanted no part of coaching. I had seen too much. I felt more secure in my job as a scout.

Everything indicated the Knicks had the ammunition to win the war soon, so why disturb my peaceful existence? Besides, I had just seen McGuire go through hell. I wanted no part of that because I had already been through it many times in my own way.

I had enough personal satisfaction watching the players prove that my judgment of talent was not bad at all. I had played the game. I had coached the game. Why go back?

I'll tell you why. I was talked into it. Irish and Donovan did a job on me. I was a convenient replacement to them. "You are all we have," I was told. I was in-house and they didn't have to conduct a search right away. I knew the players and they knew me.

What they didn't know was how I would coach. They were ready to gamble. The talent that had taken so long to accumulate was ready for takeoff. All it needed was someone to point it in the direction of a championship.

In the final analysis, the Knicks made me an offer I couldn't refuse. I didn't have a bargaining position. They could fire me if I said no.

That's a major consideration to anyone whose daily bread depends on someone else. That someone else controls your time and sometimes your life. I guess that's one reason I preferred to remain a scout. More freedom.

It didn't pay much and the traveling was tough. It wasn't even easy finding the places I visited on a map. It all added up to a good situation for me—maybe nobody else but me.

So I took the job but made sure I retained one bargaining chip. I didn't sign a contract. I would be free at the end of the season. They soothed me by raising my scout's pay to coach.

The money was great. I think it was $35,000. I had at least lasted in basketball until that money generation. I also lasted a lot longer as the Knicks' coach than I intended.

We had a fine season after I took over. We lost our first two games but went 28–17 anyway. We finished 43–39. It was the first time the Knicks had gone over .500 in nine years—since Levane took a 40–32 team to the 1960 playoffs.

It earned me a phone call from Irish. ''Mr. Felt wants to talk to you,'' he said. That's all he said. He never mentioned our agreement that I was finished coaching after the season.

I finished the season without a contract and didn't intend to ask for one. I didn't realize how close I came to not being a part of the 1969–70 frenzy. Irving Mitchell Felt changed my mind.

I must admit it didn't take much twisting of my arm to do it. It's always good business to play tough when someone wants you. I had fortunately created a situation where the Knicks indicated they needed me. That's a lot better than when they don't want you.

I knew I had some power when I walked into Felt's office. He immediately made it clear that I couldn't leave now. The Knicks were on the verge of big things. They represented big money and prestige for an organization that had invested so much in trying to get a winner.

I finally succumbed and was given a three-year contract with a very nice raise. It was a great feeling. I was getting paid a lot of money to coach the team I had learned to enjoy so much.

It had become a fun thing once I got my philosophy over. The first thing I did was to establish some rules of discipline. I told them no more food in the dressing room. No more eating of hot dogs while the coach talked at halftime.

And especially no more kids and visitors. Management people were bringing their kids and friends into the room for autographs and socializing. That had to stop. I even started to close our practices. I wanted the dressing room and practices to be all business. I didn't want distractions of any kind during business hours.

Some labeled the practices secret. It wasn't that at all. We had nothing to hide. I just didn't want even the players to bring their kids to the workouts. I always remember one incident when Johnny Green was a Knick.

He had twin boys who were about six then. He brought them to practice one day and they got into an argument over a basketball while the team was scrimmaging. There was only one basketball and they were having a tug-of-war with it. Everything stopped until Papa Green made peace.

I established my way of doing things immediately and it worked. We became a better team right away. We not only won but we had fun from the start of my second coaching career.

One of Frazier's recollections from those days he put this way: "How could Bradley get hit by a car in New York?" That brings me back to the end of my first day as Knick coach.

It had been a full hour and a half of preparing for the Lakers. They were coming to the Garden the next day. Remember, those were the days when the Lakers and Celtics dominated the league.

With Russell and the Celtics in the East, Chamberlain and Baylor in the West, I had enough on my mind. The phone rang that night and woke me up around 11. I am an early-to-bedder by habit.

It was Donovan. He told me I wouldn't believe it but Bradley had been hit by an MG driven by a young lady. It wasn't serious but Donovan thought he had better let me know right away.

It wasn't serious to Bradley, either. He laughs when he looks back at it. He was living near the old Garden on 50th Street and 8th Avenue and was crossing the street in the rain.

"I suddenly saw this car coming at me as I stepped off the curb," he recalled. "I tried to jump out of the way."

He took a glancing blow on his hip. He hurt his wrist and cut his ankle when he hit the ground—no real damage. Lucky for us and, as it turned out, also for the country.

Dr. Kazu Yanagisawa, our team doctor at that time, told me that Bradley was fortunate it was raining. "His hand slid because of the rain when he tried to break his fall. It might have been serious otherwise."

That reminds me that I have only two sad recollections of that entire time. Dr. Yana, as we called him, and Nate Bowman have died. The doctor never lived to see the Knicks win their first championship. Bowman contributed and is the only Knick from that team who has passed away.

All the players still remember the day of Dr. Yana's funeral. He had been the house doctor for the Knicks and Rangers for many years. He had had such a strong relationship with the Knicks that Emmette Bryant came down from Boston for the funeral. We had traded Bryant to Boston and he even had a game that night. He remembered that Dr. Yana had removed cartilage from his knee and prolonged his career.

All the Knicks met at the Garden to go to the funeral in New Jersey. There were three limousines and a private car to be driven by Tom Hoover, who used to play for the Knicks. He had Bryant, Bowman and Dave Stallworth in his car when we all left.

By the time the limos got to Bergenfield, New Jersey, there was an urgent message to call the Garden. Donovan called and came back to tell us Bowman, Stallworth and Bryant wouldn't be showing up. They had been arrested.

It turned out to be something out of a Marx Brothers picture— maybe the funniest thing that ever happened to that Knick team.

Stallworth had his own car parked at the Hotel New Yorker, a block from the Garden. Bowman had borrowed it that morning and put it back in the hotel garage but left the ticket in his room.

While Bowman went for the ticket, the others waited in front of the New Yorker. Along came a police car. It stopped when the police spotted the wrong inspection ticket on the windshield of Hoover's car. It was last year's blue instead of this year's green.

By the time Bowman made it back to the car, the cops were grilling Hoover, Bryant and Stallworth. They asked for Hoover's license and he gave it to them. They asked for the car's registration but Hoover didn't have it.

He explained he had borrowed the car from a friend and forgot to get the registration. They were all taken to the precinct but couldn't figure out why no registration was that serious.

They found out at the station house that the car had been stolen almost 11 months ago. They had to stay there until the friend from whom Hoover had borrowed the car verified his story.

I can still hear Bryant saying: ''I come down from Boston for a funeral and wind up in jail.'' He was living in the Bronx while playing in Boston, so he asked: ''Who's going to drive me home?''

Hoover grinned and said: ''You want to ride with me?''

Bradley was the subject of many funny stories. It made him feel like one of the guys, that he was accepted despite all his glittering credentials, despite the way he grew up and where he was educated.

His father was vice-president of a bank not far from St. Louis, so everyone assumed he was wealthy. After he became a Knick and they saw how he dressed, they wondered and teased him.

He'd wear these button-down oxford shirts with more holes in them than a golf course. Barnett would kid him about his ''cement shoes.'' And then there was his raincoat. I think Peter Falk borrowed it for his TV series. Or it wound up in the Smithsonian Institution as a relic. The players would needle Bradley about the worn-out coat and he'd just smile.

''He never was annoyed at us,'' recalled Frazier. ''And when we won the championship, we took his old trench coat from him and bought him a new one.''

It was on the road and his teammates got tired of Bradley's breaking their dress code. Everyone dressed in shirt, tie and jacket in those days. "Red was always on him about that trench coat and we'd ball it when Bradley wasn't looking," said Clyde. "Bradley liked that. It made him feel a part of the team."

DeBusschere remembers telling someone to take the laces out of Bradley's shoes after a road game. I think it was Mike Riordan. He and Barnett were Bill's key needlers.

Bradley came out of the shower, dressed and slipped into his shoes without blinking. He went all the way to the airport without saying a word. When he got off the bus, he paraded to the plane with all of us—still without shoelaces but wearing a smile.

DeBusschere joined the Knicks shortly after we reached .500 in 1968. It's important to note that our team already was coming together. We were doing very well just before we got him and there was no panic to make a trade.

We were becoming so good, teams were calling and offering to do us a favor. They would take Bellamy, Komives or even Frazier off our hands. We knew we needed more help but we weren't in a hurry. We could afford to wait for the player we wanted.

I had eyes for only one player. That was DeBusschere. I remember him telling me shortly after I took the job: "I can help the Knicks." I assumed he was unhappy in Detroit so I put that little piece of information in my memory bank.

DeBusschere had been the Pistons' player-coach and was re-placed by Donnie Butcher, who was replaced by Paul Seymour. That was hard to take for a person as proud as he was. He had gone from a Detroit hero and untouchable to just another player in management's eyes.

Jim Karvellas remembers those days very well. He had gotten his first NBA job as public-address announcer for the Chicago Packers. It was then that he established a friendship with DeBusschere in a unique way.

"Here's how that happened," recalled Karvellas. "My father owned a grocery store on the South Side of Chicago. I grew up working in that grocery store. Two blocks away was the Picadilly Hotel.''

That's where some of the White Sox players stayed. They used to shop in the Karvellas grocery store. ''Guys like Luis Aparicio and Nelson Fox,'' continued Karvellas. ''As a kid, I was beside myself. I didn't know whether to ask for autographs or weigh up two pounds of tomatoes or oranges for them.''

He was star-struck as any kid might be with the famous Sox second-base combination. His father wasn't. ''I would sit there and my father would tell me to pay attention because I would ring up the wrong things,'' recalled Karvellas.

One day a new phase of his life began. He said: ''Fox brought in this guy Dave DeBusschere into the store. I had heard of DeBusschere because, by that time, I was the PA announcer for the Packers. It was the 1962 season.''

DeBusschere had been just drafted by the Pistons and by the White Sox as a pitcher. He had pitched for Indianapolis when he got out of school and then the White Sox brought him up. That's why he was in Chicago and staying in the hotel near the Karvellas grocery store.

''This was before DeBusschere reported to the Pistons,'' Karvellas explained. ''So Fox brings DeBusschere into the store. They were a strange matchup. An odd couple. Nellie was a quiet guy with a big cigar and DeBusschere was a personality guy. But they both liked to drink beer. They found each other.''

That's how Karvellas became close to DeBusschere and later learned, in confidence, that he was unhappy and anxious to leave Detroit. DeBusschere told him so the season before we got him. Dave even indicated he would be interested in Baltimore. Lucky for us nothing happened with that.

Jim met a lot of the Pistons through DeBusschere. Dick McGuire was the coach and he shared an apartment with two of his players: Kevin Loughery and Bob Ferry.

''I couldn't believe it,'' said Karvellas. ''The coach and two of his players in the same apartment. They only had two beds. They had to flip a coin to see who would sleep in the Murphy bed. Loughery lost and that's how he came up with the name Murph.''

We finally accommodated DeBusschere by trading Bells and Komives for him. That, as everyone knows, was the final piece in the puzzle. We made that deal on December 19, 1968. As I've said, the Knicks were heading in the right direction by then.

New York wasn't really excited about us yet, but we had established a flow that satisfied me. I was the only one familiar with the nuts and bolts and felt good about the way the Knicks had progressed. We were 6–13 in November of the 1967–68 season and 18–17 on December 19.

4

December 18, 1968, was particularly meaningful because we beat the Celtics in Boston. We were already talking with the Pistons about DeBusschere. Conversations had been going on for a couple of weeks.

Paul Seymour needed a center and he was willing to take Bellamy back. In fact, Bells was the player he wanted. We eventually had to throw in Komives. The Pistons wanted to make the package look better. They were taking out insurance against the certain criticism for moving the popular DeBusschere out of Detroit.

That victory in Boston was important to us because the Celtics still had Russell. He was in his final season of unprecedented success. Imagine, 10 championships in 12 years to that point and always a Knick-killer.

Everything at that time was measured by the Celtics. We were always among the also-rans who rarely beat them. All Russell had to do was show up and the Knicks would lose.

Of course, it had its fringe benefits. If the Knicks hadn't finished so badly in those days, we never would have gotten the choice draft picks that led to the championship.

So beating the Celtics that night in Boston was a huge turning point. I don't recall all the details, but I do remember what Bellamy did in what was to be his final game for us. "You can look it up," as good old Casey Stengel used to say. I did.

Bellamy shot only 4-for-15 but played 48 minutes and went to the foul line 14 times. He made 10. It was another good team effort against Russell but this time we won.

I remember another fine Bellamy game against Russell around that time. That one was in our Garden. Bells had 11 rebounds and 11 points in the first quarter. That was unheard of against Russell by anyone.

Bellamy wound up with 29 points and 24 rebounds. He should have gone straight to the Hall of Fame in Springfield. Sam Jones, another Celtics Hall-of-Famer, explained why he didn't.

"Bellamy can play like that," said Jones, who quit at the same time as Russell after Bill's 11th title in 13 seasons. "If he comes to play like that all the time, the (Knicks) record could be reversed. He'll get up for Russ and Chamberlain and Thurmond but he also should get up for Finkel."

Jones was referring to teammate Henry Finkel. He was the Celtics' backup center, who was destined to become the answer to this trivia question: "Who played center for Boston after Russell retired?"

Jones wasn't telling us anything we didn't know. If Bellamy had played like that all the time, he would've been a franchise center and we might not have needed DeBusschere.

We made the deal the day we flew into Detroit after our big "upset" in Boston. We were in the hotel at the airport when Donovan phoned and said: "We got a deal."

The sweetest music I ever heard, but it almost upset our plans to go to the races at Windsor across the river in Canada. The racetrack, any one, was our ritual home away from home. Players would shop, go to movies and even be cultural like Bradley but the racetrack was my escape.

The road can be awfully lonely and boring. Our way of killing time was for me, Whelan and the press to go to the races and pool our money. We would put up $2 each and it would be group handicapping. Big gamblers.

I never handicapped. It was too much of a brain drain. There were far more important decisions ahead now that we had DeBusschere. Don't get me wrong. The news was great when it came but it threatened our night at the track. That would have really been disastrous.

One serious problem developed. We had to wait until Knick management put its stamp on the deal. It wasn't official, either, until the league office was notified by conference call with both teams and gave clearance. That's the procedure in all trades.

I think it was around five o'clock when I got the news. You would think upper management would say lock it up before Detroit changed its mind. There was a delay. I don't recall how long but it was interminable under the circumstances.

We could have blown the deal. I hate to think of that even now. Donovan finally called back. It was a go. I had to inform Bellamy and Komives. The writers had to create their Pulitzer Prize stories fast because the Daily Double closed at eight and the caravan had to drive across the border to Canada.

I dropped by Bellamy's room and hardly interrupted his TV with the news. He said: "That's the way it is," without even getting out of bed.

I also had to get in touch with DeBusschere after Detroit contacted him at home. He recalls getting the news while hanging a painting in his living room. The painting showed him driving around Bellamy in a game with the Knicks.

He was interrupted when the phone rang. It was Ed Coil. The general manager of the Pistons informed DeBusschere he had just been traded.

I sometimes wonder about that painting on the wall. It showed DeBusschere and Bellamy passing in the night. Did it have some eerie influence on the deal that brought DeBusschere to New York and two championships?

Crazy things like that happen in sports and everywhere. It's now well known what DeBusschere did the following night when the players changed uniforms. He played like he had just gotten out of jail.

The trade created a few change of directions in my game plan. I told Reed that he was going back to center, Bowman that he would be Willis's backup, Riordan that he would get more playing time now that Komives was gone, and Frazier that he was starting. It really didn't matter right away but it was the making of the Knicks.

I had scouted Dave and had always wanted him but couldn't get him. Nobody could but Detroit because of the territorial rule in those days. Come to think of it, maybe that's why I roomed him with Bradley. Maybe it was subliminal since both were territorial picks.

I figured he was a great player. As I've said, he could do everything. His leadership quality, an intangible, was even better than we expected. He was an inspiration for the other players. He gave us a hard day's work.

These things happen with all teams—both ways. You never really know how good or productive a player is until he performs in your situation. Reed and DeBusschere were perfect examples.

I never stop thinking how close we came to not getting Willis. I know this: If we hadn't, I wouldn't be here recalling the 1969–70 championship excitement and the impact Reed in particular had on NBA history.

None of that ever would have happened if someone had drafted Reed ahead of us. I was sitting at the Knicks' table with Donovan. In those days, every team had a table on the floor and the individuals making the picks sat there. That has drastically changed like everything else.

It's more sophisticated because of electronics. Now the selectors remain in their home cities and relay their picks to Commissioner David Stern in New York over a national phone hookup. What are they going to think of next?

After we picked Barnes, we couldn't believe it as every team passed on Reed. It's interesting to look at these first guesses by the others (though not in this order): Atlanta, Jeff Mullins; Detroit, Joe Caldwell; Golden State, Barry Kramer; Los Angeles, Walt Hazzard; Philadelphia, Luke Jackson; Washington, Gary Bradds and Boston, Mel Counts.

I turned to Eddie and said something like: "Is it possible, I hope?" We agreed the Celtics had to take Willis. They had just won another championship and had the last pick. When we heard them announce "Boston selects on the first round Mel Counts of Oregon State," we slammed the table.

I'm not saying we knew what Reed was going to do for the Knicks but he was a bonus pick for us. We got lucky. He fell in our laps. We, at least, were better prepared to know Reed's qualities.

Looking back, I say to myself: "What would have happened if the Celtics had taken Willis Reed?" There's no telling how many more championships they might have won after Russell retired in 1969.

That's when we began our championship run because of Willis. I shudder when I think how great the Celtics were with Russell and how close they came to getting Reed. And what the Knicks would have been without him.

We said: "Willis Reed" almost before Commissioner Walter Kennedy announced the Knicks were up first in the second round. We wanted to get our pick on the record fast. Who knows? The way the Knicks were going then, a bomb might've gone off and wiped us all out.

Let's be honest. In the back of our minds was the possibility we could have made a mistake on all three guys: Barnes, Jackson and Reed. There have been far fewer guarantees from the draft than mistakes.

We were sure Reed was going to be an outstanding player but who knew how outstanding? It was better to at least know he was going to have the opportunity to play for the Knicks, not against us.

Also, remember there were only nine teams in the league then. There is no way we would've gotten Reed today. A lot of things have changed. The Reed thing is similar to the Jerry West shot against us in the 1970 series—the one he heaved over 60 feet to send the third game into overtime. Just think, if that happened today, he would win the game because it's a three-point shot. We couldn't have gotten Willis on the second round of a draft that now has 27 teams.

That's what makes history revisited so pleasant. There's no way we could have accomplished what we did without Willis. He was our leader. He was our franchise.

Reed showed us he was the franchise pretty quickly. We lived with him for about two weeks in his first camp and discovered he was even better than we thought. He had good hands. He made good decisions. He had a strong body and will.

> *"DeBusschere immediately solved a major problem. He played the power and scoring forwards who were hurting the Knicks."*
>
> —Red Holzman

He is the only player who ever asked me for a rule book. He was the politest and nicest young man from the first time I met him at Grambling. The immediate thing about him as a Knick was his poise on the court. He knew how to play. He had all the right instincts. It made me wonder how we and all the other talent experts had miscalculated so badly.

Timing is everything in life. Reed and DeBusschere proved it to us. DeBusschere also came along just in time. He asserted himself from the moment he put on a Knicks uniform.

DeBusschere didn't need any help that first night. He tore his old team apart in Cobo Hall. Our championship-to-be team was born right there. I started him, played him 37 minutes and he hit 9-for-15 with 15 rebounds.

We won 135–87, the widest margin of victory in the 21-year history of the Knicks. DeBusschere sure made me look like the coaching genius. He fit us like one of my Brooks Brothers suits. We never even missed a beat on defense, where timing is so important. We held the Pistons to 87 shots, a very low number in a sport where the arms go first.

I remember us taking some heat for the deal. They couldn't understand how we could give up a 7-foot center, a precious commodity, for a 6'6" forward. They learned.

They never turned my head, though. Remember, I was the guy who kept telling the players: "Never turn your head on defense." Besides, we knew Reed's natural position was at center. Despite his lack of size, we didn't have the slightest doubt that he'd be a better one than Bellamy in the long run. We never hesitated to make the deal because of Willis.

We also knew that DeBusschere was a fine scorer and rebounder and an intelligent player. But we really didn't find out how good he was until he began playing for us.

Somehow the New York bas-ketball fans seemed to know all that before we did. He got a tre-mendous welcome two nights later in the Garden. He stood there with a smile on his face and realized he had found a home. As I said, he still lives in New York, where he works in real estate.

> *"The arrival of DeBusschere had been the missing piece in the puzzle, the finishing touch to a great masterwork of art."*
>
> *—Willis Reed*

DeBusschere responded his first night in the Garden as a Knick by scoring 26 against Seattle. We won the first eight games he played for us. He considers that introduction as a Knick not far off our NBA record 18 in a row the next season year.

We had now won 10 straight and sent a serious message to the rest of the league. We didn't know it at the time but DeBusschere put us over the top. The Vietnam War was still top priority throughout the country but the Knicks were operating in another world. We did have Cazzie and Riordan to remind us of the disturbances that ripped the country apart. They were in the reserves and subject to being called up at any time. They were playing and serving.

It was hard to forget the war because the papers were full of demonstrations against it. Cazzie, for example, was called up with his unit at one time. Fortunately it was during the summer so he was back when camp opened for the 1968–69 season.

This was the headline in a New York paper that greeted me as Cazzie and the others gathered in Farmingdale, New York: "Caz Recalls Showing a Knick Pal the Ropes." And this was the story that was printed:

Cazzie Russell was standing with his M.P. outfit in the midst of the recent Chicago demonstrations at the convention when he spotted a familiar figure.

"I waved my billy club at him and told him to get behind the ropes," Caz said, but Phil Jackson never recognized him.

Russell was there because his 233rd M.P. outfit of the National Guard had been activated. Jackson first insisted he had not been there in Chicago when they were demonstrating at the site of the Democratic Convention.

"He's trying to tell me he wasn't in Chicago," said Cazzie. "How many 6-8 guys are there with sideburns? He was with the hippie group. He was wearing James Bond glasses and this handlebar mustache. I saw him on Michigan Ave. at three o'clock in the afternoon when they (the hippies) were out there at their fullest."

Caz acknowledged that Jackson never could have recognized him. "He'd never know me in my uniform," said Russell. "I was wearing my M.P. outfit helmet over my eyes and I had a bayonet, M1, handcuffs and a licking stick."

Russell insisted he waved the licking stick at Jackson and he got behind the rope. "He followed my instructions," said Cazzie as he and Jackson were drying off after showering.

Phil finally confessed. He had been in Chicago at the demonstrations and didn't recognize Cazzie. "You had a gas mask on," Jackson reminded Cazzie, who nodded.

"Come to think of it, Caz, you never looked better in your life," ad-libbed Jackson. They laughed.

"He said he was passing through, so he thought he would stop off," said Cazzie. "I came to observe," said Phil.

"He was the cause of my being activated and having to spend four days on the street and live down in the armory for eight days," insisted Russell, nodding at Jackson. "Thanks a lot, Phil, for spoiling my summer."

Cazzie refused to discuss the Chicago demonstrations any further. He had been on duty and military people have a tendency to dislike and discourage loose talk.

"It was bloody," he conceded. But he added he was not involved in any of the serious confrontations.

End story. An interesting one when I read it, except it turned out to be a hoax. Cazzie and Phil staged it for a beat writer. They couldn't resist. It was their kind of humor.

Cazzie was in the National Guard and had served in Chicago. The rest was a put-on. Cazzie started talking and Phil eventually caught on and embellished the story.

Jackson was one of my favorite people. I guess it's because I "discovered" him in the boondocks of the country.

He was a strange combination: a hippie son of a minister. He played both parts very well. He had a

> *"If I had to pick one representative aspect of Red Holzman's basketball philosophy, it would be the structure of the Knicks' offense. The opposing team would never be sure where the ball was going when the Knicks were down to a clutch shot. Bradley, Frazier, DeBusschere, Reed and Barnett were all great pressure players and none of them were afraid to take the big shot."*
>
> *—Phil Jackson*

knack of having strange things happen to him. One day he was walking in midtown New York when he spotted a cameraman.

Jackson followed his first impulse. He made a face and waved. "I saw the camera and just reacted," he explained. "They stopped filming right away. I didn't even know what they were shooting."

He found out that night. It turned out to be a TV news segment of a policewoman working as an undercover prostitute. He was in on the final shot.

"A lot of people asked if that was me waving in the background," he said. DeBusschere told him: "I knew it had to be you." Jackson was a character in his own way.

He was a peaceful man by nature. He still is, though I see him stamping his feet and glaring at the referees when they don't treat

Michael Jordan and the Bulls fairly. I wonder how many know he once set a NBA players' record for a fine.

Phil got angry and shoved Earl Strom, who was known to get into some extracurricular incidents of his own. For example, there was the time we were playing the 76ers during the playoffs at the Palestra in Philadelphia. Earl got upset at a regular heckler sitting behind a basket. He kicked the fan.

Strom then exercised his authority by having security kick the guy out. He hit Jackson with two technicals and also threw him out on the Night of the Record Fine.

Walter Kennedy was the commissioner then and he was responsible for Jackson making NBA history. It was $200 tops for fined players at the time. Kennedy hit Jackson for $1,000—the stiffest player rap in history then.

That was a huge amount of money in view of the salaries the NBA was paying. It was an expensive way for Jackson to make the record book. I'm not at liberty to say how he paid it. But when Charles Barkley is fined $10,000, don't feel sorry for him. It's petty cash.

I still feel sorry for Jackson because he missed the 1969–70 championship season. I know we gave him a ring and a full players' playoff share. He also received another ring when he helped us win, again, in 1972–73. And he's now got the two he earned as a championship coach with the Bulls.

It's still not the same as watching all that excitement go by while recovering from back surgery. He broke down as we were heading toward the 1968–69 All-Star break.

We were in San Diego, the last stop of a five-game swing through the West, when Jackson said he couldn't play. We sent him to a San Diego doctor. That's when they found the slipped disk. It ended his season at 47 games and he was gone until 1970–71.

That was some night in San Diego. The entire Odd Couple missed the game. Frazier couldn't play because of the flu. I told Danny Whelan to put the roomies on a plane and get them back to New York right away.

I had paired Frazier and Jackson since they were rookies. I don't know why. They got along despite different personalities, so I just did it. I seem to remember Donnie May rooming with Frazier for a while, too.

Frazier reminded me that he did room with May after we picked Donnie on the third round of the 1968 draft. "He was so immaculate," said Clyde. "When he used to take out his toiletries, they were always symmetrically in place."

Frazier confessed he used to be sloppy. "Then I roomed with this guy and he got to me after a while," he said. "He drove me crazy trying to be neat like him. He was very meticulous."

I never did ask Clyde if, when he went to the bathroom late at night, he'd come back and find Donnie had made his bed. An old joke that I guess should remain an old joke.

May was so neat, all the players kidded him about it. DeBusschere, Bradley, Riordan and Bill Hosket took Donnie out for a few drinks one night. I had given May permission to leave training camp the next day to get married back in Dayton.

When the players returned from hoisting a few, Riordan turned to Donnie and offered him $20 to jump into the pool at our motel. The four players would chip in $5 each.

"With my clothes on?" May inquired. "You can take your shoes off," was DeBusschere's spontaneous concession.

Donnie was dressed neatly, as usual, with a nice suit, shirt and tie. The players never figured he'd do it. He said: "Give me the money," because he didn't trust them.

They handed him the $20. He took off his shoes and dove. That was indicative of the chemistry—as they call it today—that we had going into the 1968–69 season. A lot of laughs, a lot of hard work and a lot of victories were just ahead.

The Odd Couple reflected our teamwork on and off the floor. Players do not necessarily socialize with each other. They have different tastes and dislikes like anyone else.

Frazier and Jackson were a good example of how personality opposites can get along. Clyde was laid back, Mr. Cool. Jackson was more outgoing, the extrovert type.

They preferred to room together because they had made a smooth transition from their personal habits. "Phil always liked the room cold because he was from North Dakota," explained Clyde. "I liked it warm because I was from Atlanta."

They compromised by having the windows open when they went to bed but closed when they were walking around. Frazier liked to run right out and get something to eat while we were checking into hotels. They settled that with Jackson acting the bellhop and lugging the bags to the room. Anything to save a tip.

Jackson's reasoning was logical: "That way I got into the room first and threw open the windows as wide as I could."

No one ever criticized Phil for not being a thinking man. He's proving it even more with the way he is coaching the Bulls.

Phil would purposely try to deep-freeze his roomie. "He liked it so cold, you could see your breath," was the way Frazier put it. Then there were the TV and phone.

Jackson made the supreme sacrifice with the phone. "He was always on it," explained Phil. "His long-distance calls were immense. His home was in Atlanta and he went to school in Southern Illinois and he was always calling someone."

Besides, Jackson was a late sleeper. Frazier was always the first one awake, so he got squatter's rights to the phone. I assume Clyde paid the bills. I guess he did because I never got any complaints from Phil.

Danny Whelan would leave two wake-up calls for everyone when we were on the road. Clyde would leap out of bed first, while Jackson preferred to linger.

Frazier would shower, shave and dress, then wake up Phil in time for him to beat bus departure and fines deadline. There were times when players missed the bus. They had to pay for a cab on top of a fine because promptness was one of our team disciplines.

The Odd Couple's teamwork broke down one time in Canada. We were all on the bus but Jackson, while Frazier had just made it. The door was about to close after Phil was the last to arrive, when Clyde yelled: "Hold it!" He leaped out without explaining why.

He was gone in a flash and back in a flash. My trusty watch was in my hand. He returned carrying a pair of alligator shoes. I always sat in the first seat on the right so I could nail the stragglers. It also enabled me to be first off the bus.

As soon as Clyde put his foot in the door, I said: "Give Danny five dollars." I was letting him off cheaply but sometimes I liked to give the impression I was a coach with a heart. It was all part of the fun game we developed with fines.

"It's worth it, Red," said Frazier. "These shoes cost me a hundred dollars, so I figure I just made ninety-five." Clyde didn't even insist that Jackson pay the fine for seriously violating their ground rules by not finding his shoes as the last man clearing out the room.

Frazier would always pack before going to bed, but Jackson waited until the last minute. Clyde would be downstairs 10 minutes ahead of time, while Phil would always be in a photo finish.

Therefore, they worked it out that Jackson's responsibility was to inspect the room as the last one out. Phil would check the closet, the bathroom, the drawers, under the bed. Once in a while he found something.

They settled the TV problem easily. Clyde couldn't sleep unless it was on, so he kept it on. That was fine from his viewpoint but not necessarily Jackson's.

Phil made the concession for the sake of teamwork but with a foul claim. Jackson said the trouble was Clyde didn't really care what was on TV as long as it was on. Frazier would fall asleep and snore. Meanwhile, Jackson was hooked on the TV he didn't care to watch in the first place.

We were just one big, happy family. That is until that night in San Diego when Jackson, Frazier and Russell couldn't play. Cazzie had been called up for reserve duty.

We were down to nine against a San Diego team that had Elvin Hayes, a hard-nosed Don Kojis and a player named Pat Riley. The Lakers were dominating the West but the Rockets were competitive and tough at home.

It was hardly the time to be undermanned. On top of that, Bradley informed me he was sick. He was sick to his stomach. He said he could play but I wasn't sure.

Bradley had to sit on the bench no matter what. Teams had 11-man rosters and we had to have at least 8 in uniform. What a night.

He brought it up—if you will pardon the expression—while we were looking back at those days. "Hey, listen," said Bradley. "Did you see the president [Bush] passing out and vomiting on the floor? It reminded me of me in San Diego."

Bradley was so persistent about starting, I gave the guy who came into our dressing room this lineup: Bradley and DeBusschere at the forwards, Reed at center, Barnett and Riordan subbing for Frazier at guard. It was the first start for Riordan, our find as the 128th pick on the 12th round in the 1967 draft.

Just as the referee was about to toss the ball for the opening tap, Bradley ran toward our bench. He never made it. He upchucked onto the shoes of one of our writers at the press table.

I said: "Bill, Bill sit down." He said, "No, no, I can play." He grabbed a towel and went back.

"He had turned white," was DeBusschere's recollection.

"He turned green," said Whelan. "If they had that on video, I tell you . . ." Bradley didn't let him finish. It was his story and he wanted to tell it.

He resumed with "Every time I go to San Diego . . . you know where the paper is in San Diego, the *Union* right across from the Mission Valley Inn . . . every time I go past there I think of that damn tuna fish sandwich I ate."

My brilliant response to that 24 years later was: "Why the hell didn't you buy a steak for yourself? You were saving meal money that day?"

Whelan had been in the middle of the mess and was entitled to give his own description. It went this way: "You know what happened just at tipoff. They were ready to start the game. Bill goes like this: He puts his hand over his mouth and he starts walking off towards the press tables and our bench. And then he did it."

Whelan was rolling. "When he came off the court, he sat down for about a minute and then said he wanted to get back in it."

Bradley sat next to me and I sent in May, his first start. In all my years, I have never seen a "starter" miss an opening tap. Bradley made my record book that night.

I sent him in three times and each time he had to run off the court. He was a remarkable competitor, though. He actually played 37 minutes, had 11 assists and 9 rebounds.

We won 105–102 with seven and a half players. DeBusschere came through for his roomie with 26 points, while good old Willis picked it up with 36. We survived that crisis but ran into more trouble right away.

Actually, it was four games later and just after the All-Star break. That's when Cazzie broke his ankle and joined Jackson on the injured list. We were playing Seattle in the Garden and there were only two seconds left in the third quarter.

DeBusschere rebounded a shot and tossed Cazzie a long pass. Bob Rule of the Sonics deflected it. Then Joe Kennedy dove for the free ball, clipping Cazzie and breaking his ankle.

It was an oblique fracture of the distal right fibula. It was an oblique fracture of our team's progress. At least that's the way it looked at that moment.

But you never really know. I thought at the time that Cazzie's loss would be disastrous. I had created a team rhythm. Cazzie was starting, Bradley was backing up and now it was interrupted.

There was only one option. It didn't take a rocket scientist to decide Bradley would be the starter. The loss of Jackson and Cazzie at the same time put an awful lot of pressure on our bench.

Everyone had to move up without any effect on the way we were playing and winning. The Sonics were shocked by the freak accident. "Too bad, they were going so good," said the Seattle coach, Al Bianchi, who was destined to become the Knicks' general manager in a different era.

Cazzie and Jackson wound up in the same hospital at the same time in rooms across the hall. Once the shock of surgery wore off, the fun and games resumed for them. They even started a two-man wheelchair league in the hall.

It's strange how things happen in life. The loss of Cazzie hurt badly but it did solve a problem with which I was wrestling. I had inherited it from McGuire. It was the Cazzie-Bradley thing.

5

We drafted both Cazzie and Bradley as guards. McGuire moved Cazzie to forward and I switched Bradley after I became the coach. That turned out to be their most productive position.

Neither was fast enough to handle the smaller and faster guards. Cazzie's strength was his uncanny ability to heat up fast. He was instant offense.

Bradley had the sounder all-around game. I had the advantage of hindsight. I was able to watch them while McGuire was handling the team. I had the luxury of studying them against the best in the NBA.

I watched Bradley go up against the speed of the guards. It exposed a weakness of his. He could have gotten by against a lot of them but he never would have been as productive within our team structure.

He turned out to be an excellent small forward though he was relatively slow and only 6'5". He compensated with his intelligence. He could move without the ball. He was an exceptional passer with a natural instinct to make the play.

The other small forwards, many bigger, had to cope with him. He had the outside shot and the ability to move off screens. He was struggling at guard, so I moved him to exploit his strengths.

Cazzie was at small forward first and that complicated it. I just couldn't walk in and dispossess him. He had earned the right. I realized that.

I still couldn't overlook the reason why I was there. My priority was to get maximum mileage out of everyone. It became clearer and clearer that Bradley wasn't as good at coming off the bench as Cazzie.

> *"Cazzie was a pure shooter, and, boy, he could fill it up when he got hot."*
>
> —Walt Frazier

Cazzie thought otherwise and I couldn't blame him. I had been a player and I knew just how he felt about starting. I had to make the switch but I was very careful.

I knew that Cazzie would help the team more by coming off the bench blazing. He was great at it. He never saw a basket he didn't like and didn't need any time to get accustomed. Bradley just couldn't do that.

I had to be discreet. So I used the practices. I'd use Bradley with the other starters at times to see how it worked. That was standard operating procedure.

I never discussed it with either Cazzie or Bill. It was a simmering situation I hoped would not boil over and hurt the team. I didn't want any clashes among the players and never had any—I think.

The Bradley-Russell thing was the closest. It was resolved when Cazzie broke his ankle that night in the Garden. I remember how I ran onto the floor with Whelan, and Cazzie was in pain and hoping it wasn't broken.

He was back just before the regular season ended. By then Bradley had the job locked up and was enjoying it. So was everyone on the team as we kept winning.

We were in a winning rhythm. If it ain't broke, don't fix it, as the experts keep saying. Bradley was not only performing, his enthusiasm was catching.

His attitude was great. He would play anyone I assigned him, mismatch or not. Some guys going against John Havlicek would say: "That guy's a pain in the ass. He's too busy." To Bill, defense, especially against the Havliceks, was an honor and the ultimate challenge.

He would irritate the man he was playing. He would always have his hand on Havlicek's chest to check and annoy him. He'd try to keep the ball away and bump Havlicek away from where he wanted to go. Bradley was a perpetual agitator in motion.

He was a pest and he loved it. Havlicek was a great talent, which made the matchup one to remember. I think everybody loved and respected Bill but he was such an irritant on the court. He could get under your skin. That's why I liked him.

He planned it that way and then gave you one of his innocent who-me looks. He used to drive Rick Barry crazy. He would push and pull Rick, a rough man to cover who didn't like to be touched. Barry would get mad enough to fight.

There were some skirmishes but you know basketball fights. Barry was a shooter and not a fighter. Havlicek moved too fast to hit. Bradley did have some exchanges with Jack Marin of the Bullets. They traded a few slaps but none of their bouts are in the Ring Record Book. They were two intense players in a matchup of skills and the will to win.

Bradley always had another severe test when I'd assign him to Bob Love of the Chicago Bulls. I did that because DeBusschere had to play shorter Chet Walker, a terrific one-on-one shooter. Love was 6'9″ and could shoot and run like a sonofagun.

Bradley also had to block out the bigger Love under the boards. He'd take quite a beating but never complained. The only time I heard him beef was when we weren't playing team basketball. That drove him crazy. He was a perfectionist.

I never even heard him complain about injuries. We had some tough guys that way—Bradley, Reed, DeBusschere, Jackson and Riordan, especially.

Riordan would ignore being hurt because he wanted to play so badly. I don't think Mike ever asked Whelan for even a Band-Aid. He was one of those gym rats who never got tired of practicing or playing.

You know how some players like to shoot around when they get to the arena. Well, Riordan was the only player I ever knew who worked out and then took a shower before every game. He had the perfect temperament to sit on the bench and seldom play.

How else would he tolerate my using him only to give fouls during our championship year? Mike was a tough New York kid who understood and accepted a role others might have resented. He considered it an important team contribution when he took a foul that a starter would have to give.

That was the unique strength of the Knick team that was about to win a championship. From Johnny Warren, the last man on our bench, to Reed, our top honcho, winning was the only thing. They were the 11 musketeers.

That's why Bradley also played through injuries. He even played the night he got hit by the car.

He wasn't all basketball, however. He had another side to him. He had a whimsical sense of humor that only the players knew because he was such a private person.

DeBusschere still tells the story of the Christmas party he and his wife, Geri, threw at their home. They had the whole team, including me, Whelan and some friends over. Bradley called that morning.

He wanted to know if he could come dressed as a priest. DeBusschere informed him it wasn't a costume party. Bradley knew but told Dave he was asking because he didn't want to offend anyone.

Bradley showed up in a black suit with his collar reversed. As DeBusschere tells it: "Our future President walked over to a guest and said: 'Excuse me, but I'm ready to take your confession.'" No, it wasn't me.

I had nothing to confess, anyway. I think I even handled the Cazzie-Bradley situation fairly. On both sides.

As I said, Cazzie was instant offense. Put him out there at any time and a second later he had a basket. Before I made up my mind on the switch, I wanted to be thorough about it. I wanted to take a good look at it.

In the final analysis, I didn't do it. The players did it. Very often a player would say: "Why did you take me out of there?"

I'd say: "I didn't take you out. You took yourself out. You were either tired or you weren't doing what you're supposed to do."

Cazzie made the decision for me when he got hurt. I never had to explain it to him. I figured he was unhappy but he understood I did what was best for the team.

I respect him for the way he accepted the situation. No player likes to lose his job because of injury. I'm sure Phil Simms felt that way when Jeff Hostetler was given his job.

Let me tell you something about Cazzie. We knew we had to trade him someday if someone we needed more came along. We finally did deal him to the Warriors for Jerry Lucas, who helped us win the 1972–73 title.

Cazzie could have left the Knicks with some resentment but he wasn't the type. He actually sent my wife a plant while she was in the hospital with a hip fracture from a car accident. He was no longer with the Knicks. It's one of those gestures that makes an old coach feel good. The plant is still thriving in our backyard.

Those are the things you always remember. Nor will I ever forget the life Cazzie pumped into the dressing room and our games. He was the first of the health-food nuts. He introduced vitamins and his own teakettle to our dressing room. And he'd carry his golf clubs along on our trips to warmer places.

We had to go on without him after he broke his ankle and I was surprised how well we did. We actually won 11 in a row. We were 33–19 when Cazzie got hurt and Jackson was lost. We were 21–9 after that.

Donovan and I talked about some replacements. I didn't want anyone just to fill space. I was using seven or eight players, anyway. I never worried about things I couldn't control, so I simply moved Bowman, Hosket, May and Riordan up on the bench.

We played with nine men the rest of the way and did very well. We were existing on beer and soda in the dressing rooms. Even Bradley was learning how to drink beer by then.

DeBusschere gave him a crash course. Pretty soon Bill was one of the guys. He'd pack a bottle or two or three in his bag and lug them back to his room. We weren't a tough drinking team as drinking teams go. Just tough to beat.

We finished the season with a flourish but in third place behind Baltimore and Philadelphia. The Celtics and Russell sneaked into the playoffs in fourth place. We were remarkable considering the circumstances.

We had sent a message that the Knicks were coming even without Cazzie and Jackson. We know we would have done a lot better that season with them. We might have beaten the Celtics in the playoffs and made the final instead of them if we had had our full lineup.

> *"If we win you will have a lot of free time; if we lose you belong to me."*
>
> —*Red Holzman*

Russell had gotten older and slower. His "last legs" still were younger than those of most of the other centers. Let me tell you what kind of competitor Russell was if you don't already know.

We had played the Celtics near the end of the regular season and he wound up in the hospital. He went up for an alley-oop and flipped over someone's back. He hit the floor hard and lay there from shock and exhaustion.

He was 34 at the time with little mileage left on his odometer. Yet he grabbed his clothes and sneaked out of the hospital so he could prepare for the playoffs with the 76ers.

The Celtics won and we were next for them. I remember Gene Shue, who was coaching the first-place Bullets, saying the Knicks were capable of winning the NBA title. He mentioned our defense, shooters and especially Willis.

We had just swept his team 4–0 in our opening series. The Bullets were like the Knicks then. We were about in the same stage of development, although the Bullets had done it quicker.

The addition of Unseld and Monroe had turned Baltimore, now Washington, around overnight. It went from a last-place 36–46 to a first-place 57–25 in one season.

Shue was right about us, only he was a bit premature with his prediction. We were close to winning it all but not yet ready. We had key players missing for the 1968–69 playoffs, but we scared them anyway.

Cazzie did make an unexpected return for the final five games of the regular season. But he was in no shape to be a real contributor in the playoffs. We played the Celtics too shorthanded to spoil Russell's last games against us.

We had to get by Baltimore first, and especially Unseld, who had been voted Rookie of the Year and MVP. Only Wilt Chamberlain had accomplished that. I can still see Wes grabbing a rebound and flinging an over-the-head two-hand pass the length of the court.

I hope you realize what kind of strength that takes. How far do you think Dan Marino can throw a football that way? Without being intercepted, of course. We never could intercept Unseld's unusually long passes.

We managed to do enough in other areas to sweep the Bullets. I must admit they weren't the real Bullets because Gus Johnson had torn up a knee. Also, Kevin Loughery had to take cortisone shots for a groin injury in order to play.

Shue's strategy was to minimize Reed. He even used Unseld to bring the ball down at times in order to draw Willis away from the inside, where he anchored our defense.

Those things always look good on paper. Reed destroyed the theory with 32 points in 40 minutes in the first game. We spread it around as usual. DeBusschere had 23 rebounds with no Gus Johnson to contend with, Frazier was 11-for-18 and Barnett was 9-for-17.

Earl Monroe answered with 32 points as his rivalry with Frazier took on legendary status. The Pearl had 29 in the second game and Clyde 23, 12 assists and 7 rebounds.

In game three it was 26 points, 17 assists and 7 rebounds for Clyde but Reed was the big gun. He produced 35 points and 19 rebounds. We were one game away from sweeping the series between the two acknowledged heirs apparent to the Celtics.

I remember Unseld's words to this day. He said the Knicks had no key man. He thought it was Frazier, then it was Reed, then DeBusschere, then Bradley. I don't understand how he overlooked Barnett.

That's the story of Barnett—always overlooked and underrated but one of the smartest players I ever had. I guess it was his laid-back nature. While everyone was watching DeBusschere, Reed and Frazier, he'd be quietly doing damage.

It reminds me of that old story of the exhausted fighter sitting on his stool between rounds. His face was battered and bloodied when his manager said: "Keep going. This guy can't hurt you." And the fighter said: "You better watch the referee then because someone's beating the hell out of me."

> "We weren't the tallest, fastest, or best jumpers. We were just the most intelligent team I've ever seen."
>
> —Walt Frazier

That was Barnett. He did the damage that no one noticed but the coach. I'd use him on West and Monroe at times because he was such an excellent one-on-one player but no one noticed. That's because everyone was watching our other four guys.

DeBusschere, Reed, Frazier and Bradley are all in the Hall of Fame now. Barnett is not. He's still the unnoticed player who, in my coaching opinion, deserves to be enshrined in Springfield with the other Knicks.

We have retired all five of their numbers. They hang in the Garden as a tribute to the greatest team in Knicks history—a team that also moved the NBA to another level with the excitement and drama of the 1969–70 season.

We were on the verge when we became the first team in history to sweep a division winner. Reed took 25 shots, unusually high for him, and made 15 to put away the division champion Bullets. "It's unbelievable the way they hit the open man," said Marin when it was over.

That not only was descriptive of our offense. It also probably inspired *The Open Man*, the title of the book DeBusschere wrote after we won the championship the next season.

The NBA has never seen such an explosion of books. Everyone but the ballboy wrote one after the 1969–70 championship. His agent probably demanded too much. The Celtics had won 11 titles in 13 Russell years but never produced as many books as the Knicks did from one season. I guess that's what happens when you succeed in New York.

It's a time out and you have only one minute to remind everyone what we must do.

Only Danny Whelan, our trainer, had the right not to listen.

All photos copyright © George Kalinsky, Major League Graphics.

Bill Bradley strolls toward the bench for the constant reminder of what the coach wants done.

Dave DeBusschere and Walt Frazier escape to the peace and quiet of the trainer's room for a pre-game taping.

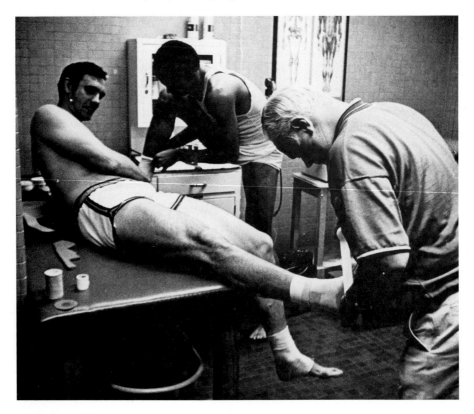

A crushing moment for the Knicks as Cazzie Russell is helped off the court after breaking his ankle in a game with Seattle.

Our instant offense man is soon back shooting with the cast still on his leg.

Earl Monroe and Walt Frazier engage in classic confrontation during heated Knicks-Bullets battles.

Notice tricky Clyde has his hand on The Pearl in the photo above, while in this photo he pins Monroe to the floor by standing on his foot.

Bill Bradley tries to shake Jack Marin in a match-up that produced many sparks and some little fires.

Wes Unseld and Willis Reed were the heavy hitters off the boards.

Kareem Abdul-Jabbar rises above everyone as we surround him, hoping for the rebound.

Willis Reed challenges Jabbar and tries to get it back at the other end.

It wasn't all scoring for Jerry West.
Sometimes he had to play defense
against Walt Frazier, too.

Our defense has perfect rebounding
position as Willis Reed goes way up
to swat Wilt Chamberlain's shot
away.

Dave DeBusschere's job against the Lakers was to keep Elgin Baylor from hurting us.

Dick Barnett is too elusive and quick for Dick Garrett as he hits a jumper.

We played out the 1968–69 season by losing to the Celtics 4–2. Russell the player-coach went from there to carry his fourth-place team to his 11th and final title.

That's the series that ruptured Russell's long relationship with Chamberlain. They were so close at one time, Russell used to have Wilt over for dinner when the 76ers came to Boston. Their hot rivalry eventually melted the friendship and the championship series was the final blow.

One game did it. Wilt hurt his leg in the seventh game at the Forum. He took himself out. Bill van Breda Kolff, an original 1946 Knick and Bradley's coach at Princeton, was the Laker coach and didn't like it.

When Wilt felt he was okay, he wanted to return for the final minutes. Van Breda Kolff ignored him. They haven't spoken since. Neither have Wilt and Russell, who criticized Chamberlain after the Celtics took the series, 4–3.

As I've said, the 1968–69 playoffs was the last we would see of Russell. His leaving moved us closer to the top. He was, in retrospect, a missing link in our winning the whole thing.

Chamberlain's teams would have been dominant if not for Russell. People always ask which was the better player. I'm not exactly known for getting involved in controversy or argument. I prefer to play it safe.

I've already said it, anyway. What Russell did for defense, Chamberlain did for offense. The thing that separated them was that Russell's teams won 11 times while Wilt's teams won only twice.

Chamberlain dominates the record book. I still consider him the greatest scorer ever though Kareem Abdul-Jabbar owns the statistic: 38,387 points to 31,419.

"I remember Russell very well," recalls Bill Hosket, one of our Minutemen. "We went six and one against Boston in 1968–69. A lot of times it was New York–Boston as the TV Game of the Week. Our team was starting to mold."

Hosket sat and watched most of our final regular season game in 1968–69 in Boston. He finally got his chance. So did Donnie May.

"It's the tail end of the game with all those special lights they put in for color television,'' recalled Hosket. ''Donnie made a steal and Russell's still on the floor. He's back on defense. We must have thrown more passes on that fast break because neither one wanted to shoot it.''

Neither one wanted to challenge Russell and suffer the embarrassment of having the ball stuffed down his throat on national TV. ''I think we gave the ball up more then than in our whole senior year in high school,'' continued Hosket, referring to when he and May were teammates. ''Boom, boom, boom. Back and forth.''

Hosket almost went over the end line with the ball, still refusing to shoot. He finally dealt it back to May. ''He had nothing to do but shoot and he just lays it in and Russell just looks at him,'' said Hosket. ''Nothing. He just stood there looking at both of us. I get the assist and May gets the bucket.''

Now it was playoff time. We beat Baltimore four straight and the Celtics eliminated the Sixers 4–1. Hosket picks up his story from there.

''They come to New York City for the first game of the playoffs. We had the home-court advantage but we were never in that game. They took over from the opening minutes. Here is Russell, a guy that May and I had gotten a layup on a couple of weeks before, and Willis couldn't get a shot off. I can still see Willis running into the corner to shoot. Russell was absolutely phenomenal in that playoff.''

Hosket didn't play with us long. We lost him and May to Buffalo in the expansion draft but his view from the bench was interesting. He came to the Knicks with the 1968–69 season in progress because of the Olympics.

I always roomed our top rookie with Willis. He had the patience and liked it. He knew how to break them in. Hosket explains why Reed was an unusual team leader and why my choice was perfect.

''Rooming with Willis was a great experience for me,'' he said. ''He had such dignity. He was so patient with someone who didn't know the way around the league. I caddied for him. I made sure he got to all the games on time.''

There were some fringe benefits. ''Willis didn't like to eat alone.

He preferred eating in the room,'' said Hosket. ''I said that was fine with me if he bought. He always did. I had to carry his bag and run errands, like all rookies, but he was a great guy.''

Hosket hasn't forgotten the first time in our dressing room. He recalled walking in and seeing May. ''He said: 'Boy, am I glad to see you,' and I said: 'How ya doing?' and he said: 'How am I doing? I'm the worst player on the team. These guys can really play.' ''

That was some greeting from an old high school teammate Hosket hadn't talked to for quite some time. ''I couldn't believe that,'' said the man everyone on the Knicks called Hos. ''I always had a lot of respect for Donnie's ability. He was the Most Valuable Player in the NIT. And Donnie always played with the competition. As tough as the competition was, Donnie always rose to the occasion.''

That was exactly why we drafted May, and Hosket as well. We liked the way they reacted to the caliber of the competition. They were winners on winning teams and that's a trait I always looked for when I was scouting.

While they weren't as good as most of the Knicks we already had, they had the attitude and competitive quality that fit. Hosket learned for himself quickly. Not that he wasn't familiar with most of the players.

We had Bellamy at center when he arrived. We hadn't made the DeBusschere deal yet. ''Bellamy, to me, was the bad guy who played against Jerry Lucas in college,'' recalled Hosket. ''And Bradley is the guy I had gone down to see play in Cincinnati Gardens when he came in there with the Knicks.''

That was in Bradley's rookie year and Hosket, who was from Dayton, was anxious to see him as a pro. So he went to the game with a friend. ''That was the only game that Bradley didn't get in,'' said Hosket. ''I watched him warm up. I watched him shoot but never got to see him play.''

Riordan laughs when he recalls that first game for Hosket in the Garden. Says Mike, ''I was sitting next to him during the introductions and his name was misspelled on the board.''

Hosket recalled that they had put ''Bob Hosket'' on the message board. Riordan says: ''I think there were two mistakes. I think they also spelled it Hoskett with two t's instead of one.''

That was quite a first night. Hosket enjoys a few nice memories, such as the night he was credited with six baskets on five shots. He was on a break with May and tossed a pass that hit someone on the head and bounced into the basket. ''I should have gotten an assist and a basket,'' he insisted later.

The way I see it, Kareem is the top scorer in history but Wilt was the greatest so far. Kareem played six more years, 515 more games and 9,587 more minutes.

Wilt has the most impressive statistic. He averaged 30.1 to Kareem's 20.6. You can hardly turn a page in the NBA Guide without seeing Chamberlain's name. His only weakness was at the free-throw line.

Teams would deliberately foul him. Yet only Jerry West made more free throws than Wilt in a season. West made 840 in 1965–66. Wilt had 835 in 1961–62 and Michael Jordan's best so far has been 833 in 1986–87.

Wilt still shares the record with Adrian Dantley of 28 free throws made in a game. Wilt did it in that 100-point performance March 2, 1962, against the Knicks in Hershey, Pennsylvania.

No one has come close to his stats that night. He was 28-for-32 at the foul line and 36-for-63 from the field. I was scouting for the Knicks but I wasn't at the game.

I was at his first game, though, against the Knicks in the Garden. It was 1959 and Wilt was streamlined then, not the Man Mountain of Muscle he became from lifting weights. I was years younger and my hair not only was redder, but I had some.

Wilt was 23 and still had the body and quickness of the high school track star who used to run the quarter mile. He hit 20-foot jumpers from the top of the key. He wound up with 43 points and 28 rebounds.

Fuzzy Levane was the Knick coach and he turned to me and said: ''You mean we have to face him twelve more times?'' There were only eight teams then so Knick fans got to see Wilt in the Garden six times.

That's another thing that has changed radically. Expansion has limited appearances at the Garden. The Los Angeles Lakers, for example, who established a hot rivalry with the Knicks in our championship era, now come into New York only once a season.

Chamberlain was to carry on long enough to play an important role in our first championship. We closed out 1968–69 in Boston with a sixth and final game for us.

We lost the series in the first game. We had been beating the Celtics by pressing and not giving their offense a chance to get off. We were confident we could keep doing that. We had the home-court advantage. A win in the Garden and we would be home free.

Russell had other ideas, as it turned out. He still had some mileage left in the old machine. He must have changed the battery and spark plugs because he played 48 minutes and we lost 108–100.

We made one good run at them after they got off by 15. We cut it to 78–73 and the Garden was rocking with ''Dee-fense! Dee-fense!'' That was our secret weapon. The fans were our shock troops and they would come to our rescue whenever we were charging.

I remember Frazier saying when it was over: ''When I take thirty-one shots, we can't win. I don't take that many in practice.''

I don't know what happened to us in the second game. When at a loss, say Russell. We were looking for him too much. We weren't loose and hitting the open man. We were, as Hosket says, too aware of Russell's presence under the boards.

We actually missed 30 of 33 shots in one stretch. We were 9-for-47 at the half and lost the second game at the Boston Garden 112–97. We came out of it with only one plus. Cazzie was back.

I managed to give him a little playing time but he wasn't going to be a factor. He was gone too long for his instant offense to have any effect on Russell. We won the third and fifth games at home with the idea we could still win it all.

We might have if Frazier hadn't suffered a groin injury and become practically useless in the final game. We lost by only a point, 106–105. We are sure, as we look back today, we would have won with a little luck.

The fickle fingers of fate cost us a healthy Frazier and Cazzie at crunch time. We might have gone all the way if we had everyone available for the playoffs of 1968–69.

A championship team has to be good and lucky. It can't afford to lose a key player. I don't care how good a team is. The Celtics were a perfect example. They might have had 12 championships in a row if Russell hadn't been hurt in his second one.

Boston won in Russell's first season but lost to the St. Louis Hawks in the next season when he played injured. Pettit, Hagan and Macauley were on the Hawks. They were coached by Alex Hannum and the ballboy was Max Shapiro.

Shapiro was later to make a major contribution to sports. I believe he originated the baseball fantasy camp concept that's so popular. The kind Mickey Mantle and Whitey Ford run in Florida.

I guess that puts Shapiro in the NBA Ballboy Hall of Fame, along with Marv Albert, who used to be a ballboy for the Knicks, and Joe Graboski, the ballboy of all ballboys, who was the only one I know to have played in the NBA.

Graboski was a ballboy for the original Chicago Stags. He played for them from 1948 to 1950, moved to the Indianapolis Olympians for 1951–53 and finished with the Philadelphia Warriors in 1961.

So much for sports trivia. That last game in Boston wasn't trivial. It convinced us that 1969–70 would be our season. Everything fit. We even had Dave Stallworth coming back.

Donovan told me that the night we eliminated the Bullets in the playoffs. Knick fans remember how Dave the Rave had suffered a heart scare late in the 1966–67 season. McGuire was the coach at the time and the team was playing the Warriors in Fresno.

The date was March 7, 1967, to be exact. Stalls complained about a knot in his chest after making a left-handed hook. He saw a doctor in Fresno and nothing was detected. The Knicks went to San Francisco for another game with the Warriors, and Stallworth saw another doctor.

He received the same diagnosis. Nothing detected. McGuire was afraid to play him but the doctor advised Stalls: "You can play. But if you have any sign of distress, get right out."

McGuire played him 11 minutes and took him out when

Stallworth got kicked in the thigh by Nate Thurmond. That was a stroke of luck, as it turned out. When he got back to New York, they discovered that he had had a myocardial infarction.

It was a heart attack and we were frightened for him. He was only 23. There are all kinds of heart attacks. This one turned out to be mild enough for Stalls to return and make a big contribution—especially in the fifth game of the final series with the Lakers when Willis got hurt.

The Knicks had kept him on the payroll while he was recuperating. He had earned the right to be treated as an important part of the team. He was a delightful person, a happy-go-lucky guy always smiling and showing that gold upper front tooth.

There were many times when we thought of Stalls and his heart attack out in Wichita, Kansas, while we were indulging in fun and games. We were given progress reports but we never expected him back.

They had told him he would never play again, but that didn't mean a thing to him. He had too much energy and enthusiasm to quit just like that.

On April 2, 1969, the night we eliminated the Bullets, he dropped into our dressing room. He had come to New York for another examination. He left with Donovan to walk down the hall to the doctor's office.

That's when he learned he could probably play again. The doctor suggested he keep it quiet for a while but Stallworth couldn't. He had to tell someone, so he informed one of our beat writers and it was all over the place.

6

We had come a long way and very fast since the days when Frazier and Bradley were coming off the bench. I remember McGuire saying, at the time he was experimenting: "Just think. I'm sitting between Bradley and Frazier."

Clyde remembers. He reminds me that he and Bradley were roommates for a while. That was before I came in and paired Bradley with DeBusschere.

"No one had any animosity towards Bradley because he was such a nice guy," recalled Frazier. "But he was strange to room with. It was the first time I ever saw a guy sit in front of a TV and never finish a program."

Clyde doesn't know why he was given Bradley. Neither do I. Those were the days when players doubled up. We eventually gave them singles. Today, they probably all have individual suites or own the hotels they stay in.

"Bill would just sit there and keep turning channels," explained Clyde. "It was before the flicker or remote control. He was one of those guys who never watched one program. Just as I got interested in one thing, Bill turned it off. I was too fascinated to ask why he kept switching stations like that."

Those were the things that helped create such great relationships. So were the card games on the planes. Barnett was always the middleman. "I bankrolled him," said Reed.

"Yeah," said Clyde. "I bet Dick still owes him a lot of money.

Barnett's favorite line was he'd pay when his brother straightened out and he was a hunchback."

There was another time when Charlie Pride, the country-western singer, got on the plane. "We were on a flight with him," said Reed. "Barnett was having his usual card game going. I was his personal banker. I always backed him in all his games."

Reed chuckled as he recalled how Barnett always used his favorite line about the hunchbacked brother on him, too. "His brother was never going to straighten out," continued Willis. "Anyway, for some reason, we're going somewhere and we had to make a stop like Oklahoma City. That's when Charlie Pride gets into the card game."

It was poker. I'm sure Jackson was in it with Barnett. They were poker freaks and always started games.

"Well, Charlie Pride talks himself into the game," said Reed. "He won all the time. I guess he was a pretty good player and they'd figured they had a sucker. He said: 'If I didn't have this concert, I'd travel with you all the time. I'd probably make more money.'"

Barnett also was deeply into chess. He had postcard games going on with friends around the country. They'd mail each other moves. He went to Fordham and got a doctorate in economics not long ago.

He was our good-humor man—the life of the dressing room. He liked to tell self-deprecating stories—for example, the one about the time he bought a new Cadillac.

"I drove it to Harlem and parked," Barnett said. "I went around the corner and pretty soon two guys came up and asked if I'd like to buy a set of new tires for a Cadillac. They turned out to be mine."

True or not, a good story. It reminded Frazier of a similar one: "He told us about the time a couple of guys asked if he wanted to buy some nice new shirts cheap. They opened a box and showed him the collars. When he bought them, the only thing in the box was the collars."

Bill Russell ended our season on April 18, 1969. We considered the year exceptional despite being knocked out of the playoffs. We were becoming the toast of the town.

The Jets, however, owned New York at the time. They had just upset the Baltimore Colts and New York went wild. That was the game where Joe Namath predicted the Jets would beat the NFL champions who had the great John Unitas at quarterback. It was some shocker, especially since the merger with the NFL was new and AAC teams were being laughed at.

Later that year, New York did it to Baltimore again when the Mets upset the Orioles in the World Series. Mayor John Lindsay threw a victory party for them at Gracie Mansion to which the Knicks were invited.

I never understood what we were doing there with Tom Seaver, Jerry Koosman, Nolan Ryan, Ron Swoboda and Tommie Agee. We had just started the 1969–70 season. I guess we were window dressing. We were part of the New York sports scene so Mayor Lindsay wanted us there.

We knew we were good. We just didn't know if we were good enough to win the championship. New York had been waiting 23 years for that. That's a long time for emotions to build.

Basketball was the New York City game and the Knicks were the only team that hadn't won a championship. The Yankees, Dodgers, Giants (baseball and football) had all done it. Not the Knicks.

Even New York, which was considered the Sophistication Capital of the World, was ready to explode. We recognized the burden we were carrying from the moment we opened training camp. The whole city was looking at us to do something big.

I had no special rules about reporting to training camp. Remember, this was almost 25 years ago and the conditioning was easy. I would write a letter to each player and tell him he had to be ready the first day he showed up.

No one approached conditioning then as they do today when they even hire special coaches. Players used to lay off all summer and play themselves into shape. Trainers wouldn't let athletes lift weights because they said it would make them muscle-bound.

Today they spend fortunes on weight rooms. They have equipment I can't even spell. Everyone looks like Arnold Schwarzenegger. The only thing I ever picked up was checks.

I remember one time at the annual Maurice Stokes Game at Kutsher's Country Club in Monticello, New York, Jerome Kersey and a Portland teammate had just finished 36 holes of golf after breakfast.

Kersey spotted Danny Schayes lounging at the pool. It was a hot summer day. But Kersey asked Schayes: "Do they have a weight room here?" That's not how I prepared the Knicks.

We didn't even have stretching exercises. I think the only one who did them was Frazier. I wasn't hung up on conditioning like Gallatin. I guess I never forgot what happened to him.

I always told our guys to be in shape when they came in. We were going to do some hard drills and scrimmage right away. I must admit the way they condition players today is better. Of course, the investment in the players is so much greater.

In my playing days, we got into condition by playing. We played a lot of exhibition games when I was with Rochester. If we didn't play a league game, we'd be playing an exhibition someplace. We'd play every night.

Actually, Les Harrison was way ahead of the times. Les took us to universities, where we'd work out every day against the colleges. You were allowed to do that then.

He'd take us to North Carolina State, where Everett Case was. They'd beat the hell out of us because they were in great shape. As we went along, we started to beat the hell out of them. We'd scrimmage every day for two hours and for about a week.

We went to Toledo and Seton Hall when Bobby Davies, my teammate with the Royals, was coaching. We never exercised or indulged in conditioning except play. We didn't even have a shootaround the day of a game as they do today.

I think Bill Sharman started that when he coached the Lakers. They were pretty successful and everyone started doing it. I never thought it was of any value but it got to be a mental thing.

The players got to expect it. If you weren't doing it, you weren't a good coach. You have to keep players happy about certain things. I didn't like the shootaround before the game because I thought it took the edge off the players.

I guess it's okay if you don't get too carried away and work for an hour. That can happen. All of a sudden the coach is yelling and turning it into a full workout.

I was the only coach when we began training camp in 1969–70. I was the only voice. I ran the practices. We'd never heard of assistants.

We had veteran players and I wanted their input. DeBusschere, Bradley, Reed, Frazier and Barnett were very intelligent. Why shouldn't they contribute? They knew something.

I was only dealing with 12 guys. It wasn't like baseball, where there are 25, or pro football, where there are 45. I always told the guys if they knew of a play they liked, we'd put it in. They were my assistants.

"Red was the boss of the defense," said Frazier, looking back. "We'd spend about eighty percent of our time on it. He'd also run the offense and put in plays. But if Bradley or DeBusschere or anyone had any suggestions, he'd listen. Bradley and DeBusschere happened to be very good at it."

I had a lot of free coaches, so why pay for more? I even studied my own films. Now they have a full-time specialist for that. The NBA has grown so huge economically, they can afford it now.

> *"You guys have got to play together, and the guys who don't play that way won't play."*
>
> *—Red Holzman*

DeBusschere was the only player I was concerned about. He always went to camp heavy. I remember Clyde once saying that we were winning because "DeBusschere had come to camp only fifty pounds overweight this year."

He would normally blow up to 260. One summer, when he was with Detroit, he actually came to New York out of shape to fool around in a charity game. He broke his ankle.

He was much more serious when I asked him to come in at 240 for the 1969–70 season. It was 15 pounds less than he'd carried into the Pistons' training camp the year before.

He made it by working with a doctor all summer. He hated training camp. He liked to ease himself into shape. I made sure DeBusschere didn't retain any of his old habits.

The actual start of our camp for everyone was September 13, 1969. There was turmoil all around us. People were still mourning the loss of Rocky Marciano, the retired unbeaten heavyweight champ. Marciano died in the crash of a private plane near Des Moines the day before his 46th birthday with two friends. He had been on a speaking engagement. He was buried in Fort Lauderdale, Florida.

The Mets were on the march to their first World Series and they had just rewarded Gil Hodges with a new contract. Hodges, then 45, had come back from a heart attack the previous season to lead the Mets to first place in their division. They boosted him to $75,000 a year.

A hot war was being waged between the NBA and ABA. There was a report that Sid Borgia, once a top NBA ref but then supervisor of officials for the new league, was raiding the older league. Borgia was said to be close to signing Norm Drucker, John Vanak, Joe Gushue and Earl Strom.

That would have been a coup because the four referees were among the best in the NBA. Commissioner Walter Kennedy fired back with: "They [the ABA] have flatly refused to ever halt for one day, when negotiations are going on, the raiding of players . . . nor consider a moratorium of their anti-trust suit."

There were bigger news stories and headlines. "VP Agnew Raps Integration Busing," read one. Others were: "Middle East: The Brink Again," "Israel and Egypt Exchange Artillery Fire" and "Woman Killed by Terrorists' Bomb in Gaza."

President Nixon announced that at least 35,000 troops would be withdrawn from Vietnam by December 15. And on the home front, Mayor Lindsay was locked in a reelection fight with Democrat Mario Procaccino, who was charged by Lindsay people with conducting a "racist campaign."

That was what was making news when I introduced DeBusschere to my favorite conditioning drill. It was his first camp and I broke him in easy—at least in the morning because it was picture day. It's a ritual that lets the newspapers refill their files with fresh pictures.

Then it was on to the Holzman pickup drill in the afternoon. I had 16 players in camp and split them 8 apiece at the endlines. Each player ran at top speed and picked up a basketball I rolled onto the court. He would have to scoop it on the dead run and finish the play with a layup.

The player then took the ball and flipped it to Dick McGuire, who was on the other side of the court, and he rolled it to a player going the other way. To complicate it we used four basketballs, not one.

I wanted constant action and agony. I wanted the players not in shape to regret it. DeBusschere asked Reed how long the cruel and unusual punishment would go on. Willis told him only about 10 or 15 minutes.

They all survived, as I remember. We were a team that came together quickly. Cazzie was back ready to play and so was Stallworth. John Warren of St. John's was the only rookie in camp destined to make it.

The excitement was there real early. Stallworth epitomized it when he played his first regular season game in the Garden. He got a standing ovation when John Condon, the voice of the Knicks, announced: "Number nine . . . Dave Stallworth."

> *"Ballhandling was to be one of the trademarks of our team that went so far because of its ability to hit the open man."*
>
> —*Red Holzman*

Stalls displayed another of his dimensions we had missed when he said: "I was embarrassed. I didn't expect anything like that. Maybe a generous hand but not that." Modest and humorous.

He had overcome his fears. He had overcome our fears. I didn't pamper him once the team doctor certified he could play without any risk. He was to play all 82 games in his comeback year and was a major part of our quality depth.

I still can't believe how Stallworth came back and what he did for us. I was always a little wary because even the words "heart attack" are scary. Also, the Knicks had already had two experiences with heart conditions and were extremely careful.

Back in the 1950s, the Knicks signed John Gardner of the Harlem Globetrotters. He was a lean and quick power forward. He never played because they discovered he had suffered a silent heart attack somewhere along the way.

Then there was Solly Walker. He was an outstanding forward on the St. John's teams—also in the early 1950s. The Knicks were interested in him. They intended to draft him but he failed the physical because of a heart problem.

I decided to use Stallworth behind DeBusschere. It would be a nice change of pace. DeBusschere would wear you out and then Stalls would come in with his speed and run you ragged.

The authors were already lining up—yes, at training camp. They suspected it was going to be the Knicks' year and how right they were. Truthfully, so did I.

We had a rousing start. We put together a winning streak that every Knick still considers a highlight.

The streak started with Detroit and ended with Detroit. We beat the Pistons 116–92 at their place with superb defense from Reed and DeBusschere.

That game not only started the streak, it helped establish a motive for the rest of the season. It became the trademark of that Knick team to go out and keep the other teams under 100.

"Dee-fense! Dee-fense!" got louder in the Garden every time we played. We really heard it when we beat the Bullets 128–99. It was a one-sided game but the fans were screaming to hold the Bullets under 100.

We failed to hold the Hawks under 100 the next game but we came close. We won 128–104 for three straight. Richie Guerin, then the coach, was impressed with his old team. "When they were up by twenty-five, they applied the pressure on defense, didn't get selfish and played like a team," he said.

I had to remind Frazier not long ago of No. 4 in the streak. It was against San Diego in the Garden. We won another one-sider by 13 and Clyde got 43 points. They raised the roof when I took him out with three minutes left after he had scored 23 in the second half.

It was the first time he had gone over 30 in a regular season game. I told him I was sorry for not putting him back when the fans chanted for him. "That's all right, Red. I missed enough shots out there," he told me.

Someone suggested he was supposed to be the Knicks' passer. "Red says I'm supposed to hit the open man. Well, tonight I was the open man," he responded. He talked as sharply as he dressed. That's why the writers flocked to him after our games.

Next was our first regular season game against Alcindor. In fact, it was back to back: first in the Garden and then in Milwaukee. We won a squeaker 112–108 at home with Bradley's two free throws clinching it.

It was all Reed for six in a row the next night. Willis muscled the 7–2 rookie Milwaukee center into a terrible performance. Reed overpowered Alcindor for four baskets in one stretch and outscored him 35–17—which only shows that size doesn't mean everything.

Reed was almost six inches shorter and couldn't jump over Alcindor, so he went around or shot over him. "He's too big but I don't concentrate on him anyway," said Willis, adding: "We needed the ballgame."

That's what made that Knick team special. Everyone was capable of stepping up when we needed a game. They were all in tune now. Every game became like one big symphony orchestra playing Carnegie Hall. Never a sour note.

There was almost a fight that night. Riordan challenged Alcindor after taking an elbow in the face from him. Then another Milwaukee player went for Mike and Reed stepped in.

Willis informed everyone that if there was going to be any fighting he'd do it. So much for that. Riordan broke up everyone by saying: "They should've let me take a punch at Lew. I just would've hit him in the hip."

Phoenix was next and No. 7 was easy. We ran into our old friend Dick Van Arsdale as well as Connie Hawkins and won 116–99. Gail Goodrich incited the Phoenix crowd by getting tossed and we paid for it. We were showered with hot dogs, ice cream cones and coins. The only thing I regretted was I like my hot dogs with sauerkraut.

So much for the peace and quiet of a retirement area. Hawkins had 39 points, 17 from the foul line. It was on to San Diego and No. 8. Another easy one. People were beginning to expect us to win big.

Winning on the road has always been tough but we beat the Rockets 129–111. Los Angeles was our next stop and we loaded the plane with pizzas from our favorite restaurant, Casa del Baffa.

First there was bad news. A newspaperman informed us after the San Diego game that Chamberlain had ripped up a knee and was facing surgery. They had to repair tendons that tore away from his kneecap.

He faced a serious operation, especially for a huge guy like Chamberlain whose knees supported 275 pounds. They had to reconstruct the knee area and strengthen it. What a crippling blow to the Lakers.

It was early November and the doctors said it was impossible for Wilt to come back that season. They didn't know Wilt. He said he would return. Guess who was right? He arrived back in time for the championship series with us in April.

Frazier knew it all the time. ''He's trying to psyche us with that story about coming back so fast,'' was his response to Wilt's prediction. ''He sounds like General MacArthur with that 'I shall return' business. But if I know Wilt, he'll probably be back fast. He's probably practicing his free throws right now in bed.''

Joe Mullaney was the Laker coach and he used Rick Roberson against us as we went for nine straight. He was a 6'9" rookie center who hardly played because of Wilt but he made an immediate impact. On DeBusschere's nose, that is. Roberson broke it during a rebound battle.

DeBusschere passed out. His nose was squashed and he was bleeding badly. He almost fainted again when Dr. Robert Kerlan, the Lakers' team doctor, tried to push it back into shape.

''DeBusschere was the kind of guy who would almost faint when his nose broke,'' says Frazier. ''Reed had his nose broke many times but he'd go to the bench and tell Danny to shove it back into place and he'd go right back and play.''

Willis had great tolerance for pain, I guess because he had so much of it. DeBusschere was tough but pain was the only thing I knew that could overcome him. He spent the rest of the game listening to us win 112–102 on the car radio heading for the hospital.

Willis scored 35 and had 16 rebounds. Barnett pressed West into 13 misses on 18 tries but Jerry hit 18 in a row from the foul line. And DeBusschere had his nose twisted back into place after Dr. Kerlan gave him a shot to kill the pain.

DeBusschere wore a grotesque safety contraption for a while to protect his new nose and good looks. He had an aluminum splint covering the nose and tape all over his face. I think it was Barnett (who else?) who told Dave: ''You never looked better in your life,'' when he showed up for our next game in San Francisco.

We were nine in a row and counting. DeBusschere was remarkable. He was very good despite the handicap. He had a sensational second half: 16 of 24 game points and 10 of his 12 rebounds. Not bad for a guy who could hardly see.

Bradley paid his roomie this tribute after the game: ''He sleeps quieter now. He used to snore. It's the only reason I'm glad he has a broken nose.''

We won 116–103 but that wasn't the big news that night. The Royals had traded Jerry Lucas to the Warriors. They now had some front line with Lucas, Nate Thurmond and Clyde Lee. They also were in a position to trade Lucas to us later.

We were 15–1 coming home and people started to run to the record books. Another win and we would tie the best start in NBA history. The Warriors had been the only team to beat us and we had just taken care of them on their court.

That one defeat in the Garden looks so much bigger today. Otherwise we would have won our first 26 that season. It would have been another well-deserved tribute to a group of players who revolutionized the way team basketball was played in the NBA.

Red Auerbach didn't seem to think the Knicks were so great. He said we were lucky. I assumed he was basing it on the Celtics' having won 11 titles while we hadn't won one, yet.

He didn't think we had accomplished much after we beat the Bulls 114–99 at home to tie the record. It had been set by the 1948 Washington Caps, who were coached by Auerbach.

> *"Boston games are like heavyweight championship fights, people can't wait until the buzzer rings."*
>
> *—Walt Frazier*

Auerbach had remnants when he accompanied the Celtics to the Garden for our game. Henry Finkel was no Bill Russell, while John Havlicek, Jo Jo White and someone named Don Nelson failed to stop us. We held the Celtics under 100 and won 113–98.

We were dominating. Our defense was making the most noise but also we were shooting almost 50 percent. Remember, all five of our starters hit from outside.

A writer asked why the Knicks were shooting so well. I gave him one of my better ad-libs: "How the hell should I know?" I don't know any coach who can claim credit for his players' shooting well.

Cincinnati was next at home. There was trouble on the team. The Royals had existed on the talent of Lucas and Oscar Robertson. Now

Lucas was gone and there were rumblings that the Big O was unhappy with the coach, who happened to be Bob Cousy.

Oscar wanted to leave. He was a future Hall-of-Famer but had never won a championship. He was 32 and couldn't see that happening unless he played with a team that had a super center. It seems to be the same thing Charles Barkley was saying in Philadelphia before he was traded.

Oscar was to find a pretty good center in Milwaukee the next season. He teamed with Kareem to win the 1971–72 title. Then Kareem gave the Bucks a trade-me-or-lose-me ultimatum that landed him in Los Angeles. So much for a Milwaukee dynasty.

Oscar was to Milwaukee what DeBusschere was to the Knicks: the missing link. That was the season after Cousy had been given the job of breathing new life into a Cincinnati franchise in serious trouble.

It was survival time, a time for radical ideas, and Cousy came up with a surprising one right away. He would play as well as coach.

Cousy applied for reinstatement as a player. He had retired in 1963 and was 41 when the 1969–70 season started. One thing held it up. Auerbach claimed the Celtics still owned the rights to Cousy and wouldn't give them up for nothing. He insisted on compensation.

Cousy had to get an official release from the Celtics to be eligible to play. He explained it this way: ''I sent Arnold a telegram and a copy to the Commissioner's office. He [Auerbach] is supposed to send me a contract. I want to know when I'm supposed to become a free agent so I can negotiate [as a player].

''I want to play for two reasons. One emotional. We're trying to build a new image and we're trying to excite the fans and, I'm not being egotistical, I think I can draw some people. The other reason is I think I can help the team by playing four or six minutes a game while Oscar is resting. Like a relief pitcher role.''

He did announce he had activated himself the day of the Royals game with us. It wouldn't take too long for the Knicks to discover what Cousy had in mind as a player. However, it wasn't the night we beat the Royals 112–94 for 13 in a row.

After that game, I was asked what was wrong with Oscar. He was the ultimate ballhandler but the other guys were doing it. Something strange was going on.

I discreetly ducked that fast one. I had enough trouble answering my own coaching questions. So they went to one of their favorite Knick spokesmen and Frazier responded.

"He was never in the game," said Clyde, referring to the Big O.

"They're not playing their style of ball," said Reed, another of our top spokesmen.

Cousy didn't get into uniform that night. He was waiting for a spot that was soon to come. We headed for Philadelphia and a 76er team that had finished second ahead of us the previous season.

The Sixers still had a strong nucleus of Billy Cunningham, Luke Jackson, Hal Greer and Matty Guokas—yes, that Matty Guokas who became coach of the expansion Orlando team. We escaped by the skin of my balding head.

We won 98–94 but were leading by only two with five seconds left. Jack Ramsey was the coach and he called time. Cunningham had just scored a big basket, so I told our players to watch him and Greer. It was purely coincidental that they were the 76ers' best scorers.

I always admired Ramsey as one of the smartest coaches in the game. He figured we would be looking for Cunningham on a variation of the play on which he had just scored.

So Jack used Billy as a decoy. He faked as though coming for the pass-in but set a pick for Greer. He almost got away with it.

There was a third coach on the floor—DeBusschere. He spotted Darrall Imhoff lining up differently than on Cunningham's scoring play.

DeBusschere told Bradley to watch the middle for the screen. His roomie dropped off Guokas as soon as the pass was made and helped double-team Greer. He missed and Reed wrapped it up with two free throws after grabbing the rebound.

It was a tough one for the 76ers, who were 5–11 at the time, while we were now 19–1. They accused the refs of stealing one for not calling a foul against Barnett on Greer's shot. They were bewildered by the way we had read their last play.

DeBusschere guessed right. We were a thinking man's team in every respect. Still, Cunningham couldn't believe it and said: "How did DeBusschere know that? It was the first time we ever used that play. He's a sneak. He goes down and listens in our huddle. He's cheating."

Cunningham was kidding but it hurt—the Sixers, not us. We were now three games away from equaling the record but no one was talking about it. Players can be superstitious that way.

Not the writers—they were getting excited. The fans were getting excited. My butcher was getting excited. The Knicks?

"We thought we'd never lose again," recalled Frazier. "Everyone expected us to win big," said DeBusschere, also looking back at the Knicks' hottest streak.

Why not? We spoiled everyone by making it 15 straight 128–114 over Phoenix in the Garden. I began feeling like a push-button coach.

We were frisky as colts while we were making everyone feel old or older. Connie Hawkins, then an NBA rookie, went 40 minutes against us and said: "My ankles, my arms, my wrists and even my face is tired."

This time it was Reed, DeBusschere and Barnett doing the damage. Willis had 15 rebounds and 37 points against Neal Walk, then a rookie, and once leveled Paul Silas on a slam dunk. DeBusschere had a season-high 25 and Barnett contributed a career-high 12 assists.

We were one away from tying the record when we beat the Lakers 103–96 in the Garden. It was to be the Roberson-DeBusschere rematch but Rick was hurt and didn't play. He had to sit on the bench in uniform because there were only seven healthy Lakers and a minimum of eight players had to dress.

West almost ruined us, naturally. He only got 41 points and we had to come from behind to win. We had really spoiled the fans. Some actually booed when the Lakers went ahead by six in the third quarter.

We headed for Atlanta and the Georgia Tech gym the Hawks used in those days. That was always a rough place because there never were any New York fans there. It's been enemy territory ever since General Sherman marched through Georgia, I guess.

Only the Frazier family rooted for us. He was from Atlanta and his mom led the "Hey, June" shouts from one small area of the stands. He was Walt Frazier, Jr., therefore "Hey, June."

Otherwise, the people didn't like the Knicks from the last picture. They never forgot a brawl in which Reed swung at everyone who threatened him. It wound up with Bowman and Bill Bridges wrestling into the floor seats.

"I heard about it but I wasn't on the team when they had that," said DeBusschere. "I was," said Bradley. "It was November 1968. I was there. Bridges and Willis. What happened was some fans grabbed Bowman and started hitting him. It was Bridges and Willis in the major event. The other events were look out, I might hit somebody."

That was the background as we visited a year later. For the first time since the streak started, I noticed the players were tense. They realized they were a step from NBA history. It was the dressing-room mood of the playoffs, although only our 25th game into the season.

I couldn't help noticing the difference because our players always were relaxed and kidding each other before the games. Both sides knew this was a special game because of the streak.

No team ever wants to be a contributor to any streak. The Hawks were also motivated by the background of our heated games. Bridges informed Barnett of the Hawks' intentions when they met before the game in the toilet the teams shared.

"You guys aren't going to set any records against me tonight," he warned Barnett. "Why not?" said Barnett. "Aren't you playing?"

"Let's go get 'em," yelled Frazier. Boy, did he get 'em.

"I remember that," Bradley said to me when we met to reminisce. "It was in the old Georgia Tech Fieldhouse."

DeBusschere interrupted Bradley. "I remember Clyde was very

effective," he said. "But if I'm not mistaken, I thought Barnett did a helluva job on Joe Caldwell. He wouldn't let Caldwell touch the ball."

I never saw a second half like that one. The Hawks couldn't get the ball past midcourt. We kept stealing it. I sent Riordan, Stallworth and Cazzie into a close game and they opened it to 66–61 at the half.

DeBusschere was sitting but he remembered one particular play. He almost fell off the bench when Stalls bounced a perfect pass between a Hawk player's legs to Cazzie, who bounced the ball to Willis for a jam.

What a coach. Then came the third period, a defensive dream. All the hours we had put in on defense came together. I've never seen anything like it. We outscored the Hawks 32–5 in the last nine minutes of the quarter.

Clyde was in a revolving door. We were pressing all over and the ball always seemed to land in his hands. He'd grab it, head for the basket and we'd score. He'd run back, get to midcourt and there he was going the other way again.

"I remember saying to Walt Hazzard: 'Dammit. Hold onto the damn ball. I'm getting tired,'" recalled Frazier, who is now on the Knicks' broadcasting team.

We won 138–108 and the Hawks were shell-shocked. "That's the most embarrassing twelve minutes I've ever spent as a player or coach," said Guerin. "Frazier showed the best individual effort and the Knicks the best team effort I've ever seen. That Frazier stole everything but our jocks."

That was when Guerin challenged Komives after the game, saying: "You're a tough guy, you want to fight, well, fight me."

"Richie was a tough guy," Bradley added.

Guerin was fearless. He let everyone know he'd be intimidated by no one. Joe Lapchick, who played with the original Celtics before he turned to coaching, used to say: "They ask you the question right away and, if you don't give the right answer, you're in trouble."

They asked Guerin the question as soon as he came into the league. He answered with two wild-swinging fights. One was a brutal battle with Bill Sharman. The other was with Adolph Schayes, who had a cast on a broken right wrist and used it as club.

"The best fight I'd ever seen—well, it wasn't really a fight," said DeBusschere. "The best punch I've ever seen. I was in Detroit my rookie year. Ray Felix, God rest his soul, who had been with the Knicks, was finishing in LA." DeBusschere stopped to laugh. "This was in sixty-two. Coming off the floor after the game. Nothing's going on during the game, you don't see anything. I was walking right behind Walter Dukes as he's going to our locker room."

It's important to remember that Felix and Dukes were Knick teammates at one time.

"Ray comes past me . . . here comes Felix . . . taps Wally on the shoulder, Wally turns around and Ray goes boom! Down Wally goes and Felix turns around and walks away."

I asked DeBusschere what was it all about.

"Dukes gets up and walks to the locker room," he explained. "I said to him: 'What the hell happened?' and he said: 'Ah, he was ticked off because I stole his girlfriend from him.' And that was the end of it."

Dukes was a character. One time he traveled to Europe with the Harlem Globetrotters. They went on their usual tour and wound up back in Paris. They all left from there except Dukes.

He never made the plane, so he had to pay his own fare back. Abe Saperstein asked how come he missed the plane and Dukes explained he had to wait for his clothes to come back from the tailor.

Another time, when he was with the Knicks, I believe, some thieves broke into the trunk of his car. He filed a claim for 9 or 10 trench coats. Can you imagine the cops looking for someone trying to peddle trench coats for a seven-footer? He wound up as an attorney.

On to the Cincinnati Royals and our attempt to break the record. We left Atlanta for Cleveland, where the game was to be played. That indicates how poorly the Royals were drawing at home.

Of course, when the Royals scheduled the game, they had no idea they would be involved with a New York team creating so much excitement. There's no doubt they would have played the game at home—which, as it developed, might have given the Royals just enough of an edge to prevent us from winning.

We had our Thanksgiving turkey dinner in Cleveland, the day before the game. That's one of the penalties you pay in sports. While everyone is at home for the holidays, you are on the road somewhere thinking of home.

Danny Whelan did his usual nice job of arranging dinner for the players and the press traveling with us. It was cozy and warm. Just one big, happy family.

November 28, 1969, was our date with history. DeBusschere recalls being worried about the game. "Oscar can go one-on-one and kill us," he told Bradley.

I was worried about the players not being in a mood to play.

It was the perfect situation for a letdown. I know I never felt like playing a road game on a holiday. The arena itself wasn't inspiring. It was the same broken-down place the Cleveland Rebels used as one of the pioneer teams. I also felt that a lot of our energy was left in Atlanta after our incredible third quarter.

I was right. We got off to a very bad start. We were playing in slow motion and the Royals were off to a seven-point lead at the quarter. I had to change the pace of the game, so I sent in the Minutemen—Stallworth, Cazzie and Riordan.

They were always hungry to play. I never had to motivate them. They were the heart of a tough bench. People always seem to forget that when they evaluate what that 1969–70 team accomplished.

Those three missed only 4 of 16 shots and we led 55–52 at the half. I went back to DeBusschere, Reed, Bradley, Frazier and Barnett and they still were on empty. DeBusschere remembers how I yanked him entering the fourth quarter.

We were, again, losing by 78–77 and he had made only one basket. I had never seen him so futile. I didn't send DeBusschere back until late in the final quarter. The Royals were still leading but I wasn't going to lose with one of my best players on the bench.

I'll let the players take the dramatics from there. It was their ball game so they are entitled to explain how they overcame a five-point lead in the final 16 seconds.

"I thought we played a very listless game for a team that was going for that kind of record," recalled DeBusschere. "We just weren't in the game. We were flat."

"It was that arena," said Bradley. "It wasn't exactly an arena. It was like playing in an old 'Y.' The locker room was dark, cold. This arena was about fifty years old. And the hotel across the street was one of the worst."

It wasn't very inspirational. They didn't have fancy scoreboards. They didn't have animated TV message boards. They didn't even have any rooting interest, which surprised us when 10,348 showed up for a neutral-site game. What didn't surprise us was that most of the fans were for Cincinnati.

Actually, the only thing exciting about the game was the finish. The first thing that comes to mind was that we were trailing 101–98 with 1:49 left. Cousy put himself in when Oscar Robertson fouled out after killing us with 33 points.

I remember how Cousy stood in front of the bench and looked at his players. He was searching for someone who was suitable for that critical moment.

The guy Cousy was looking for turned out to be himself. He had the courage to put himself into a game that was on the line. He had been away for many years but the first thing he did was hit Norm Van Lier with a cross-court pass that led to a jumper.

"What was the situation? We were six points down with about a minute to go?" asked Bradley, indicating what time can do to anyone's memory. I reminded him we were losing 105–100 with 27 seconds to go.

It became a five-point game because we fouled Cousy to stop the clock and he stepped up and made 2-for-2. I still don't believe it. But that's the kind of player he was—great in the clutch. His hand never shook.

We made him pay for it, though. "What I remember is bad. What I remember is he makes some mistakes," said Bradley. "He

[Cousy] has not played the whole game. So he puts himself in and he's the guy who throws the in-bounds pass. It's intercepted.''

Every little thing becomes big in a situation like that. Every play, every tick of the clock is huge. Reed, for example, looked like he saved a ball going out of bounds but the officials ruled he stepped on the line.

That was the possession that led to Cousy's two free throws. We rushed the ball downcourt and Reed was hit by Tom Van Arsdale on a jumper. That put the Royals over the foul limit and Willis had three chances to make two.

That was the rule in those days. We needed two from Willis to give us some shot at a tie. He missed the first but made the next two just as we were about to die. Nothing ever rattled him. We were back within three with 16 seconds on the clock.

Cousy took the ball out and we pressed him. We kept everyone from meeting the ball so he had to call his last time-out—a smart move under the circumstances.

Now Cousy could set up a play and, as well, pass the ball in at midcourt. That pushed us farther away from our basket, which is always a coaching consideration with little time left. We both used the time-out to set up our strategy.

We were ready for the situation. We always did our homework in practices. We were prepared for anything and everything. I didn't need to sketch the plays or the moves on paper like they do today. All we did was review assignments in the huddle or discuss a variation. That was it.

I didn't have to draw X's and O's for Reed, DeBusschere, Bradley, Frazier and Barnett. I simply reminded them to overplay everybody. The idea was to close off the passing lanes and steal the ball if possible.

Cousy was thinking with us. He put Connie Dierking, his tallest man, back in. He figured we would be overplaying, so he wanted Dierking as an escape for a lob pass should he get stuck.

I put Riordan in to press Cousy because Mike was quick and active enough to bother the pass-in.

"I was guarding Van Arsdale," said DeBusschere. "I figured if

Cousy lobbed the ball over my head, Frazier was overplaying Van Lier and he'd pick it off.''

As I was saying, those were the things we worked on in practice, so we knew what to do in any game. I didn't have to draw diagrams and tell them "You go here, you go there and you stay here."

DeBusschere knew exactly what he had to do. He said: "Whoever the guard was went the other way and Van Arsdale came running up from the forward position. I saw Cousy was in trouble. I knew he only had about another second to throw the ball in."

Reed had cut off any pass to Dierking, so Cousy flipped a bounce-pass toward Van Arsdale. It was all he could do.

"I took a chance. I cut between him and Van Arsdale," said DeBusschere.

DeBusschere stole the ball and put us within one point. "If Cousy had delayed just a fraction, my momentum would have carried me past him and over midcourt," he said.

Cousy figured his five seconds were running out. Little things like that are what history is made of.

With six seconds to go, it was 105–104. I didn't have to wave everyone to move up on defense but I did. I had to make my small contribution to history.

Cousy got the pass in this time and Van Arsdale dribbled upcourt. All he wanted to do was eat up some clock by getting the ball past midcourt and we would have to foul. He never made it. He was triple-teamed before he got there.

DeBusschere was right with him. Reed moved over and so did Frazier. I think it was Willis who knocked the ball loose. I know Clyde picked it up and drove for the basket.

"I could have passed to DeBusschere but I was afraid of the clock," said Frazier. He stopped at the top of the key for a jumper and missed. It bounced right back to him and he missed again.

"A bad shot. They win the game on a bad shot," was the way the Big O described it when it was over. Maybe. From his place on the bench, Oscar could see that Frazier might've had time to drive closer for a better shot.

It all became academic when Van Arsdale fouled Frazier on his second miss. Clyde had a 3-for-2 with two seconds to go. "I had to make them both and I did," he said. "The first was the tough one. When I made it, I clenched my fist and said: 'Whew!' It was some relief."

It also was a tie game. He was Mr. Cool when he made the second and put us ahead by one. Now all we had to do was press and keep the Royals from matching our miracle. Everyone on the bench was thinking: "No mistakes now."

The Royals made it, again. Reed stole the pass-in. The bench went wild. It was over. Wait a minute. Not yet.

You know what I remember about that game? Willis got the ball and I thought he fouled the guy. For some reason, Willis took a shot. It was a reflex action but he barreled into Van Lier. He hammered Van Lier with his knee and Norm went flying onto his back.

It was an obvious foul. Everyone froze. It was like pressing the pause button on your VCR remote control. Confusion reigned. I panicked. "Why did he do that? The game is over. He puts his knee right into the guy's chest. Go home. Take the money and go," I say to this day.

Reed remembers. "We won the game but I think that was a mistake. I shouldn't have shot." He laughed when he thought of it. "In my mind, I thought the game was basically over. That's the reason why I shot it. There could have been an offensive foul called. They could have gotten possession."

There was confusion. Someone pointed to the game clock. There was a double zero. Bob Wolff, our TV commentator, was telling the audience back home: "Hold it! Hold it!" He finally informed everyone on hold back in New York: "It's over! The Knicks win one-oh-six to one-oh-five!"

"I knew I screwed up," said Reed, forgetting the plays he had made to save the game. "I'm looking and hoping there's no more time, causing us to lose the game and the record."

Everyone was elated when it was over. "I remember all of us running off very jubilantly," said Frazier. "'Let's get out of here before they change their minds.'"

He was kidding but I remember an exhibition the Knicks played with Philadelphia when I was scouting. We had won and were in our dressing room when the refs called us back. There had been some mistake. The game went into overtime and we lost.

That's the only time in my memory when a team lost a game it had won. "That's the most unbridled I ever saw that Knick team," said Frazier, recalling the record-breaker. "We acted like high school kids after that win. Normally, we were very professional. When we won a game, we showed very little emotion."

It was strange to see those Knicks act like that. By then winning was a habit. We never expected to lose no matter how bad it looked. Frazier calls it the greatest emotional moment of that Knick team.

"Everyone was hugging each other running into the locker room," he said. "Even in the two championships, we never displayed that kind of emotion. We weren't that excited. It was amazing."

Frazier was reminded of the closing seconds of the seventh game with the Lakers for the first title. Everyone on the bench was up and erupted when it was over. "We were drained," said Frazier, referring to the starters. "There wasn't much left after that. When we ran into the locker room, we weren't as jubilant as that game in Cleveland."

He said the 18-game celebration was like his high school days at David T. Howard in Atlanta. "It was out of character for that team," he said. "We were so unflappable. The guys were old pros."

That record streak doesn't look like much now. Milwaukee won 20 straight the next season and the Lakers went wild for 33 in 1971–72. I think that's like Wilt Chamberlain's 100-point game and Joe DiMaggio's 56-game streak.

I can't see anyone winning 34 in a row. But that's what I thought about 17 in a row when we broke the record. Remember, Babe Ruth's 60 homers looked unbeatable before another Yankee named Roger Maris came along.

We still cherish that 18-game streak and consider it one of the highlights of an extraordinary year. We had a game in the Garden the next night and I will never forget the reception we received.

I don't know how long it lasted but it seemed like forever.

Komives and Bellamy were back in the Garden for the first time and they couldn't believe it. The Detroit players were looking around and wondering why their fans didn't treat them this way.

There's only one answer to that: You must be a winner.

Which we weren't that night. We lost. We had our 19th straight in sight but the Pistons outscored us 35–20 in the final quarter and beat us.

Bellamy and Komives had their revenge but I still wouldn't trade DeBusschere for them.

Our fans gave us another standing ovation when it was certain the Pistons were ending our streak. They started it before the final buzzer and finished a minute or so after the game had ended. It was their way of showing their appreciation for what we had accomplished.

It was only the beginning but we had a solid grasp on everyone's attention. We had played only 25 games and were leading the Bullets by 6 games with our 23–2 record.

We ran it up to 26–3 before we lost again. By then we were the hottest thing in sports. We were in every magazine but *Playboy*. Even Auerbach was convinced.

He prefaced his quick reevaluation by mentioning we hadn't done anything yet. He meant win a championship. "They can go to the end and if Willis Reed gets hurt, what have they won?" he pointed out.

Then he got positive. "Right now, I don't know of any center more valuable than Reed," he said, which was nice of him since he had passed on Willis in the draft. "He does everything that has to be done. He rebounds. He shoots. He's the leader out there. He's a fantastic athlete. He's a superstar."

I couldn't have put it better. Those were the very things I had noticed in Willis when I was scouting him. He was even more than that to me once I became the coach.

I used Reed to reach the players because of his leadership

qualities. He was my shock absorber. I would get on him. He was the captain and the best player, so I created a team balance by showing the others that Willis wasn't getting preferential treatment.

I wasn't taking any chances. I knew Willis from the first time I scouted him at Grambling. I knew he wouldn't get angry if I picked on him. He had the temperament. He was not a prima donna.

Frazier was next on Auerbach's list. "Frazier is what I call a complete ballplayer," he said. "He's a fine passer. Not great but good. He's a wonderful defensive player. He gets people jittery by guarding them. They don't have a guy who's going to be blocking shots but they've got a scrambling type of defense that enhances Frazier."

> *"You know Clyde. It's his show. It's his ball; he just [lets] us play with it once in a while."*
>
> *—Willis Reed*

Clyde was our quarterback. He was a natural quarterback, having played that position in high school. He became our key man once he captured the rhythm of the game.

"I was his key man, all right," said Frazier. "You know how you walk out of the hotel rooms without leaving your key. Well, Red played this little game of putting his key in your pocket and saying: 'You're my key man.' I was his key target."

There had to be some levity. You can't expect players to handle the tough talk if they don't respect you. A sense of humor makes people understand there is a human side and softens the serious part of the business.

Yes, I had to yell at times but I couldn't have gotten away with it if I hadn't worked at creating mutual respect. I was dealing with adults who were star athletes and expected to be treated like men, not kids.

I was fortunate to have a group of players who understood there was a time for fun and a time for business. It's amazing how so many different personalities blended so well.

They were the jewels and I was the little old watchmaker. They recognized and accepted my message of intent on my first day. I made it very clear what I had in mind for them and myself.

A team can't win unless its members show respect for each other—for instance, by being on time and treating everything with importance. I wanted the Knicks to start recognizing all the things it takes to become a winning team such as discipline, unselfishness and total dedication during business hours.

Auerbach understood that's what it took for his great teams. It can be more than just outstanding talent. That's what Red had begun to recognize in the Knicks as we started to dominate the league.

His new look at us continued: "DeBusschere is a tower of strength. He makes few mistakes." I considered that an accurate but far too short analysis of DeBusschere and what he did for the Knicks. He was the catalyst who accelerated our dramatic change into a championship team.

He took many shots for us on a nose that was broken seven times in his long playing career but it never changed his attitude. "I had my nose broken in college, I had it broken when I played with the Pistons, I had it broken by my daughter," he remembered. "Roberson's was the worst. He put my nose on the side of my face."

He had only one nose to give the team. On the other hand, his fondest memories of his baseball and basketball days were with the Knicks—no contest.

His baseball career was brief. Two years in the minors and two years with the White Sox. I don't know how many people remembered he pitched in Yankee Stadium.

"I faced the good players that were there in the early '60s. Mantle, Maris," he recalled. "I know they never hit any homers," he proudly added. "I probably walked them."

He is not on Maris's 1961 record list of 61 home-run pitchers. He pitched against Jim Bouton in the Stadium. "I remember batting against him. I know I didn't get a hit. That's all I remember," he said.

He considered the blanking of the home-run bats of Maris and Mantle his supreme baseball accomplishment. "Mantle and Maris weren't like Harmon Killebrew," he adds. "It seems every time I faced him he hit one. He listed his ten longest home runs one time and I was in there twice. Two years of pitching and I was in there twice.''

DeBusschere said the Knicks were special players for a special time. They were champions but not arrogant. Clyde and Cazzie were flamboyant in their own way but that never disturbed the chemistry of the team.

''The critical thing with the team was that everyone had a lot of personal pride rather than egos. There was no arrogance,'' he pointed out. ''They thought very highly of themselves, which is good and you should. The consensus of what the team was all about was we were more afraid to lose because that was more embarrassing. It's the old saying: 'Losers are afraid to win and winners are afraid to lose.' ''

We were lucky in that respect. Our players had enormous pride but were totally unselfish. We didn't have an ego that had to be satisfied. It had to be massaged a little but that was part of the game. Everyone needed it yet everyone had to be treated differently.

Back to Auerbach. On Bradley, he said: ''He was one of the great passers in college and, when I said that, people didn't believe me. He's proved what I said. He's done everything.''

Finally, on Barnett: ''Everyone figured he was the type of guy who would concern himself only with what he scored but he's fit right in.''

As for the Minutemen, our bench, Auerbach put it this way: ''They have so many people.'' Put them all together and the Knicks had become not only the best and smartest team but the most exciting draw in the NBA.

People around the league came not just to see our interesting style of team basketball, they came to see us beaten. That's what happens to the heavyweight champs and we were on the way to becoming that very early in 1969–70.

We went to play the Bullets, for example, and we were greeted with ''Kick the Knick'' buttons. We had become a crusade—especially in Baltimore because of what the Jets and Mets had done to its teams.

Our players grabbed some of the buttons and put them on their uniforms in the dressing room. A few wanted to flaunt them on the floor but I wouldn't let them. I took all NBA games seriously and didn't believe in demeaning the sport. Besides, who needed Baltimore to become madder at us New Yorkers than it already was?

I wanted the players to concentrate on the game because it's a game of concentration. The winners have it, the losers don't. We showed that when we set the record in Cleveland. We never would have won if we hadn't focused on the last few critical seconds.

We also learned for the thousandth time that no lead is safe in pro basketball. That went for our team and all the others. We proved it once more when the Bullets zoomed 13 points ahead early in the game on their court.

It was a typical Knicks-Bullets battle. We had the added motivation of those Kick the Knick buttons and they were carrying the honor of a city humiliated by New York in baseball and football. Also, we were two young teams fighting to lead the NBA into a new era with Bill Russell gone.

Thus, a relatively insignificant game so early in the season was another war between us. Our shock troops turned it around and eventually won it for us. Someone on the Bullets helped with an awful mistake. He got Reed mad.

I already had removed Bradley, DeBusschere and Barnett for Cazzie, Stallworth and Riordan when we fell behind. I was about to send in Bowman for Reed when a Baltimore player jammed Willis's finger.

It was an accident but Willis got angry. He scored six points, grabbed four rebounds and stole two passes just like that. That's what I mean by concentration. That's when I sent in Bowman to let Whelan treat Reed's finger.

We were within six at the half and won 116–107. It was our seventh straight over the Bullets, our closest competition and rival in those days. It was a solid win on their court that put the city of Baltimore in an even deeper depression.

"Their bench brought them back and I was amazed," observed the Bullets' coach Gene Shue, who had played for the Knicks at one time. I wasn't amazed because I was convinced we were that good. There simply were some teams that were late finding it out.

We went to 26–2 against Milwaukee the next night at home. We had reached another milestone because the 1966–67 Philadelphia 76ers had gotten off to a similar start on their way to a record 68 wins.

Our whole team talked about streaks after the game. Warren, our Quiet Man, stopped everyone with this contribution: "I was four-and-ten at Far Rockaway High and then two-and-twelve."

That Sixer team was voted the best in NBA history because of its 68–32 finish, though the 1971–72 Lakers were to set the 69–31 record that still stands. Both teams had one common denominator: Wilt Chamberlain.

His name always pops up in the history of the league. That's why I can't say enough about him. I wonder why people minimize his contributions simply because Russell won more titles. Wilt is still the most powerful force the game has ever seen.

He was an outstanding all-around athlete whose one regret was that he could never compete in the Olympic decathlon. Pro football teams drooled at the thought of him playing for them. One offered him the opportunity to be a goaltender: Stand in front of the goalposts and swat away field goals.

They even discussed a heavyweight championship fight with Muhammad Ali. "It was serious," Wilt reminds those who might think otherwise. "They talked about a million dollars for me. My father told me to forget it and work on my foul shooting."

I believe that everyone has been so carried away by Wilt's size and strength, they've overlooked the quality of his game. I never saw him play in high school or college. My experience with him began when he came into the league with Philadelphia. He was the Stilt then.

I know he prefers to be called the Dipper. Anything you want, Dipper. He was never given enough credit for his knowledge of the game. He was a real basketball player, not a scoring freak or specialist.

He could do everything. He could do everything Russell did. He was a great shot blocker, although they didn't keep those statistics then. They've overlooked that, just as they've overlooked a lot of what he's done.

He was the top rebounder 11 times, while Russell managed only 4. He still owns the NBA record with 55 in one game. He finished with a 30.1 scoring average that included the 100-point game, five in the 70s and 26 in the 60s. He averaged 50.4 in 1961–62 and no one's come close to that and never will. I know never is a long time but I believe I'm safe with that prediction.

Wilt could do anything he wanted. One year, he was determined to show he could make the play and led the league with 702 assists in 1967–68. He was on the 1972–73 Laker team that won those 33 in a row and the championship—a tough competitor in every respect.

I know Wilt has been given a lot of credit because he owns about every record in the book. He had a massive impact on the game. Looking back, I believe the league has never had a player of his size and talent who came close to him.

I have to thank Bill Russell for something, though. I never forgot that alley-oop against us the previous season when he got hurt. He didn't make the basket because the pass was not perfect but it impressed me. So I borrowed it.

We put it in our repertoire, so to speak. We worked repeatedly on Frazier standing at midcourt, Barnett picking the opposing center and Reed releasing for the alley-oop.

''It never worked in practice,'' said Clyde, who just couldn't lob the long pass in perfect position for Reed to jam it through. The timing was always a bit off until we played DeBusschere's favorite team—the Pistons—on Christmas night in the Garden.

We had just tried the alley-oop against Atlanta but failed as we lost 125–124 in overtime at home. It was our third straight defeat and people were beginning to wonder if our fantasy bubble had burst.

Someone on our team always had a capable answer in situations such as that. This time it was Clyde, who generally did. He suggested: "The way we're going, we may have to pull another trade and send DeBusschere back."

He was feeding the newspaperman a line of convenience because DeBusschere had just blown a couple of last-second foul shots. He tied the game with one and then missed the second that sent it into overtime.

I called for the alley-oop with the Hawks leading, again, by one in overtime but Joe Caldwell deflected the pass-in. Riordan grabbed the loose ball and fired long to DeBusschere but he missed a jumper. We lost a tough game where every one of our starters had scored at least 17 points.

DeBusschere got it back in Chicago on the first anniversary of his trade to the Knicks. I knew he was still bleeding over the Atlanta game so I kept him out there 46 minutes. Also, I was anxious not to let the losing streak go on too long, so I altered my pattern of substituting and, also, kept Reed on the floor over 40 minutes.

DeBusschere celebrated his Knicks birthday by hitting 10 of 12 shots for 23 points. When he got hot, he got hot. Willis had 25 points and 25 rebounds. Besides, they both did some defensive job on the Chicago shooters and we won 108–99.

I remember closing the dressing room for a long time that night. I usually let the press in within a minute or two because I recognized that deadlines had to be met. I always felt that if there was something I had to say to the players, it could wait until tomorrow.

That night I had to deal with a little tyranny. I guess it was the losing streak that had us all a little edgy—especially me. I didn't like the way some players had reacted to my suggestions from the bench.

I couldn't let that pass. I had worked too hard—and so had the players—to establish great chemistry and wasn't about to lose control. I wanted to nip it before it got serious.

As things turned out, it never would have happened with that group of players. They were too confident and professional. However, it seemed like a flash rebellion toward my authority at the time.

I had to deal with it right away. Deadlines had to wait. I reminded the players that no matter what I said, I was right whether they liked it or not. Today, I guess the players would have me fired.

I hated to do it but it had to be done. Bradley was one of the players and it bothered me because I wanted it to remain fun and games. I had been trying to nail Bill with a fine for a long time and had just gotten him for being late for practice.

I didn't want to interrupt the rhythm of the team. We survived with the end of our losing streak. By then, we were celebrities in New York. We were celebrities whom the celebrities were flocking to see. Los Angeles didn't own the copyright.

Dustin Hoffman sat behind our bench. Robert Redford, Neil Simon, Elliott Gould, Woody Allen and Bill Goldman, the screenwriter and novelist, also were regulars. They were impressed. We were impressed. The Bill Hoskets were carried away.

Pat Hosket remembers the excitement of New York in those days. The celebrities they met. The parties they attended. The fun they had.

"We were just two kids from Ohio," she recalled. "The first time we were in New York, we went to the Knicks' office in the Garden. The first person we saw was Phil Jackson. He was in a *Guys and Dolls* suit. I said to myself what big shoulders he had."

Her husband, Bill, was our first-round choice in 1968. He had been on the United States team that had just won the Olympic gold. He had been a Dayton high school teammate of Donnie May, whom we also picked on the third round that year.

May had gone to Dayton University while Hosket played for Ohio State. We had reunited them, primarily to sit and give us bench strength. The players paired them as an entry and they adapted to the role. One didn't move without the other.

"I remember one time at the start of the season," said Frazier. "They were sitting on the bench discussing what they were going to do in the summer. I almost fell off the bench. Here the season was just starting and they're already making plans for the summer."

Dustin Hoffman got friendly with Hosket and used to throw peanuts at him. "We got friendly because we were always sitting on the bench in front of him," said Hosket. "We'd go out to dinner with him. I remember the time we went to a New Year's party at his place. When New Year's came, Patty just happened to be standing next to Dustin and he kissed her. She hasn't washed her face since.''

Hosket was a new face around the Garden. No one really knew him. On his first game, he had trouble getting through the employees' entrance, where all players enter without a pass. Security didn't recognize him, so they wouldn't let him in.

"There was this guard standing there and he asked me where I was going," recalled Hosket. "I told him who I was. I said: 'I'm Bill Hosket and I play for the Knicks. He said: 'Get out of here.' He called over another guy and I told him who I was and he said the same thing: 'Get out of here.' I didn't know what to do.''

What did he do? "Well, while we were talking, I happened to look at someone reading a paper near the entrance," he said. "It was the New York *Post*. It had my picture on the back page. It said: 'Newest Knick.' I said to the guards: 'Look. I'm Bill Hosket.' And that's how I got in.''

It happened to me one night in the Garden. I always came out of the dressing room late. The players would go out first to warm up. Danny and I would fool around for a few minutes and get to the floor a few minutes before the introductions.

It was the same routine all the time. This night, I was stopped by an usher. "You can't come through here without a ticket," he said. "I'm Red Holzman. I'm the coach," I said. So much for recognition.

Oh, yes. The alley-oop that finally worked. It was against the Pistons, who had just gone ahead on a lay-up by Bellamy with a second to go. We were lucky there was enough time left to get a time-out. Another tick and Bells's shot would have won the game.

As someone once said: "It's not over until it's over." Thanks to Yogi, we won that game. All I did in the huddle was to say: "The one-second play," and review assignments.

I wanted to remind Barnett that he was the key man. He would have to take his man down low, then swing around a screen to get behind Bellamy and set a pick. Everyone else knew what to do because we had simulated exactly that situation so many times in practice.

That's what I mean by being prepared. I didn't have to draw X's and O's for the players. I never coached with a notebook or one of those magnetic boards in my life. I never even used a computer, which showed how old I was even then.

It worked perfectly. Barnett picked off Bellamy to release Reed going to the basket. As Willis leaped, Frazier timed a perfect pass about a yard from the hoop. The clock doesn't start until the ball is touched so Reed's hand had time to sweep it through in one motion.

We won 112–111 and the Pistons were stunned. Every game with us was a mission because of the DeBusschere deal and we had just stolen one from them. Reed got all the attention.

It was a heartbreaker for Detroit. Cazzie fell on the floor in the dressing room yelling for a doctor as he faked a heart attack. Reed had to describe every minute detail for the historians of such deeds.

Frazier just sat on his stool and smiled. These were the moments he enjoyed best. He was on stage after another exciting win in which he had played a major role.

They gathered around him and now it was his turn to dramatize his contribution to the One-Second Play. His eyes twinkled. He milked the opportunity for a few seconds and then said: "I was trying to make the basket." Sitting in the stall next to Clyde was Willis, who then said: "I'm glad I spoiled it."

The winners make jokes and the losers say: "Deal." That's something I learned from the card-playing days on all the bus and train rides. We were winning, so the dressing room was always light and lively.

Barnett was the main man. He had a droll sense of humor that always had the players laughing. I didn't know that side of him at first. I only knew him as a fine player I had scouted when he was at Tennessee State and ripping up the NAIA tournaments.

I had him high on the 1959 draft list I discussed with Eddie Donovan, then the Knicks' general manager. I was struck by Barnett's intelligence. Underneath all that scoring flair was a brainy player. He could play any style of game and excel.

So why didn't we draft Barnett when he became available? We were going to draft him. It was my first input as Knick scout and we were picking sixth. Syracuse was right ahead of us. The Lakers picked fourth.

Barnett and LaRusso were the top players on our list. When the Lakers took LaRusso we were hoping Syracuse wouldn't take Barnett. They did. We took Johnny Green, who gave us six years of good service.

I was always a Barnett man. That's why we grabbed him when he became available in a trade and let Van Arsdale go in expansion.

> *"Don't let up, die out there if you have to."*
>
> *—Dick Barnett*

Barnett and I shared many memorable moments when he became a Knick.

I made him an assistant coach after he retired. And he stood next to me when the Garden retired our numbers—12 for him and 613 for me, which represented my total Knick victories. We joined Frazier's 10, Reed's 19, DeBusschere's 22 and Bradley's 24.

We celebrated my second anniversary on the job by flying out at midnight for a seven-thousand-mile trip of three games in three nights. Too bad they didn't have Frequent Flyer programs in those days. I would have owned United.

First stop was Los Angeles and we arrived at 6:30 A.M. New York time. We got in front of the Lakers by 18 in the second quarter but ran out of gas or sleep or something. Jerry West buried us with 40 points and 10 assists as we lost 114–106.

On to Vancouver and up at 6:45 to catch an 8:30 flight. I knew the players were tired, so I pulled out one of my better clichés. I told them: "Sometimes when you are tired, you are loose, so go out and win." We did by two points.

DeBusschere had a tough night. He got hit with a technical for telling the referee what we were all thinking about the job he was doing. It cost him $25 and that really hurt.

The players didn't go to bed after the game, they collapsed. There was a 6:45 wake-up call for the 8:30 flight to Phoenix. It took six hours because we were apparently on a milk plane. We went by way of Portland, Los Angeles and San Diego. The pilot must have been visiting his girlfriends.

DeBusschere couldn't keep his eyes open, which is why he probably hit his first eight shots. We trailed by five at the half but won going away. Willis took charge with 20 points in the third period.

I remember telling someone after we had logged exactly 7,172 miles that some people don't travel that much in a lifetime. New Year's Eve was around the corner and we were 33–7. I felt great about the old year and was wondering why it couldn't keep going just a little longer.

Hosket got involved with the DeBusscheres the night of the Dustin Hoffman party. Bill and his wife had no concept of how to get around New York, so Dave and his wife, Geri, elected to lead them to the apartment on Central Park West.

Hosket recalls dragging along with DeBusschere to Riverside Drive, where some drunk insisted Dave was Wilt Chamberlain. Now that's a drunk.

Competition was finally rearing its head at that time. Milwaukee was coming on. Alcindor was maturing quickly and the Bucks had won 9 of their last 10. We were 11–7 since our streak ended.

I sensed we were in trouble when I picked up the papers and read what the Bucks intended to do to us. It was a nationally televised game and the place was sold out. Alcindor had turned Milwaukee inside out in its second season in the league.

Reed's stomach and knees were bothering him and he played sick. I guess we left our game on that long plane trip. Alcindor killed us with 41 points and we lost by 13.

We had given the Bucks grandiose ideas. They had beaten us for the first time in the existence of their franchise and also were the closest team to us in the standings.

It was January 2, 1970, and no way to start the new year. We began playing mind games around then. We were sure we'd make it to the playoffs in first place. That never bothered us because by then our defense had held the other teams under 100 in 20 of our 44 games.

The players were rooting for Milwaukee to finish second. Kind of strange unless you understand that first played third and second played fourth in those days. Baltimore looked like it would be third and we had handled the Bullets so easily the season before.

But we still had a long way to go. Atlanta was stepping up in the Western Division, where it was a two-horse race with Los Angeles.

Chamberlain was still out but West and Baylor were carrying the Lakers. They were hanging in on the 50 points West and Baylor guaranteed every night. Those two were solid-gold Hall-of-Famers but they had never won a championship.

Too much Bill Russell. They just couldn't get past the Celtics. Only two teams did during Russell's regime: the 1957–58 St. Louis Hawks and the 1966–67 Philadelphia 76ers.

Here is a bit of NBA trivia: Alex Hannum coached the Hawks and 76ers, thus becoming the only coach to win championships with two different teams. And there is a footnote to that trivia.

I was indirectly involved in Hannum's destiny, which eventually led him to at least one of those titles. I happened to be coaching the Hawks when the Syracuse team dropped Hannum.

He was a hard-nosed, smart player and I talked Ben Kerner into signing him. Kerner had just moved the Hawks to St. Louis from Milwaukee, hoping Bob Pettit would stimulate more business.

Hannum was there when Kerner let me go because the Hawks still weren't winning or drawing attention. It was virgin pro basketball territory and Pettit hadn't yet established any excitement.

History has a way of creating its own tricky bounces. In this case, Kerner turned to Slater Martin as my replacement. It was in season and Kerner didn't have any time to look around.

Martin had been part of the Minneapolis Lakers' championship era. He had been traded to the Knicks and came to the Hawks in a trade for Willie Naulls. Dugie, as they called him, was in his twilight days so Kerner targeted him to run the team.

Martin had other ideas. He didn't want to coach and told Kerner to get someone else or he would go home to Texas. That's how Hannum got the job. When Kerner cornered Martin and asked who he thought could do the job, Slater said: ''Hannum.''

Hannum still says if I hadn't brought him to St. Louis as a player, he would have quit and gone home to California. That's like saying if I hadn't helped bring Bradley to the Knicks he might never have had the chance to be President some day.

Baylor and West met the Russell Celtics in five finals and never won. Four of them went to seven games. The first was in 1961–62 when West shot 30.8 for the season and Baylor 30.3. Boston won the seventh game 110–107 in overtime at home.

West and Baylor had captured the hearts of Hollywood by then. It was the second season after the Lakers had been moved from Minneapolis to Los Angeles by Bob Short.

Short had purchased the Lakers from their original owner, Max Winter, who was to own the Minnesota Vikings. Short later was to sell the Lakers to Jack Kent Cooke and buy the Washington baseball team.

The Lakers moved to LA in 1960 because they no longer could pay their bills in Minneapolis. Everything was downhill after the George Mikan era. West already had been the top pick in the 1960 draft but never saw Minneapolis.

He became an instant hero in Los Angeles at a time when it craved for more sports. The Rams had moved there from Cleveland and the Dodgers from Brooklyn. Now Hollywood had another favorite son.

West became one of LA's own very fast because he had no previous identity elsewhere. Only one thing stood in the way of West, Baylor and the Los Angeles sports fans: a championship.

In 1962–63, the Celtics won in six games and the next season in five. It went to seven games in 1965–66 and it was getting even more frustrating. The Lakers won the first game in Boston 133–129 in overtime but lost the final 95–93 in Boston.

They were back at each other two seasons later. By then the Lakers had added Chamberlain to West and Baylor. They represented almost 100 points in scoring averages. Chamberlain finished at 30.1, West at 27.4 and Baylor at 27.0.

No team has ever had that awesome firepower. Yet when they

met the Celtics in 1968–69, the Lakers still lost. The Celtics had almost missed the playoffs for the first time in 20 years but it was the same result. The Lakers lost the seventh game at home by two points. Don Nelson helped win it with a lucky bounce on a jump shot that went up and in off the rim.

I point that out because it was an important part of the background when we faced the Lakers for the 1969–70 championship. They were on top of the Western Division without Chamberlain, who got back in time to play against us.

It was a little rocky that Christmas. We weren't very smooth and we suspected Reed's stomach problem was an ulcer. Everything that happens under those conditions tests your patience.

We had to stay in Windsor because a convention in Detroit had taken all the rooms. We had two days of practice before the game. We had to go back and forth through Customs at the bridge. Each time they stopped our bus and inspected the team bags.

Leave it to Frazier to lighten our dark mood. After going through all the socks, jocks and other things the players carried, an inspector wondered if we were a team. Clyde hit him with one word: "Sometimes."

Cazzie hasn't forgotten that trip, either. He had left early on our second day of practice to visit the University of Michigan, his alma mater.

"I had gone up to Ann Arbor and was on my way back to practice and I noticed a roadblock," he recalled. "They stopped me. At that time, I had grown a mustache and they said they were looking for a guy with a mustache."

It turned out that the police were on a manhunt for a guy who had killed a sheriff. He had escaped while being taken to jail. They told Cazzie to get out of his car.

He had no idea what was going on. He asked why he had to get out of the car. The cop put a pistol to Cazzie's head and another leaned on the hood of the car and aimed a rifle at him.

"I guess when I went to the glove compartment to get the registration, they thought I was reaching for a gun," he said.

He asked the policemen what it was all about. "Someone in your race committed a murder,'' was the answer. "He had a slight mustache and he was six-three, six-four.''

Cazzie had a slight mustache and was 6'5". He handed the policeman his license, issued to Cazzie Russell. "I'm sorry, Cazzie,'' the cop said and they let him go.

"Obviously, you take a different perspective of it now,'' he said. "At that time it wasn't particularly funny. I got the impression that all black guys looked alike as far as they were concerned.''

He recalls getting to practice in time to avoid me fining him. "I had given myself enough time,'' he said. "I left almost an hour and twenty minutes before practice. The drive was just forty-five minutes. Of course, the police ate up twenty minutes of that time. I got there with about ten minutes to spare.''

Cazzie was in no mood when practice started. He had been shaken up and the cops' apology didn't exactly compensate for his embarrassment and anger. So he took it out on his teammates. Willis finally calmed him down.

It worked. Despite the trauma of his day with the police, Cazzie saved the game with the Pistons when DeBusschere came up with leg cramps, which occurred frequently with him. There was 2:23 to go and we were leading by only one.

Cazzie came off the bench gunslinging as usual. He hit two quick baskets and we were home free. I have never seen anyone who could generate instant scoring quicker or better. It reassured me that I'd been right when I'd decided he was better than Bradley coming off the bench.

I coached the East All-Star team and Willis was voted MVP. That was the good news. The bad news was that they announced the day before the game that there was going to be expansion, again.

Buffalo, Portland and Cleveland were being added right away, while Houston was to enter in 1971–72. That was to turn a two-division league of 14 teams into four divisions of 18. It also meant we would lose some players.

Hosket, May and Warren were most vulnerable. They were at the end of the bench in that order. Hosket was getting the most playing time. He was a big-man backup at 6′7½″ and was a good basketball player.

As Riordan remembers it: ''We all knew our roles. That was one good thing that Red did. We all knew we'd get some playing time, that's why there was no fighting or complaining about it. I knew I was going to go in and give a foul. Sometimes I gave two and even stayed in longer if I was contributing something.''

We had one rough stretch where DeBusschere's back began bothering him. He didn't help it any by fixing his own flat tire on the way home one night. Stallworth and Hosket stepped up and it wasn't too eventful until we went to Philadelphia.

It was January 30, 1970, at the Spectrum. The success of the Knicks resulted in many of our fans showing up at games in Philadelphia. We had a lot of them in the crowd that night, which added up to a hostile situation.

We were losing 50–49, so it was nice and quiet. Then we erupted to a 90–72 lead behind Frazier, Barnett and Cazzie. They couldn't miss as we hit 14-for-19. Neither could two guys behind our bench when they started swinging at each other.

Beer was involved. One guy was griping about beer spilling over him. Next thing I knew, two guys were swinging and headed for our bench. We staged our fastest break of the season as we cleared out. The best basketball fights are always in the stands.

The perpetrators were two New York transit cops who had come down to see the Knicks play. They were getting sloshed and didn't realize, or care, that their slippage was annoying the Sixer fan. It ended with the transit cops being escorted out—after someone spotted a gun on one of them.

As I was saying, all fun and games. In the confusion we won the game. We had forgotten the trading deadline was February 1 because we had no intention of making any changes. We were set for the rest of the season.

We went to Detroit and found that some teams had other ideas. Willis got 30 points off a young center named Otto Moore and we wondered where Bellamy was. Why was Moore playing so much?

We found out after we won that our old friend had been traded to Atlanta.

That hurt because the Hawks were a team we figured to meet in the playoffs and they needed a center badly. Then there was the news that Oscar Robertson had been dealt to Baltimore for Gus Johnson.

Before I could digest that, it was over. The Big O exercised a clause in his contract and refused to go. We were always interested in Oscar. We all considered him the best all-around player in the game and some still do.

At that time, however, we were solid in our backcourt and didn't want to change things—even for Oscar Robertson, who was 32 at the time. We particularly didn't want to disturb Frazier, and the addition of the Big O would do just that.

I assumed Oscar would have come to the Knicks if we had been interested. He wound up satisfied with going to Milwaukee and getting a championship ring there. We wound up with the same group of players who would take us to the championship.

Oscar wasn't in uniform when we got to Cincinnati a few games later. He was waiting for the Royals to accommodate his desire to leave, which they eventually did. He sat in street clothes at one end of the bench while Cousy sat at the other end.

It was like cat and mouse. That reminds me: We were in the dressing room before the game and I was about to address the team with one of my brilliant speeches. I looked up and there was something running along the pipes.

"It's a rat!" I screamed. Someone said it was only a mouse. "Let's get out of here!" I yelled. So much for the Life of the Rich and Famous.

A mouse had also run across the floor during our 110–96 defeat in Atlanta the game before. Two mice in two straight games has to be an NBA record. They split a win apiece when we walloped the Cincinnati mouse 135–92. For some reason, the team never missed my dressing-room speech that night.

We made our final decision on Phil Jackson at that time. He had been rehabilitating his back after his surgery and was progressing.

It wasn't that simple then. Expansion was coming up and we had to officially freeze our roster—which meant someone would have had to be dropped if Jackson had been activated.

We decided to go as we were. We promised Phil a full playoff share. We made him an offer he couldn't refuse. We sent him a $12,000 check after we won the championship.

I made him my unofficial, part-time scout on occasion. He'd go to some off-night games with me because I respected his knowledge. He was a thinking man who knew the game.

That was our last major player decision of the season. We were 51–13 with 18 games left and Milwaukee was 45–20 with 17 to go. We looked like a lock.

11

Decisions, decisions, decisions. Sometimes they are easy, sometimes difficult. For me, the toughest thing to do was to cut someone. Anyone who has played the game will know that.

The Cazzie trade was difficult. So were the ones that got us Bellamy and then enabled us to get DeBusschere. It wasn't easy to inform players who had provided good services that they were gone.

I think one of my toughest assignments was letting Freddie Crawford know we were releasing him. He was out of St. Bonaventure and we had taken him in the fourth round of the 1966 draft. We were 31 games into 1967–68 when I had to make a roster move.

It turned out to be a beautiful, sunny day in San Diego and I had to tell Crawford he was being dropped—that he had to fly all the way home alone. I knew that really hurt. He was from New York and had worked hard to stick with us. He came that close to being a championship Knick and sharing all that has meant.

It's like Cazzie now says as he looks back at being on that team. "It's history," he explained. "We played the last game in the old Garden and the first game in the new. A championship ring. Played with great guys."

He smiled and added: "I played in a city that really knows basketball. A small city used to winning. That doesn't believe it's ever supposed to have a bad year."

Crawford never got an opportunity to share that excitement. He was a typical sub who can never feel secure. They live in a revolving door in every sport.

"Nate Bowman was my roommate," recalled Crawford. "I think it was a question between Nate and me. We had been discussing the reality of the situation at the time. Bill Bradley was coming back."

I think I called Crawford to my room. I don't think I told him it was because Bradley was coming back, but that didn't really matter. I had to make a move and Crawford went because we were overloaded in the backcourt.

"The essence of it was that it was a tough decision for Red," said Crawford. "To the best of my recollection, we had Dick Barnett and Clyde was coming on. My attitude's always been let's see what happens next."

What happened next was that Crawford wound up in Los Angeles. He flew home to New York and there was a message from Butch van Breda Kolff, the Laker coach.

"The Lakers had picked up my contract," said Freddie. "In a way, I was better off. It was a blow to leave the Knicks. Yet there had been a lot of pressure on me being a New York guy. My buddies used to come down and yell: 'Put Freddie in!' . . . also [there was pressure to get] tickets and everything."

He considered the move to LA a breath of fresh air—which is nice to hear now. There was something else about that situation that I didn't know until now. It's another piece of the Crawford story.

"I turned right around and I went out there," he continued. "My thought was I could've stayed out there and gone right from San Diego to LA but I didn't get the message until I got home. I fit in very well with the Lakers."

One day he got into a conversation with van Breda Kolff. It was then he learned why the Lakers had grabbed him so quickly. He discovered someone had recommended him to Butch.

"It was Bradley," said Crawford, who today works in mental health services in New York. "Bradley and I were close and van Breda Kolff had been his coach at Princeton. He told me that Bradley had called as soon as he learned I had left the Knicks and recommended me."

How about that? I never knew that until Crawford told the story almost 25 years later. Bradley, obviously, felt bad about displacing another player so he went out of his way to help him. Now that's class.

I learned something else not long ago. I was always aware that the referees were paid far less than the players. They worked for slave wages in the days when teams were struggling for survival.

Basketball is a tough sport to officiate and there's so much travel involved. I had my share of disputes with the refs but didn't really appreciate their hardships until a Knicks Legends Game at the Garden.

Earl Strom and Norm Drucker came out of retirement to work the game. They were two of the best referees the NBA ever produced. We all know that refs can make or break a game. Yet the pay was awful in the early days of the NBA.

"I started to work in the NBA in 1953 for forty dollars a game," recalled Drucker. "I worked like sixty or sixty-five regular season games. The second year they told me I have an automatic five-dollar raise and I'm now making forty-five dollars a game. The third year they told me I've got a five-dollar raise and I'm making fifty dollars a game."

He was then working 90 games and his total money for the year was $4,500. Compare that with today's $115,000 regular season salary for top officials plus $35,000 extra for the playoffs. That offers a good insight into the changing times.

"I called up Mr. Podoloff, the commissioner, and made an appointment to see him," continued Drucker. "I had prepared my figures. I'd ask him for a ten-dollar raise instead of five. Podoloff was rotund and short and had a tremendous big desk. When he sat behind it, I couldn't see his head. I kept getting out of my chair to look at him.

"Whaddya want?" said Podoloff, according to Drucker, who answered: " 'Mr. Podoloff. I've been in the league three years. Last year I made fifty dollars a game and this year I'd like to get, instead of a five-dollar raise, a ten-dollar raise.' With that, he pounds the desk, gets up and says: 'You want to bankrupt the NBA?' To this day they don't know that I took only a five-dollar raise and saved the NBA.''

Strom had a similar experience with Podoloff. "I'm getting forty-five dollars, fifty dollars a game and the next year fifty-five dollars," he recalled. "Mendy Rudolph and I were about to work an entire championship series because they couldn't agree on officials.''

Those were the 1961 final playoffs when the Boston Celtics beat the St. Louis Hawks 4–1 for the title. "At four o'clock in the morning Podoloff, Ben Kerner and Red Auerbach are in this room," said Strom. "They still can't agree on who was going to work the series.''

Podoloff decided to give Kerner and Auerbach a list of officials. They would cross off the names of those they didn't want. "Podoloff told them whatever names weren't crossed off, they would work the series. If all the names were crossed off, we'd cancel the series.''

Podoloff had no intention of doing that but it was his Solomonic tiebreaker. Mendy's name was on one list and Earl Strom's on the other, which is how they got to work all five games. There were no gripes because Kerner and Auerbach had handpicked the refs.

"After the playoffs were over, I came home and called Mendy and told him I was going to call Mr. Podoloff," continued Strom. "I was going to get more than a five-dollar raise. I said I was going to ask for twenty-five dollars because I had refereed the entire championship series. Mendy said that I should stick to my guns and I'd get it.''

Strom admitted he was scared to death of Podoloff, who was a little Napoleon, but was determined. "I went to his New York office," said Earl, who is from Pennsylvania. "He said: 'What can I do for you?' and I told him I'd like more than a five-dollar raise for the next season. He asked what I was thinking of. Now I'm thinking of Mendy.''

He remembered how Mendy had advised him to be firm and stick to his guns. "I say: 'Oh, well, Mr. Podoloff, I'm thinking like twenty-five dollars a game more,''' said Strom. "He said: 'Well, I was thinking more like fifteen dollars' and I said: 'I'll take it!' and ran out of there fast.''

There was not much left to the regular season except Bradley tore up an ankle and was out a month. We weren't playing good basketball and Bill's absence had a lot to do with it. My concern was to get him back long enough before the playoffs for him to get into game shape.

Bradley rejoined us when we needed one game to clinch. We were going to Portland and it was a reunion for him. That's where he had played his last college game. He had set an NCAA tournament record of 58 points against the Wichita State team of Dave Stallworth and Nate Bowman.

I drove Bradley from the airport to make sure he was comfortable and got to the hotel safely. He took a ribbing for that from Hosket for being part of management. Hos asked Bill if he and I had made out the expansion list yet.

Everything was ready for the clinching. We had champagne on ice and the Garden had arranged a special TV date so that all New York could be in on it. We even had Phil Jackson fly out with us for the celebration.

We had to win that night or the home fans would be shut out because there would be no TV coverage over the weekend. They talked me into putting a camera in our dressing room, which I ordinarily wouldn't allow.

I told Danny Whelan to keep the champagne quiet and hide it because I didn't want the Portland guys to think we were cocky and arrogant. I wanted it to be low-key in every respect, which was my style.

I even cautioned my inquiring reporters. I told them that all the talk about champagne was presumptuous because nothing had happened yet. I didn't want anyone to get worked up about popping corks.

We did an excellent job, I think, except we lost the game. Lenny Wilkens, then the player-coach, killed us with 28 points and a big mouth. He just couldn't keep a secret.

Bob Boozer squealed. He was a former Knick whom we had used

to get Barnett from the Lakers. "Lenny told us they brought the champagne tonight," he said after contributing 23 points. "Maybe he was trying to get us fired up."

The defeat brought out the best in our team philosophers. I think we led the league in them. "It wasn't one of our best games," I said.

"There's always tomorrow," said Reed.

Up stepped Frazier, our cleanup man, and he said: "To hell with another day. I want to win it and get it over with. Don't put off until tomorrow what you can do today. I didn't want to celebrate in Portland, anyway. It's like the fox who couldn't get the grapes and said they were probably sour anyway."

So we left the champagne in Portland and later discovered that the maintenance men in the arena had a helluva celebration at our expense. Knick fans probably will remember we clinched the next night in San Diego.

Which was fine with me because I always liked San Diego. There were no racetracks but there was one across the border in Tijuana.

We broke open the game with a 14-point lead in the first five minutes. I managed to give Bradley five minutes after he had missed 14 games and was assured he would be ready for the playoffs. I knew I had to give him some playing time in the remaining games.

Our dressing room was described by one of our writers this way: "It had to be the wildest celebration since VJ day in Tokyo." The players sipped beer and sodas while Reed asked me where was the champagne.

It was an uneventful night until we got to the airport for a flight to Los Angeles. That was our routine after every San Diego game. It was a short run and the players could get a good night's sleep.

It was the last flight to LA. We discovered the plane had a flat and none of us had our AAA cards. We hung around the airport for two hours. We ate the pizzas our favorite Italian restaurant had delivered while Cazzie and Stallworth entertained us with a wheelchair race.

DeBusschere took Riordan and Jackson to the bar for a few beers. "Have a drink," DeBusschere said to the bartender.

"Why?" was the response.

"We're celebrating. We won a championship," said Dave.

"Everyone expected that," said the bartender.

We wound up going back to the hotel and reclaiming our rooms. We flew to Los Angeles the next day and received the news that Chamberlain was coming back. He even showed up at the Forum and watched us lose. The Lakers were still fighting for first place and home-court advantage.

It was March 16 and we had only four games left to get our tired bodies and minds ready for the playoffs. We received word that Willis had been voted MVP by the players—the first and only one for the Knicks, so far.

> *"I had enormous respect for Willis's game, but I tried not to let him know it."*
>
> *—Bill Russell*

Willis was first, Jerry West second and Alcindor third. There were some protests but not from me. The Knicks were his team. Everyone on our side agreed.

I don't know how he was able to perform in such pain. If it wasn't his knees, it was a shoulder or a hip or a leg. He led the league in only one statistic: won and lost.

I remember Richie Guerin sent us a few bottles of champagne after the Hawks beat us that night in Atlanta to clinch their title. I sent it back. I promised our players champagne when we won the NBA championship.

I had to get them to win it. So, after the final regular season game in Boston, I said: "There are two things we can do now. We can lie back and enjoy what we've done and call it quits or we can go out and send Baltimore back early." Clever?

That was not going to be easy. First of all, we had lost our last four games and that's always a concern. Second, our matchups with the Bullets were the toughest. We were made for each other.

DeBusschere and Gus Johnson; Bradley and Jack Marin; Reed and Wes Unseld; Barnett and Fred Carter; Frazier and Earl Monroe. Oh, yes, Holzman and Gene Shue. A tale of two cities whose rivalry transcended all others.

The Bullets were still seething from our four-game sweep in the 1968–69 playoffs. The city of Baltimore was fuming over the 1969 baseball and pro football humiliations that had just taken place. Now we were seeking the hat trick for New York.

I had no way of knowing exactly how deeply the Baltimore people felt about us New Yorkers. Someone did. It was Jim Karvellas, who was the voice of Baltimore sports in those days.

His was a professional experience from a Baltimore viewpoint. He was there when the Jets and Mets beat the Colts and Orioles. He was in the unique position of understanding the emotional impact on a city that saw the Bullets as its team of vengeance.

He hooked into the Bullets first as an announcer. Then he was hired by a beer company that owned the Orioles and also had the radio and TV broadcasting rights to the Colts.

"In fact, I replaced a guy who came to New York, Frank Messer, who left to become a Yankee voice. There was an opening, so they put me in there," he explained.

So he was around for all three Baltimore–New York sports confrontations that had a 1969 imprint on them. Though we finished our playoffs in 1970, the season started for us on October 14, 1969. I even remember an early game in Chicago and watching the Mets clinch the World Series with the Orioles on TV in our hotel at the airport.

"I did the Super Bowl the year that the Jets beat the Colts. I did the Bullets when the Knicks beat them," continued Karvellas. "And I also did the regular season when the Mets beat the Orioles but not the World Series."

He understood how the Baltimore people felt about New York. He recalled: "The thing about that whole scenario was that it was an incredible time. A Tale of Two Cities—Baltimore and New York. I thought it really started back in 1958, when I wasn't there. That was when the Colts beat the Giants for the championship in what was said to be the greatest game ever played."

That's when Johnny Unitas quarterbacked the Colts to a last-second tie and then Alan Ameche won it in overtime. It was a smashing victory that put the Colts on the map.

That was the beginning. "Then, the next year, Baltimore defeated the Giants, again, in Memorial Stadium in fifty-eight–fifty-nine,'' said Karvellas. ''So they won two championships in a row over the Giants. I remember Baltimore in sixty-three–sixty-four and hearing those stories everywhere I went. That it was the greatest game ever played and Baltimore had beaten New York.''

He couldn't understand it at first. He understood the elation over a championship but what was this Baltimore–New York business all about? He soon found out.

''I remember talking to a columnist in Baltimore,'' he said. ''He wasn't a sports columnist. I asked him: 'Why does Baltimore keep talking about these games that happened four years ago?' He said that Baltimore has an inferiority complex. It wouldn't have meant as much if they had beaten the Green Bay Packers or the Pittsburgh Steelers. But they beat the New York Giants and Baltimore always bragged about that.''

When the Jets beat the Colts, that was the most disappointing defeat of them all. The Mets were next and the Knicks were third. ''That's the way I saw it,'' said Karvellas. ''The disappointing thing about the Colts thing was that they were the superior team. They considered Joe Namath a loudmouth from New York and they were gonna kick the hell out of the Jets.''

Karvellas worked that game and believes he knows what turned things around for the Jets. ''It wasn't Joe Namath's taunting,'' he recalled. ''On the opening kickoff, the Colts get the ball and drive it right down the field and all of a sudden somebody drops a pass. Then they miss a chip-shot field goal.''

Now it was all over and everyone was depressed. Karvellas discovered how deep the scarring was when he left the stadium that day. ''I couldn't get on the team bus, so I got on the bus with the wives,'' he said. ''When I walked on that bus it was as if President Kennedy had died again. John Mackey's wife was crying. Johnny Unitas's wife was crying. It was the most somber thing I ever saw.''

It was devastating to the whole city, apparently. ''They had a chance to heal until the Mets came along,'' continued Karvellas. ''The Orioles also were a better team but the Mets had a series that was unbelievable. Tommie Agee and Ron Swoboda made catches, the pitching was exceptional. I'm not sure but, at some point, that even started affecting the Orioles.''

He was referring to the New York–Baltimore syndrome. ''It was like we had just lost our father and now our mother dies,'' he added.

Now I know why Johnny Unitas and Frank Robinson used to show up at our games in Baltimore. They were fans with a greater mission. I assume if the Bullets beat us, they might've been on the floor carrying the coach, Gene Shue, off on their shoulders.

There was another big incentive as we were about to face each other in the opening round of the playoffs. We were 5–1 against the Bullets during the regular season. This is the way it had gone:

October 25—We win at home 128–99. ''The guards are controlling the ball too much,'' says Gus Johnson after his backcourt accounts for 57 of 99 shots. Bill Bradley shakes Jack Marin for 10 baskets on 19 shots behind screens. Dave DeBusschere holds Johnson to 9 shots. Our defense deflects the ball and steals it all over the place. ''They were tremendous. They have an excellent defense,'' says Gene Shue.

December 5—We win the first game in Baltimore 118–107. They have five players in double figures and outrebound us 64–47. We break the game open with a 37–24 third quarter. This is the Kick the Knicks game. Mike Riordan steals the ball twice from Wes Unseld in the closing minutes.

December 20—We pile up a 41-point lead in the Garden and win 128–91. ''Yeah, I would say a team can get a complex,'' says Shue after we record our seventh straight over the Bullets. He then adds: ''I'm not saying my team has a complex. The Knicks have beaten us easily three times this season and it doesn't make sense.''

Unseld gets four personals early and that doesn't help the Bullets. Shue goes to three guards early to change the pace but we handle that. Walt Frazier has a huge game with 29 points, 14 assists and 8 rebounds, while Dick Barnett shoots 12-for-19 for 26 points.

January 6—We win again in Baltimore 119–99. Shue says again: ''It just doesn't make sense. It can't keep up. The season is long. We'll turn things around. One of these days we'll perform well against them.''

Shue starts Leroy Ellis on Bradley, has Johnson pick up Frazier on defense. "I just fronted him," Bradley recalled about Ellis, who towered over him at 6'10". "I forgot about his rebounding and just boxed him out."

Sometimes Ellis plays DeBusschere. Sometimes Unseld brings the ball down and Jack Marin plays guard. Shue tries everything he can think of and explains it this way: "The Knicks just beat our brains in. It's silly for the coach to do the same things when he is losing. I've got a great sense of humor and great optimism but none of my damn moves work."

The Baltimore fans respond by giving Bradley, Frazier and DeBusschere a standing ovation when they put on a closing display of fingertip passing. I assume they are taunting their team for its failure against us.

February 24—The Bullets are at home and finally beat us 110–104. Bradley's out with a bad ankle and Riordan doesn't play because of a thigh injury. This time Shue's strategy works. He uses Marin on Frazier and Monroe on Cazzie, who starts because of Bradley.

Cazzie shoots only 3-for-17 in 19 minutes but I use Stallworth against Monroe and Dave hits 9-for-20 for 23 points. The Bullets are jubilant. They've finally ended the jinx.

Says Shue: "I can't tell you how pleased I am today." Says Johnson, who played with a pulled stomach muscle against the doctor's advice: "We haven't beaten them and I thought about it all night. Everybody said we were psyched and I wanted to get some momentum before the playoffs without worrying about the Knicks."

Monroe breaks out as usual with 37 points on 14-for-23. Frazier winds up with 30 points on 12-for-20 and Reed nails 20 rebounds.

February 28—We win the final game at home 118–101. Kevin Loughery and Mike Davis, a reserve guard, don't play and Shue uses Fred Carter with Monroe. Loughery has broken four ribs and punctured a lung running into an Alcindor knee. Carter, a 6'3" great leaper, pulls down 14 rebounds, scores 23 points and is called for goaltending once.

Bradley doesn't play, again. We're leading by four at the end of the third period and put it away with 10 straight. We shoot 49-for-92 with DeBusschere hitting 10-for-18 and Shue says: "I still think something good is going to happen to us."

He's almost right.

12

"I remember the playoffs, which went seven games," said Bradley. "The Baltimore matchups were good matchups. There was DeBusschere and Gus Johnson, Earl Monroe and Frazier, Willis and Wes Unseld. Jack Marin and me, Barnett and Fred Carter."

Kevin Loughery played hurt but Carter was the surprise and did a lot of damage with his playing time. New York fans believe to this day that those were classic matchups. They're remembered even more than those we had with the Lakers and Celtics.

They were all special with the Bullets. They were games within games. I put Bradley on Marin because they were play-alikes. They were both smart, tricky, competitive and good scorers.

I used DeBusschere on Johnson because Dave could handle Gus's power game. Gus had the quick body and Dave had a strong one for their battles under the boards. They also were both 6'6", which added the intrigue of two playing mastodons.

"For the heavyweight championship," is the way Danny Whelan described their matchup. Johnson was the more agile of the two. To the best of my recollection, I believe he was the first one I ever saw take off at the foul line and dunk the ball.

He didn't have to run to the basket as they do today. He just flew through the air like a bird and accomplished what it took Michael Jordan and Julius Erving an extra step to get done.

DeBusschere says he saw Chamberlain do that on foul shots in his early years. "Wilt would take that run from the back of the circle and dunk from the free-throw line,'' said DeBusschere. ''They changed the rule and you had to stay in the foul circle. He'd just take a run and jam it before his feet hit the ground.''

I'll take DeBusschere's word for it. Anyway, the Bradley-Marin matchup always produced the most fireworks for some reason. ''He thought I was much more devious than I was,'' recalled Bradley. ''We used to go at it. We were similar players. We both had good outside shots.''

''He'd irritate the hell out of you,'' needled DeBusschere.

''Did he irritate you, Bill?'' I asked.

''No, but he made me mad sometimes,'' said Bradley, referring to Marin's complaining about him all the time. ''I knew that I could get him angry and, if he was angry, he didn't get better—he was worse. How did I get him angry? A bump here and there. 'Too bad you missed that one.' Not a whole lot of verbal, though.''

Bradley would drive Marin crazy and I enjoyed it because it could give us an edge in that matchup. Bill knew Jack had a flash temper and exploited it. When Marin would get mad, Bradley would give him one of those innocent stares and Marin would get madder.

''What he would do was, he would think that he was fouled when he wasn't; then he'd get angry at the referee,'' explained Bradley. ''He was angry at me but it came out at the referee. He was on the floor yelling at the referee and it gave me the opportunity to sort of smile.''

DeBusschere and Johnson made silent warfare. They banged heads and bodies but never irritated each other. They had the same work ethic and appreciated each other's talent.

''There was no give and take with Gus,'' said DeBusschere. ''We hardly said anything to each other. I don't think Gus realized how physically gifted he was. He was injured a lot but he was enormously strong, very quick and a tremendous athlete.''

I was never really concerned about that matchup. Nobody ever positioned himself for rebounding better than DeBusschere. He was a natural. He'd get his body into the other guy and keep him off the board no matter how much bigger or stronger he was.

There is an art to that. Most players make the fundamental

mistake of watching the shot instead of stepping into their man first, then looking for the ball. It sounds simple but it's surprising how tough that is to teach—yes, even to the pros.

That's why I was never concerned that Johnson would hurt DeBusschere. "Gus wasn't a particularly great shooter from the outside," said Dave. "But around the basket, for his size, he was a terrific player. I just tried to keep him from the ball with my body."

Unseld and Reed were made for each other—strong, smart and gargantuan off the boards. Neither side fooled around with that matchup. There was no way of switching someone onto either one. They had to play each other.

They were a standoff in rebounding. Willis was the better shooter but Wes was awesome firing out to the fast break. I gave Willis a slight edge on defense because he was a little quicker and covered more space.

Willis also was the better scorer. There is a difference between a shooter and a scorer. Jerry West was a shooter and John Havlicek was a scorer.

Willis had a good touch from outside, which made him a shooter. Wes got most of his points in close, so he was a scorer. Willis wound up with an 18.7 lifetime average and Wes 10.8.

The Monroe-Frazier matchup was a thing of beauty. Earl was the ultimate scorer-shooter and Clyde had the fast hands and mind to play him. I preferred to use Clyde on the Pearl because that let us set up traps by Barnett.

Clyde would stick right on Earl as he brought the ball upcourt. He'd keep him busy as Earl was twisting, turning and doing his thing. Meanwhile, Barnett would sneak off his man and attack Monroe from the blind side.

Our strength was our defense. I had structured the team that way. Basically, it was designed to guide the players and the ball where we'd like it to go. We used it as an attacking weapon rather than sit back and let the other team go where it wanted to go.

"I must say when I watch Chicago play defense these days, I see our defense," said Bradley. "Phil's put in our defense. Out of that defense, came our offense. I always felt that Red ruled the defense with an iron fist. On offense, he'd allow some creativity on the part of the players. In terms of what they'd suggest and what they wanted to do.''

The thing that set the tone was always the defense. Show me a winner and I'll show you a team that knows how to play defense. It's the same in all sports. I remember a New York Giants baseball team that hit, I think, 221 homers one season but finished fourth. So much for offense.

Every one of the Knicks understood that. If they didn't at first, they knew it by the time they left. Defense was the name of our game. New York fans to this day chant ''Dee-fense'' whenever the Knicks make a major move in a Garden game.

''It's funny,'' said Bradley. ''Our daughter is now fifteen and a freshman. She plays basketball and we took her out to dinner after a game. We sat down and she was saying: 'Now in a one-three-one what do you do on this?' And I found myself describing our defense. 'Well, if you go there, this guy's got to come over and you double-team this.' ''

Bradley believed that our defense complemented what he called the core elements of the team. ''If we had started with offense, it would've been a mistake,'' he said. ''First we got Willis, then Barnett, Clyde, me and DeBusschere. Then we got our defense.''

Defense is hard work and many players do not prefer that. Offense is a lot more fun. ''I think our guys liked to play defense and that's the difference,'' said DeBusschere. ''We all enjoyed it. We got results and that's why everyone enjoyed it.''

We were a unique team. We were not big but we were smart—maybe the smartest team ever put together. We also had fun—all of which is related to winning, of course.

As Bradley pointed out: ''We were an interesting group the way we played. If we'd lost we would have been interesting bums. Because we won, we were an interesting group.''

The funniest thing was that, while defense became our trademark, the fans loved to watch us move the ball. That's what the New York fans appreciated.

It was the city game most New Yorkers had grown up with in the schoolyards. They recognized what was happening when we moved the ball around and had everyone involved.

It was the game I learned at City College from Nat Holman, one of the all-time great coaches. Everyone touched the ball on offense.

Of course, the game was different back in 1969–70. We'd run a play to get a layup or to get an easy open shot. Nowadays, they run a lot of plays so a guy can get the ball and go one-on-one. You can do that anytime you want and sometimes a situation calls for it. And sometimes you overdo it.

That's what they call the post-up offense these days. Everyone's moving and moving and they give the ball to one guy so he can go one-on-one. Our offense was designed to hit the open man—move the defense so it can't dig in but must react to the ball movement.

We were fortunate because every Knick knew how to handle the ball as well as hit the open shot. "The critical thing with us was that, when we had important shots to make, the defense couldn't key on one or two of us," said DeBusschere. "Every one of our guys was willing to take the shot and could make it. None of us were afraid to take it."

There are some teams that have one or two players who want the ball and are capable of hitting the final shot. We had five in the starting lineup plus a couple on the bench. They all wanted the ball with the game on the line.

"I remember certain teams we played. I could tell you the guy I was guarding didn't want the ball when we came down to the last minute," said DeBusschere. "I could just leave him out there. He didn't want the ball. He'd be just standing there in the corner."

That was one big advantage we had over Baltimore. The Bullets didn't have any great scorers or shooters—except for Monroe, of course, and we geared our defense to stop him as best we could. Nobody had five good guys to go to as we did.

March 26, 1970, was the day of the first game. Pete Maravich had just put on a 20-point NIT show in the Garden as LSU beat Georgetown in its opener. Oklahoma was next, coached by "Jack MacLeod," as one paper listed him.

Gump Worsley, 41, had just come back to the Garden with the Minnesota Stars and had beaten the Rangers 4–2. A headline read: "Deputy Mayor Robert Morgenthau Calls on Kids to Fight Drugs." And John Havlicek, out of the playoffs after a long run, revealed when the season ended abruptly for him: "I'm taking my wife to Jamaica next Wednesday."

We were ready to put our whole season on the line against Baltimore. After 82 games and all that hard work it had come down to one series. As a starter, we hoped. Training camp and the season opener seemed so long ago.

Our room on opening night at the Garden was unusually quite before the game. We were at full strength, though I wasn't too sure about Reed's knee and Bradley's ankle. Cazzie and Riordan had missed our last practice because of a post office emergency but had disposed of reserve duty and were getting dressed.

I was prepared for the most critical ad-libs of my life up to that point. I turned to Frazier and asked how many times he had heard me say: "This is a big game."

"Eighty-two, so far," he said without a pause.

"Forget whatever I said before. This is really a big game," I said, preserving my streak.

I didn't know how it happened but the Bullets jumped off to a 12–2 lead. Actually, I did know how it happened, which is why I called time then and there. We were tight. We were forcing things instead of playing our game.

I told them to let it flow. It's a game of instincts and they were overreacting. What a coach. We came right back with a 12-point run and it was a ballgame all the way through double overtime and some wild moments.

We won it 120–117. There were enough episodes to get a 13-week run on television. Monroe was involved in one highlight at the end of the third quarter when he became confused by the clock.

Now I don't have to tell you what a smart, alert player Monroe was. Yet, with the score 102–102 on Bradley's drive along the baseline and the clock running out, Earl became confused. I guess it was all the dizzy action that got to him.

DeBusschere had just saved us from being routed with one of his typical streaks. He scored 13 points, nailed six rebounds, blocked a shot and blanked Johnson in a third quarter that wound up tied. Monroe had a shot at winning it in regulation but hit the rim with two seconds left.

We went into the first of two five-minute overtimes. Monroe saw the five on the game clock and asked Frazier what five minutes was doing there. "That's the overtime," said Clyde. "Overtime?" said Earl. "I thought it was the end of the third period."

Kevin Loughery took another featured role. He was playing with a back brace that restricted his movement but didn't do much for his pain. He had a chance to put the game away in the first overtime. He had a wide-open 20-footer with the Bullets leading 110–107 inside the final minute but missed.

We then came down and they fouled DeBusschere but he made only one. The Bullets had been isolating Monroe and Frazier but this time Clyde knocked the ball loose. Barnett scooped it up and was fouled driving to the basket.

Good old Barnett. Nerves of steel. He made two and it was 110–110 with 23 seconds left. Baltimore could run the clock and win with a final shot. That's how close we came to losing the first game.

And that was when all our work on defense paid off. Frazier pressed Monroe as he brought the ball down. Earl was twirling and whirling, as usual. As Barnett came off his blind side, Earl swung away and right at Frazier, who knocked the ball loose.

Barnett picked it up with an open court ahead. He peeked at the clock. "I was looking to see if I had to shoot or had time to drive to the basket," he explained. He had time to drive to the basket.

He went up to lay the ball against the backboard for what appeared to be the winning basket. Suddenly from behind, an outstretched hand swatted the ball over the hoop and out of bounds.

It was Fred Carter. He had chased Barnett as soon as he saw Dick grab the loose ball. He was the only one. I don't know how many yards he spotted Barnett but he nailed him just in time. An amazing play.

I was off the bench screaming: "Goaltending!" So was every one of the 19,500 Knick fans in the sold-out Garden. It sure looked to me that Barnett had laid the ball against the backboard before Carter had knocked it away. That would be goaltending.

There was one problem. Make that two problems. Referees Mendy Rudolph and Ed Rush didn't see any goaltending. What they didn't see, they didn't call.

"I caught the ball with my hand before the ball hit the backboard. It was a clean block," explained Carter, who went on to become an assistant coach for the Sixers. "My hand hit it up. I knew Barnett had a step on me but I'm quicker and I caught up with him."

Despite that, we jumped ahead by five in the second overtime. The Bullets still refused to quit. They tied it with 52 seconds to go.

We finally won when Johnson gambled by dropping off DeBusschere and tried to steal the ball. That's when Reed went in for the winning dunk. A DeBusschere free throw iced it.

It was a noisy ending to a noisy and nervous night for us. "I had a lot to yell about," contributed Hosket from his 58-minute view on the bench.

Monroe played 54 of the 58 minutes, scored 39 points and exhausted Frazier as well as himself. "I think he got tired from beating me," said Clyde. "He played a helluva game. What can you do when we double-team him and he's hitting anyway? He drove me out of my mind.

"I had my body up against him. I had my hand in his face. But I got the steal and we won anyway."

That's why we went after Earl when we discovered he was available two seasons later. He became very unhappy in Baltimore. He and management had reached a dead end and we figured he'd look good on Broadway.

The Bullets, undoubtedly influenced by what they had seen in their 1969–70 playoffs with us, agreed to take Riordan, Stallworth and cash for him. That's when Monroe joined Frazier four games into the 1971–72 season to become our Rolls-Royce backcourt.

We went to the championship final that season and lost to the Lakers. But we won it all in the 1972–73 season—not a bad deal. In fact, Barnett, Monroe, DeBusschere and Jerry Lucas, who also played on our second championship team, were the best deals in Knick history, in my humble opinion.

DeBusschere, Reed and Frazier all played over 50 minutes in that opening game and I used Bradley for 42. Unseld outrebounded Reed 31–21 but Willis outscored him 30–14. DeBusschere balanced it off the boards with 24 to Johnson's 10. In fact, Debusschere, Reed and Frazier got 56 of our 61 rebounds.

BALTIMORE

	min	fg	fga	ft	fta	reb	ast	pf	pts
Carter	49	10	17	1	2	3	2	4	21
Heaney	1	0	0	0	0	0	0	0	0
Johnson	45	3	11	2	3	10	1	5	8
Loughery	23	3	10	1	1	0	2	2	7
Marin	40	8	20	1	1	5	4	6	17
Monroe	54	14	28	11	14	4	3	3	39
Scott	27	5	9	1	2	8	1	2	11
Unseld	51	6	15	2	3	31	5	4	14
TOTALS	290	49	110	19	26	61	18	26	117

NEW YORK

	min	fg	fga	ft	fta	reb	ast	pf	pts
Barnett	51	6	16	3	5	1	2	5	15
Bowman	4	0	1	0	0	1	0	0	0
Bradley	42	9	13	3	3	0	4	4	21
DeBusschere	52	8	20	6	11	24	4	4	22
Frazier	55	7	20	2	3	11	4	4	16
Reed	54	13	29	4	5	21	4	4	30
Riordan	14	1	3	0	0	1	2	4	2
Russell	11	3	8	2	2	1	1	1	8
Stallworth	7	3	5	0	0	1	4	2	6
TOTALS	290	50	115	20	29	61	25	28	120

Baltimore	22	30	23	27	8	7	—	117
New York	23	23	32	24	8	10	—	120

"I thought the Knicks played a little scared," said Johnson when it was over. I didn't believe that but I do know the coach was scared. The Bullets had met our good defense with their good defense and almost got off first.

We played the second game in Baltimore. Frustration had the Bullets and the city almost at the breaking point. We had now beaten them in 5 straight playoff games and they had lost 10 in a row overall.

Marin expressed the mood of the whole city by saying: "I'm tired of this 'Mission: Impossible' script." He was an intense competitor with a tremendous desire to win. A fiery spirit.

The papers also were building a fire under Johnson. They were ridiculing and even blaming him because DeBusschere had just had a great game against him.

DeBusschere actually felt sorry for Gus. He told Gus before the game that the writers weren't being fair blaming him. Dave suspected Gus would be taking it out on him. He was right.

There was nothing DeBusschere could do about it. He played Gus the usual way by giving him the outside shot and protecting against the drive. As cold as Gus was in the first game, that was how hot he was in this one.

He had 20 points by the half and we were in trouble. Bradley hadn't scored. Barnett had three points and DeBusschere had only one rebound. Damn those Baltimore writers.

We were sluggish for whatever the reason. I had to do something. I went to the bench, which showed how much faith I had in it. I took out DeBusschere and Barnett and replaced them with Riordan and Stallworth.

Barnett looked tired. He had played a lot of minutes and we were losing. I put Riordan in primarily to play Monroe. The Pearl's knees were bothering him but he was still capable of breaking any game open at any time.

We immediately had more zip. Riordan went wild. "Riordan did it," said Loughery after we came from behind to win 106–99 and make it 2–0. "At three quarters they were six back. He made a couple and it was down to two. That was the key part of the game."

Riordan triggered the run that put us ahead. He scored 11 of his 13 points in the final quarter and also wound up with 8 rebounds. At another time, he would have been a starting guard for us but not when we had Frazier and Barnett.

There is no doubt that our bench, represented by Riordan, saved that game for us. Mike put us in position to win but we still needed a lucky bounce or an alert play to preserve it.

We were ahead by three just inside the final two minutes when the Bullets pressed us into a desperate shot-clock situation. Bradley heaved one of those beat-the-clock shots that hit the side of the backboard.

It was one of those bang-bang plays and the Bullets got confused when the buzzer went off. They thought time had run out. Actually, when the ball hit the backboard, the 24-second clock was reset. It doesn't have to hit the rim. So while we all froze and ignored the ref's signal to keep playing, Bradley grabbed the rebound.

He ran some time off the reset shot clock and then fired an airball. It sailed over the hoop where Unseld and DeBusschere went up for it. DeBusschere won the battle by tapping it to Reed, who jammed it home. The Bullets screamed again. In the confusion, they thought Bradley's airball had created a 24-second violation by not touching the basket.

The Bullets were slow to react. It was a second straight heartbreaker and the Bullets argued about the second Bradley call in particular. They even called time to dispute it.

"It was a wild thing," said Loughery, who was one of the first to put the full-court press on referees Jack Madden and Don Murphy. "I was just trying to get them to rule that maybe the shot [Reed's] came too late. We were looking for any kind of thing."

Bradley explained his first shot this way: "I looked at the clock and there were five seconds on it." And the second shot: "I heard Dave yell: 'Four, three!'"

"For three quarters we kicked the hell out of them," said Johnson, who had 28 points and 12 rebounds to DeBusschere's 14 points and 9 rebounds.

Loughery couldn't play that much because of his back, so Gene Shue went with six men, in effect. Unseld outrebounded Reed once more but Willis outshot him. Willis hit 11-for-19 for 27 points, while Wes was limited to 4-for-7 and 10 points.

Riordan also held Monroe to 6-for-16 and 19 points, practically a shutout against us. "Two good ball games and they get them both," said Loughery after those two games on the wild side.

We won them both but I could sense the ticking of a time bomb. I was wondering when the Bullets would explode. We hadn't exactly dominated the second game, either.

BALTIMORE

	min	fg	fga	ft	fta	reb	ast	pf	pts
Carter	37	5	17	2	3	3	7	5	12
Johnson	43	12	18	4	4	12	1	2	28
Marin	41	10	17	2	5	6	2	4	22
Monroe	41	6	16	7	8	3	4	1	19
Scott	14	1	5	1	1	2	1	0	3
Unseld	43	4	7	2	2	21	5	3	10
Loughery	21	2	9	1	1	0	0	4	5
TOTALS	240	40	89	19	24	47	20	19	99

NEW YORK

	min	fg	fga	ft	fta	reb	ast	pf	pts
Barnett	28	4	11	2	2	1	6	2	10
Bowman	5	1	1	0	1	0	0	0	2
Bradley	33	7	14	1	1	3	4	3	15
DeBusschere	43	7	14	0	1	9	1	3	14
Frazier	46	8	13	3	5	4	6	2	19
Reed	43	11	19	5	5	17	2	4	27
Riordan	23	6	10	1	3	8	3	2	13
Russell	9	3	5	0	0	0	0	1	6
Stallworth	10	0	1	0	0	2	0	2	0
Warren	1	0	0	0	0	0	0	1	0
TOTALS	240	47	88	12	18	44	22	20	106

Baltimore	26	25	32	16	—	99
New York	26	22	29	29	—	106

I closed the dressing room a little longer after the game. I cautioned the players to be careful what they said to the reporters. I didn't want anyone to say something that would go onto the Bullets' bulletin board.

That's a notorious practice in sports. What you say today you might choke on tomorrow. I wasn't really worried about our players because they were a smart group but I wanted to make sure.

Don't you think that one of the first reporters in our room asked about the Knicks possibly winning four straight? ''They're too tough'' led all our clichés.

We were in no position to be carried away. We were dominating most of the statistics but not the games. We had come too far to let some loose talk motivate the Bullets even more than they already were.

We were going home for the third game and we had the advantage—in the standings. I still remember how Reed's knee was hurting. It was remarkable how he pushed himself despite so much pain.

He had arthritis, and cortisone was the only thing that helped. Temporarily, of course. It's a medication that has to be used carefully and Reed always was under the advisement of our team doctor.

We had an off day before the third game so I excused Willis from practice. It wasn't a major workout—just enough to keep the players loose and allow them to have some fun with each other.

They needled Riordan about what Shue had said after the game in Baltimore. Gene had admitted that Mike had killed the Bullets but then suggested Riordan would be the fifth guard on his team.

That got Riordan's Irish up. He was a proud individual who had fought his way onto the team despite obstacles he didn't think he deserved. He attacked every minute of the game I gave him. He never complained. He was the hardhat worker of the Knicks.

It was understandable that he bristled over Shue's comment and the players enjoyed it. They wanted him to explode and he did with: ''If Shue has four guards better than me then why isn't he winning?''

A good question, and the answer was provided in the third game back at our place. A win at the Garden and we would be in complete command. It was Easter Sunday and the game was on national TV.

My main concern was with Willis. He was limping. I talked to him and he said he was okay. That's the way he was. He wasn't going to shirk his responsibility. He was the team leader and he had to be out in front all the time.

I knew we were in trouble right away. Unseld was beating Willis to every rebound. Reed would never ask out, so I had to remove him. He actually played only 29 minutes and we were thrashed 127–113.

On our own court, no less. You never heard such silence, if there is such a thing, from 19,500 fans. All Unseld did was outrebound our entire team 34–30. No one ever heard of that before.

All the noise was in the Baltimore dressing room for a change. "Looka this, thirty-four rebounds," said Carter as he spotted Unseld's stats in the boxscore.

"Would you believe this, the Knicks got only thirty?" said assistant coach Bob Ferry. What he conveniently overlooked was the technicals. He and Danny Whelan each got one, so we at least tied in that category.

Otherwise we never were really in it because of Loughery. He did a striptease and had Monroe help him out of the back brace between periods and we paid for it. What a relief—for him, not us.

We had the usual problem with Monroe as he scored 25. What we didn't prepare for was 17 points by Loughery in 19 minutes. He had two baskets in nine minutes before we walked off at the half leading by one and then went crazy.

What triggered it was another 24-second confusion, which had become so familiar by then. This time we were confused. Stallworth took a shot that we believed hit the lower part of the backboard as the buzzer sounded.

Referee Richie Powers signaled a 24-second violation. The clock was reset and, as we were arguing, Loughery broke downcourt and was fouled a tick before the third-period buzzer.

Kevin made those two, giving him seven straight points, and he added six more at the start of the fourth quarter. He had scored 13 of 21 Baltimore points and we never caught up.

I had to admire the Bullets' defense. That's what really wins ballgames. I know they gloated over it. They knew that was our strength so they started talking about beating the Knicks at their own game.

Fred Carter had become their not-so-secret weapon. He was the third guard and Shue was using him on Frazier alongside Monroe to give Earl a rest.

Carter was still coming off the bench and Shue said: "Fred is playing like the most valuable player in the league for us. He's giving us everything. Tremendous defense on Frazier. He's playing him everywhere."

13

It was praise from Caesar as far as Carter was concerned. Frazier had one run. He hit three straight at the end of the first period and opened the fourth with another. That helped us to a 10-point lead and we felt comfortable.

Not for long. Carter lived up to his nickname, Mad Dog, to virtually shut down Clyde. "I harass him," Carter explained, "I guess, like what he does with Earl Monroe. You don't want him to penetrate. You have to be aggressive."

Monroe was remarkable despite being in such pain; he had to take cortisone shots in his knee before the game. "The cortisone made the bumps go down," he said after still shooting 10-for-18. He was referring to knots that had formed on both knees.

I had to use Hosket at center with Reed limping and in foul trouble. Bowman, my backup center, hadn't done well but Hos contributed three baskets and three rebounds in his 13 minutes.

"We gotta play every game this way," said Marin, who found winning a playoff game more pleasant.

"We played lousy basketball compared to them," offered Barnett, our wise man.

"This series is a lot of rah-rah. It's exciting to me," said Warren, our only rookie.

"It hurts a little when you get into foul trouble," said Willis, ignoring his knee. "But that didn't cause Unseld to get all those rebounds."

What could I say? So I asked Danny Whelan if he had cursed when he got his technical. "No. I just kept yelling 'Three seconds, three seconds,'" he said. It should be mentioned at this point that our trainer led the league in drawing the referees' attention to that violation.

BALTIMORE

	min	fg	fga	ft	fta	reb	ast	pf	pts
Carter	40	7	17	9	11	6	3	5	23
Ellis	2	0	1	0	0	1	0	0	0
Heaney	2	0	2	0	0	1	0	0	0
Johnson	43	6	15	2	4	7	3	2	14
Loughery	19	6	9	5	5	2	1	3	17
Marin	38	9	14	2	2	8	3	3	20
Miles	10	0	0	0	0	0	0	0	0
Monroe	33	10	18	5	5	3	5	4	25
Scott	10	2	6	1	1	1	1	2	5
Tucker	2	0	0	0	0	0	0	0	0
Unseld	41	9	17	5	6	34	4	2	23
TOTALS	240	49	99	29	34	63	20	21	127

NEW YORK

	min	fg	fga	ft	fta	reb	ast	pf	pts
Barnett	32	7	10	5	5	1	2	2	19
Bowman	6	0	1	0	0	2	1	2	0
Bradley	33	4	11	4	5	4	4	3	12
DeBusschere	38	7	14	4	6	10	2	5	18
Frazier	42	10	22	4	4	4	5	2	24
Hosket	13	3	5	0	1	3	0	2	6
May	2	0	0	0	0	0	0	0	0
Reed	29	4	16	4	4	5	3	5	12
Riordan	18	4	5	0	0	0	0	3	8
Russell	8	6	2	0	0	0	0	0	2
Stallworth	17	6	8	0	0	1	0	0	12
Warren	4	0	1	0	0	0	0	1	0
TOTALS	240	46	95	21	25	30	17	25	113

Baltimore	27	36	32	32	—	127
New York	30	34	21	28	—	113

"We beat them at their own game," said Gus Johnson.

"They're beating us at our own game," echoed Walt Frazier.

They convinced me that the Bullets were beating us at our own game after they tied the series at home. Just in case I was tired of hearing that, Gene Shue said: ''We figured if we held them under a hundred we'd win.'' That was our own game, so to speak.

Holding teams under 100 was something our defense had popularized. We had just lost 102–92 and the Bullets, understandably, were rubbing our noses in it.

I say ''understandably'' because basketball is a highly emotional game where pride and ego have everyone on the brink. It's also a contact sport where players constantly rubbed together can cause a fire at any time.

Marin and Johnson were seething after we took the first two games. So were Unseld and Monroe, though they had better control of their emotions. Only the looks on their faces revealed the anger deep inside them.

We had humiliated them and the city of Baltimore in six straight playoff games and now they had gotten even—with us and New York City. Johnny Unitas, Frank Robinson and all the others upset by the Mets and Jets were feeling a little better.

It was Robinson who had said: ''New York can beat Baltimore at tiddlywinks.''

All the Baltimore frustration exploded when the Bullets held us to 34 points in the first 21 minutes. The fans went wild. They sounded like ours back home. They were having their anti–New York feelings finally exorcised.

There were 12,289 fans jammed into Baltimore's small arena and there didn't seem to be one New York voice among them. ''These fans never showed the enthusiasm they did tonight,'' said Loughery, a New Yorker from St. John's in sheep's clothing. ''They were screaming: 'We're number one.' I never heard that before.''

We didn't just roll over. We gave them too good a start. We fell behind by 21 before we began asserting what I considered our superiority. They were a very good team but I felt we were better. All we had to do was prove it.

We closed within six but Monroe was too much for a change. I did my best to wear him down by using Frazier and Barnett on him.

I actually gave Riordan 25 minutes, hoping the constant pressure would tire Earl.

Nothing worked. Earl hit 14 of 25 shots, some impossible for anyone but him. Shue told the Bullets to clear out and let Monroe work on Riordan in the closing minutes. Mike did a good job of forcing him away from the basket.

It didn't matter. Monroe kept us from catching the Bullets all by himself. He hit two specific fading bombs that would have been three-pointers today. He wound up with 34 points and the series was tied at two.

We just couldn't do a thing with Monroe's incredible concentration. The real super-players are like that. The more noise and pressure, the more they shut out everything and operate in their own isolated world.

Frazier was one of the top defensive players of his time and Riordan was one of the most intense. Yet they couldn't distract Earl. Said Riordan: "I'm talking to him. I'm saying 'C'mon. You got it. Shoot it.' I'm not trying to be a hot dog but we want him to shoot from out there. I had my hand in his face."

Mike said he would give Monroe "40-footers" all the time. That was players' exaggeration. Actually, Earl hit 25-footers—good enough for him, bad enough for us.

I didn't need Loughery to remind me that our defense couldn't contain Monroe in one-on-one situations, but he did. "He shoots better with guys all over him and with hands in his face," said Kevin. "The only way to stop him when he's on is with a gun."

I was considering that but it was too late to get a permit. What really bothered me was what Frazier had detected. "We're letting them get off," he said. "They're playing a more aggressive defense. They're overplaying our forwards."

That becomes conspicuous when you miss your shots. DeBusschere, Bradley, Cazzie and Stallworth proved the point by going 13-for-42. Frazier and Reed, despite a knee that was getting worse, got 45 of our 92 points.

We weren't going to win with that point distribution. We had to make our shots because we weren't getting too many seconds.

Unseld pulled down 24 more rebounds. He had 110 for four games. Too much.

Did that excite him? "I've got time to get excited," he reminded the enthusiastic ones in his dressing room. "We got two more to go. I think we realize this is for keeps. We want to stay around a little longer. I'm not ready to go on vacation yet. I know it's going to be rough. Maybe that's why I'm not excited."

Gus Johnson was the happiest man in Baltimore. "I was so elated. I wanted to jump on someone's shoulders or pick somebody up on my shoulders," said this magnificent player, who died much too young from brain cancer a few years ago.

> *"I'm convinced that basketball demands, and produces, the finest athletes of all the professional sports."*
>
> *—Dave DeBusschere*

"All you have to look at is my face. I'm ready to explode," said Marin.

We were annoyed because the Bullets had outplayed us but it wasn't the Knicks' nature to get excited over a loss—or even the two straight that helped the Bullets' psyche. Our confidence wasn't even shaken though it was now 2–2.

BALTIMORE

	min	fg	fga	ft	fta	reb	ast	pf	pts
Carter	32	4	12	5	7	4	7	4	13
Ellis	1	0	0	0	0	0	0	0	0
Heaney	1	0	0	0	0	0	0	0	0
Johnson	41	8	14	2	3	13	2	2	18
Loughery	20	4	13	0	0	3	1	4	8
Marin	41	6	19	3	3	7	4	3	15
Miles	9	0	2	0	0	2	0	2	0
Monroe	43	14	25	6	7	6	2	5	34
Scott	11	2	4	2	2	0	0	1	6
Unseld	41	2	5	4	4	24	4	2	8
TOTALS	240	40	94	22	25	59	20	23	102

NEW YORK

	min	fg	fga	ft	fta	reb	ast	pf	pts
Barnett	26	3	8	0	0	2	0	3	6
Bowman	9	0	0	0	0	2	0	2	0
Bradley	30	3	12	3	5	2	2	2	9
DeBusschere	36	4	10	4	4	5	0	1	12
Frazier	44	11	21	3	3	6	7	2	25
Reed	46	8	21	4	4	15	2	2	20
Riordan	25	3	6	2	3	5	2	1	8
Russell	11	2	8	0	0	2	0	4	4
Stallworth	19	4	13	0	0	8	2	1	8
Warren	1	0	0	0	0	1	0	0	0
TOTALS	240	28	99	16	19	48	15	18	92

Baltimore	26	27	24	25	—	102
New York	21	25	21	25	—	92

"We're denied but undaunted," said Frazier. "I still think we're a much better team," said DeBusschere. "We're professionals." I agreed but I wasn't about to supply any more ammunition to the Bullets.

Reed was in serious trouble for the fifth game. He needed cortisone but didn't like needles. Who does? Unseld was outplaying him off the boards because of Willis's knee. He still got 15 in the fourth game. Our team doctor prescribed cortisone.

We also had to do something about Monroe. He hadn't hurt us during the regular season but now he was killing us. Frazier couldn't stop him. Neither could doubling up on him with Barnett because Dick's man was taking him away from Earl.

We talked it over and decided to change our double-teaming strategy. This time the closest player to Monroe would drop off and help Frazier. That meant the other players would have to switch when DeBusschere or Bradley helped Clyde with Earl.

We worked on it at practice on the off day. We knew that Monroe didn't like to give up the ball once he had it. In fact, he came to the Knicks with that reputation—which is why everyone said we'd need two basketballs with him and Frazier in the same backcourt.

We know what happened with that. Monroe made the sacrifice in his shooting game and showed he could pass if that's what it took to win. He kept the ball in Baltimore because he was the best scorer by far. Scoring was his role in that situation. He and Frazier became one of the top backcourts in history.

Reed had made one attempt to spare the New York TV audience the full agony of the fourth game. He ran into the press table and knocked the plug out of Madison Square Garden cable. Bob Wolff, our announcer, was blanked for a few minutes but was forced to resume the unfortunate details.

What can I say about Willis Reed? I don't think to this day that people really appreciate what a great competitor he was. I know he's in the Hall of Fame but they rarely mention him in the same sentence with Chamberlain, Russell and Abdul-Jabbar.

I do. When he was healthy he could play with the best of them even though he was giving away up to six inches at times. Remember, he was a small 6′9″ but played all the seven-footers.

He's the most underrated Hall-of-Famer of all time, in my opinion. He took a cortisone shot and had a Hall of Fame game in the Garden to give us a 3–2 lead in the series. Cazzie also had to be given cortisone because his knee was bothering him.

"I don't know if I can stand it," said Frazier after our 21-point victory put us one win away from the next series. "I'd rather play one game for everything."

Mr. Cool was not enamored of the way we had allowed the Bullets to get back into the series. Remember, we hadn't as yet established anything. We were still seeking our first championship and had just blown our stranglehold on the opening playoff.

"I respect us even more because we were playing one for a lot of marbles and we exploded," continued Clyde. "If we had the championship spirit like the Celtics, we wouldn't have let the Bullets come back after we won the first two games. But that's something we'll develop. Mental toughness. The killer instinct."

Reed always had the killer instinct. He had taken the needle he hated so much in his bad left knee and then said after we won: "It's about time we got it going"—a few words but to the point. He had a message for the Bullets and he handed it to them himself, special delivery.

Willis staged a command performance that was one of the best I'd seen under those playoff circumstances. We had to win the game or go back to Baltimore facing elimination.

Somebody had to step up or we were in serious trouble—the 1969–70 championship might not have happened. Willis, the captain, appointed himself. All he did was score 36 points and grab 36 rebounds as we won 101–80.

Bradley got us off with three straight baskets that had us leading by one and he wound up with five for the quarter. We proceeded to shut down Monroe with 18 points with our special defense.

Reed also did a job on Unseld off the boards. Wes got only 15 rebounds, practically a shutout for him. Our defense was simply sensational, a word I seldom used.

Of course, Gene Shue blamed it on bad shooting. He was statistically right because the Bullets were 7-for-50 in the second half. They were 1-for-18 during one fourth-quarter stretch.

We each wound up taking 104 shots but we made 42 to their 28. "You can say I was taken out because of Willis," said Unseld after leaving the game when Shue decided not to waste him in a lost cause.

"He (Reed) moved better than I've ever seen, like a guard," said Ray Scott, who divided his time as a Bullets sub and promoter of boxing in Detroit.

I can't forget the job Frazier did on Monroe this time. I had talked to him before the game. I reminded him that Earl was killing us and asked if he could stop him. I told him to forget about his offense and concentrate on defense.

Frazier played Monroe nose to nose but still gambled at times. He knew Willis was back there protecting him. Reed was a demon cop, moving all over the place and demolishing the Bullets at both ends of the court.

Earl still scored 13 points and had his teammates within 5 at the half. We really blanketed him after that. He got only eight more shots and made only one. Baltimore got only 20 points in the third quarter. Its 80 total became the lowest for a playoff game in 13 years. Carter's jumper at the buzzer avoided a record low of 78.

Carter blamed himself for not setting a fire and making only 3 baskets on 16 shots. "Pros should hit forty percent without any trouble in every game," said Marin, who wasn't too bad with 6-for-15. "We were simply flat. We played four highly emotional games. We weren't psyched up tonight."

Our crowd sensed that and never let the Bullets out of their mood. I finally was able to take the starters out to give the fans a chance to show their appreciation. Reed, DeBusschere and Frazier took their bows. The audience went wild, especially over Willis.

I went wild over Willis and was tempted to order a new supply of cortisone. "It's not the shots that you take—it's professional pride," said Shue, referring to Reed's needle before the game. He was right.

Reed sat in front of his locker after the game counting 10s, 20s, 50s and 100s.

"Is this playoff money?" someone asked.

"That's spending money," responded the team's biggest spender. "You got to have a little cash on you."

He had just cashed a very big game and no one knew better than Unseld. "You can use any phrase you want but you can say he chased me off the court. The truth is the truth," said Wes, knowing one more game like that and it was all over for him and his team.

Leroy Ellis had a brief encounter as the third center on Willis. "You want a word for him tonight? Fantastic," he said. Reed was super-quick. He had the Bullets a step behind him all night. His shot in the knee gave us a shot in the arm—just in time.

"I was moving around tonight. It was a must game for us," said Willis.

"The intensity was there tonight and it will be there again," promised Bradley, who faded to 2-for-12 after his great start. "What wins the game is what you do on the floor. We went over our defense. We were a little more aggressive. Not reckless but bold."

"Bradley was keyed up. DeBusschere was keyed up. I was charged up but in a cooler way," suggested Frazier.

The Bullets had been needling us with the fact that they were beating us at our own game. Johnson put it this way: "Tonight we didn't play their game or ours."

BALTIMORE

	min	fg	fga	ft	fta	reb	ast	pf	pts
Carter	29	3	16	0	0	3	0	3	6
Ellis	5	0	3	2	2	2	0	0	2
Heaney	1	0	0	0	0	0	0	0	0
Johnson	37	1	14	5	6	10	1	2	7
Loughery	28	6	16	4	7	3	0	3	16
Marin	37	6	15	7	7	11	6	1	19
Miles	13	0	3	0	0	1	0	1	0
Monroe	42	7	21	4	8	2	3	3	18
Scott	10	0	5	2	2	3	1	0	2
Tucker	1	0	0	0	0	0	0	0	0
Unseld	37	5	11	0	2	15	1	4	10
TOTALS	240	28	104	24	34	50	12	17	80

NEW YORK

	min	fg	fga	ft	fta	reb	ast	pf	pts
Barnett	38	5	14	1	1	3	2	3	11
Bowman	3	0	5	0	0	3	0	2	0
Bradley	32	7	15	0	1	8	3	4	14
DeBusschere	40	4	15	5	7	12	5	5	13
Frazier	43	7	13	2	3	16	6	4	16
Reed	45	14	26	8	9	36	3	3	36
Riordan	13	4	7	1	1	2	1	1	9
Russell	8	1	3	0	0	2	0	0	2
Stallworth	16	0	5	0	0	5	0	3	0
Warren	2	0	1	0	0	0	0	0	0
TOTALS	240	42	104	17	22	87	20	25	101

Baltimore	27	22	20	11	—	80
New York	31	23	22	25	—	101

We had two days off before the sixth game in Baltimore. I gave DeBusschere permission to fly to Detroit for the wedding of his youngest sister. We worked out the day before the game and flew to Baltimore to get a good night's rest.

We were very loose. We could afford to lose and still go home for the clinching seventh game. Barnett made us laugh, as usual, when he called our attention to someone who had walked up to Riordan and told him: "You're really playing great basketball this year, Cazzie."

Mike figured it was just another Bullets fan sticking it to him. Riordan had become somewhat of a Baltimore target. I guess they didn't like his aggressive, knock-'em-down style of play. Little did any of us know that a season later he'd be in a Bullets uniform and become a hero in Baltimore.

He parlayed his popularity into Riordan's Saloon in Annapolis. He still owns it, as well as a partnership in nearby Griffin's.

For me, Baltimore in April was no time to be playing basketball. The weather was too warm and lazy. It was more like beach time. It was hard to stimulate the juices for an indoor game. I was always concerned that it would affect the players.

Give me a nice cold winter's night for NBA playoffs anytime. Like the days when the Lakers were in Minneapolis and you'd get this cheerful wake-up call from the hotel operator: "Good morning. It's five o'clock and fifteen below."

It was then that I discovered what the Minneapolis people meant when they referred to their deep-freeze as a "dry cold." Your ears dropped off without you knowing it. The one good thing about those trips was that Max Winter would get you fur-collared Storm King coats wholesale.

I changed my litany for this pivotal game. I told the players not to let the Bullets go back to New York. We had them down, let's knock 'em out.

To show you what effect that speech had on my guys, the Bullets won the game and sent the series back to New York for a seventh and final one. They won 106–87 and 60 of the points were provided by Monroe and Johnson.

DeBusschere got into foul trouble early and I suspected it would be a long day's journey for us. The first quarter was real wacky. We led 18–15 by the end of it as the Bullets shot 4-for-16.

We weren't much better but the worst part was that DeBusschere already had picked up three personals. That turned Johnson loose and he was off like a mad bull. Monroe made it a stampede, especially in the third quarter when he and Johnson scored Baltimore's first 28 points.

Monroe was a frisky colt, having taken a cortisone shot right after the fifth game in New York. On our side, Reed's cortisone had worn off, obviously. This time he shot 2-for-14 and contributed only 10 points in 45 minutes. Add 1-for-9 from Bradley and 2-for-11 from DeBusschere and you know what happened.

I had them both on the bench a long time. We actually led by two at the half but DeBusschere drew his fourth personal early in the third period. Johnson attacked him for three straight baskets and I was forced to remove Dave.

Stallworth and Cazzie preserved some of our dignity. They came off the bench with 25 points. Old Man Barnett was the only starter to play up to our standards. He was 6-for-9 in the first half but got only two shots after that. No fault of his.

We still had a small chance in the game. We were behind by only six with about 90 seconds to go when we stole the ball from Monroe. We had a two-on-one break. Loughery cut in front of Riordan in time to distract him and cause Mike to miss a driving layup. Bradley was the trailer but he failed to convert the rebound.

It was all over but the grumbling in our dressing room. That was unusual. We were a very unhappy team. Our defense wasn't bad but our shooting was awful and that can do things to anyone's nerves. Besides, we were now down to one game and coming off a bad one for us.

"We didn't take command at the start," said DeBusschere, who wound up with five personals early in the last quarter. I had to sit him, which he didn't exactly like.

"If we had made any shots at the beginning, we could have put it away," said Frazier, who was a shallow 5-for-15 himself. "It's good we're going home," he added. "It means a lot emotionally," said DeBusschere.

I would have preferred winning myself. This way we gave Monroe, Johnson and Unseld a life. No one was more grateful than Gus, who didn't like the way he was being treated. It was his last chance to make a statement.

"People have been saying I sold the Bullets out, that I have been lying down on the job," he said after his major 44 minutes, which included 14 rebounds. "Maybe this is redemption. Hell, I'm not knocking DeBusschere but we've both been pretty lousy. We were beating up on each other today and I got the edge this time. You don't know how bad I wanted to win this game. I lay awake all night thinking about it."

I couldn't figure out how anyone could play as he had without any sleep. He had been a nightmare to us and I hoped that he got the good night's sleep before our seventh game.

"Gus is an emotional player," explained DeBusschere. "He hits his buckets and starts all kinds of moves. He gets to do his stuff and he's really tough then. I was in trouble early so I couldn't play him the way I wanted today. Then I had to sit and watch him. That was the toughest."

DeBusschere hadn't been shooting well and that was on his mind as we headed into the clincher. "That's going to make it easier for Gus," said Dave, not really believing it.

I didn't believe it either because I knew how DeBusschere responded under great pressure. I didn't underestimate, though, the lift that Johnson had just gotten from this one big effort of his.

I recognized it even more when he discussed the star-shaped diamond inlay he'd been wearing for years in an upper front tooth. He said he was finally going to remove it.

"It was something different, unique you know, when I had it put in," he explained. "A star for a star. Now it's lost its purpose, so I'm going to have it taken out." He was a star who no longer needed a gimmick for recognition.

I had to admire Loughery. He had discarded his protective brace and took a great risk to play at all. He had a visible scar on his chest where they had gone in to repair his punctured lung. He could have punctured it again but played anyway.

"I was hurting the first two games. I was terrible," he said. "I couldn't shoot and you get so damned sick and tired of the Knicks beating you all the time."

He was bugged by the way the Garden fans had taunted the

Bullets after they had dropped the first two games. "The crowd kept yelling 'Four straight,'" he said, meaning a sweep. "How much of that crap can you take? I'm a professional, you know."

BALTIMORE

	min	fg	fga	ft	fta	reb	ast	pf	pts
Carter	33	6	16	0	1	5	2	4	12
Heaney	1	0	0	0	0	0	0	0	0
Johnson	44	12	23	7	9	14	0	3	31
Loughery	17	1	9	1	1	5	3	5	3
Marin	33	2	11	7	8	7	1	5	11
Miles	19	2	2	0	0	2	0	2	4
Monroe	45	11	25	7	7	4	5	3	29
Scott	7	0	2	0	2	3	0	1	0
Tucker	1	0	0	0	0	0	0	0	0
Unseld	40	2	7	2	2	24	2	4	6
TOTALS	240	36	95	24	30	64	13	27	96

NEW YORK

	min	fg	fga	ft	fta	reb	ast	pf	pts
Barnett	29	6	11	2	5	1	1	0	14
Bradley	32	1	9	3	3	2	2	3	5
DeBusschere	24	2	11	0	0	8	1	5	4
Frazier	45	5	15	8	13	8	5	4	18
Hosket	3	0	0	0	0	1	0	2	0
Reed	45	2	14	6	7	16	2	2	10
Riordan	22	5	10	1	1	1	0	2	11
Russell	12	4	7	1	1	1	1	0	9
Stallworth	28	6	11	4	4	12	0	4	16
TOTALS	240	31	88	25	34	50	12	22	87

Baltimore	15	26	30	25	—	96
New York	18	25	23	21	—	87

We received sad news the day we were to play the Bullets for the Eastern Division title in the Garden. We heard that Maurice Stokes had died.

None of our players really knew Stokes but some had appeared in the Maurice Stokes Game named for him. It's been staged at Kutsher's Country Club in Monticello, New York, since Stokes was stricken with encephalitis in 1958.

He had banged his head in a game the Cincinnati Royals had just played. He was on his way home with the team when he became ill on the plane. The brain injury left him speechless and paralyzed in the hospital.

Jack Twyman, a teammate, had himself appointed Stokes's legal guardian. The main fund-raiser for the hospital bills came from the Stokes Game, in which all the stars of the day participated. Chamberlain, Russell, Cousy and Oscar Robertson donated their services to help a former player in great need.

I knew Stokes as an outstanding college player at St. Francis of Loretta, Pennsylvania, and then as a member of the Rochester Royals team for which I had played. I was coaching the St. Louis Hawks when he first came into the NBA. And I've also coached at the Stokes Game.

His is one of the sad stories of the NBA. He was struck down in his third season of a certain Hall of Fame career. I remember him as a big, pleasant individual who loved the game and lived for it at a time when there was very little money.

Twyman knew him better. "He was always watching or listening to games," said Jack, who handled all of Stokes's affairs until he died at the age of 36. "You'll never know, meet or read about anybody as courageous as Maurice. I never heard the man complain in twelve years of lying on his back. His mind was unaffected and he wanted very badly to live."

Life isn't always fun and games for some people. I am still impressed by the way all the big names in the NBA rushed to help Stokes. I sometimes wonder if today's athletes have lost a lot of that.

We had the final game with the Bullets on our minds. We had every reason to be up for this one. New York had been looking so long for a team that could finally win a championship. We were the better team and we were playing before our friendly fans in the Garden.

All good reasons why we should win. The best one came from Geri DeBusschere, though. She bugged her husband about the necessity of winning. He reassured her the Knicks would. "Well, you'd better," she finally informed him. "We need the money for

Historic shot of Willis Reed in pain before he left the fifth game of the championship series with the Lakers.

Dramatic moment when Knick captain strolls onto the floor for the seventh game without being noticed by the other Knicks.

All photos copyright © George Kalinsky, Major League Graphics.

Our bench senses the Knicks's first NBA championship is in the record book and begins celebrating.

I get a little more animated as a happy Dave DeBusschere comes out of the game and congratulates Willis Reed for his incredible contribution.

It's all over now, and Champagne flows in the winners' dressing room.
Nate Bowman showers Howard Cosell as Bill Bradley and Dave
DeBusschere act as bookends.

Willis Reed speaks to the world, as team president Ned Irish and
Garden Chairman of the Board Irving Mitchell Felt stand by.

It is trophy time with the NBA commissioner Walter Kennedy. First he hands me one for winning the Eastern Division title.

Then Willis Reed joins in accepting the Walter Brown silver bowl for the NBA title.

Willis Reed invites the team to his weekly TV show that was another fringe benefit from the 1969–70 championship season.

Phil Jackson sees the playoffs through his candid camera, in his role as my designated team photographer.

I am voted into the Hall of Fame and visit it with two people who helped me make it—my wife, Selma, and Fuzzy Levane.

We point to a picture of our Rochester Royals team that also won an NBA title when I was a player.

Senator Bill Bradley at the Hall of Fame with wife Ernestine, at his induction.

Bradley joins sports announcer Curt Gowdy on the dais with Dave DeBusschere, who was inducted at the same time with Dollar Bill.

Dave DeBusschere's wife, Geri, and his daughter and sons look on as his Number 22 is about to be hung from the Garden rafters.

It's number retirement night at the Garden for me and Dick Barnett. My number represents my total victories as an NBA coach. Bill Bradley and DeBusschere join Barnett's wife, Irma, his son, and his mother.

the heating in our summer home and for the new carpeting in our house in Detroit.''

How could the Bullets overcome that? Of course, I didn't know that the Bullets were hearing the same thing from their wives.

''I talked to my wife in Ohio,'' said Johnson, ''and she told me to win it. There's ten grand if we do. She wanted to fly in with my sister and the trainer of my dog. I've got a champion show dog, a Great Dane. I told her to forget it, we haven't won the series yet. At least my dog's having more success than I've been having.''

We already had earned $20,000 for finishing first in our division and having the best record in the NBA. There was $25,000 more if we beat the Bullets. The loser got $20,000.

No one had to remind the Bullets how much money we had cost them the previous season. They won the Eastern Division and we sent them home with only $45,000 to split. There would be $25,000 more for the winner of our next series and $17,500 for the loser. Going all the way meant $118,000, a major incentive.

Now let's take a look at what the NBA champions get today. Chicago won it in 1991 and this was its payoff: $95,000 for the best NBA record, $90,000 as conference winner, $46,875 for winning the first round, $55,000 for the second round, $91,250 as conference champion and $545,000 for the NBA title.

That adds up to $923,125, which made the $118,000 for the 1970 NBA winner look like petty cash. But that was good money in those days. Our players thought so as they prepared to go on.

''Now the big money,'' was the Nate Bowman reminder in our dressing room before our survival game with the Bullets. ''How much do you want it?'' someone scribbled on the blackboard.

Dick McGuire, of all people, wiped the message off the board. ''They're high enough, why get them higher?'' said McGuire, who was scouting for us.

There was idle talk in our dressing room. We were all a little nervous underneath. We already had decided on a game plan. Monroe was the target. If we could stop him, we'd stop the Bullets.

We would try to keep the ball out of his hands. If not, we'd try to force him to pass but not to Johnson, if we could help it. Our defense was going to be the key to our game.

I also instructed Barnett to bring the ball up. I wanted to conserve Frazier's energy for the job of disturbing Monroe's shooting. I didn't want Clyde to even think about shooting. He could pick up Earl in the dressing room for all I cared.

I don't know how many people ever attended a Knick game in those days. The crowd would start getting noisy and applauding even before "The Star-Spangled Banner" concluded. The noise would build up like the blowing of air into a balloon, then it would explode.

That Garden crowd always was our sixth man. It could demolish the eardrums as well as the nerves of our opponents and sometimes the referees. The noise and the chants of "Dee-fense! Dee-fense!" always helped demoralize the other teams and lift us.

I must tell you a little story about that. It's 22 years later, when this book is being written, and a guy is running up Second Avenue in New York City. It's around 79th Street where the southbound-only traffic is some of the heaviest in the city during business hours.

Buses, taxis, trucks and cars are jamming the three driving lanes. Now picture this: A lone figure is running against the flow of traffic. He's dressed in jeans, sports shirt and sneakers and is waving his arms as he screams: "Dee-fense! Dee-fense!" Only in New York.

That's the edge the Knicks had at home in those days. What we didn't know then was that Monroe's knee was so bad they had given him another shot right after the sixth game. Poor guy. He only played 41 minutes and got 32 points against my best defensive strategy.

We didn't get off the way I wanted. Johnson broke loose from DeBusschere to score six of Baltimore's first eight points. I knew Dave would take care of that. He did by sneaking into the passing lane a little more.

For some reason that discouraged the Bullets from giving Gus the ball. That's when Barnett took charge. While everyone was homing in on everyone else, Dick broke the defense wide open all by himself.

He'd drive the lane and go all the way if they let him. If Unseld or Johnson moved over to help out, Barnett would drop it off to Reed or DeBusschere. Our coordination came back.

We led by 15 at the half because Cazzie, Stallworth and Bowman ran it up from the 45–40 lead we gave them. Monroe, Johnson and Marin wouldn't quit but they never overcame that assistance from our bench.

They still shot back to within six entering the final quarter. They just couldn't match our superior bench. Shue relied fundamentally on six men while we had eight or nine. They stayed close but it never was in doubt.

I always felt that close games, especially in the Garden, belonged to us. We had too many quality players to fold under pressure. Someone would get hot if we needed it. DeBusschere and Cazzie got hot and soon we were leading by 15.

We won it 127–114 and I felt proud for the Knicks and the Bullets. They had staged a magnificent series for all the pro basketball world to see. It was challenging at its best, from Monroe and Frazier to Unseld and Reed and through DeBusschere and Johnson.

We had beaten a fine team with character as well as a tough mascot. Tiny B was a little dachshund that we allowed in the Garden for Baltimore's first victory. He was back again by invitation, but the fans booed him into submission as he chased the plastic ball his trainer rolled on the court.

Even Tiny B couldn't overcome the Knicks' home-court advantage. Monroe got 32 points on 21 shots, Johnson had 23 points and 14 rebounds and Unseld yanked down a game-high 16 rebounds but managed only two points. DeBusschere and old man Barnett split 56 points down the middle and we had won, finally.

''I was waiting for Barnett to get old,'' said Carter, who had a subdued 12-point game.

"I'm a hero now," said Barnett as reporters and photographers crowded him. "On this club, it's not an individual thing. You've got to subordinate things. I shot a little more than usual tonight," he said after his 23 shots were high for the night.

Monroe was series high with 196 points, or almost 18 points a game, but he expressed his respect for Barnett. "Barnett was fantastic," said Earl, who played Dick on defense. "I tried to shade him to the right. This was the first time I ever saw him score so much going to his right."

DeBusschere reported this last conversation with Johnson: "I made my way to Gus and walked out with him. I said: 'You played a helluva game. I just want you to know you're the best defensive forward in basketball. You're a great competitor.' And he said: 'It was a good match. It was a helluva series. You're a great competitor.'"

Frazier said goodbye to Earl Monroe and hello to Lew Alcindor. "One monster. Now another," was the way he put it.

Jack Marin had the last words on our upcoming series with the Milwaukee Bucks and whoever was next. "If the Knicks don't win it all, they should be ashamed of themselves," he said after dying hard.

The last thing I remember about that series with the Bullets was Earl Monroe coming into our dressing room. He walked around and shook hands and wished us luck. Now that's class.

BALTIMORE

	min	fg	fga	ft	fta	reb	ast	pf	pts
Carter	33	6	12	0	4	7	3	2	12
Heaney	1	0	0	0	0	0	1	0	0
Johnson	45	9	16	5	6	14	1	4	23
Loughery	25	4	11	3	6	3	1	3	11
Marin	35	7	18	7	8	3	2	5	21
Miles	12	2	3	0	0	0	0	0	4
Monroe	41	12	21	8	11	1	6	4	32
Scott	11	1	3	3	4	4	0	2	5
Tucker	1	2	2	0	0	0	0	0	4
Unseld	36	1	8	0	0	16	3	6	2
TOTALS	240	44	94	26	39	48	17	26	114

NEW YORK

	min	fg	fga	ft	fta	reb	ast	pf	pts
Barnett	41	13	23	2	2	3	2	3	28
Bowman	4	0	0	0	0	3	0	2	0
Bradley	23	4	8	0	2	0	3	5	8
DeBusschere	44	12	20	4	4	13	2	3	28
Frazier	46	7	10	1	1	10	8	4	15
Hosket	4	0	1	3	3	0	1	0	3
Reed	40	6	18	2	4	14	3	5	14
Riordan	13	3	5	4	4	3	3	1	10
Russell	21	7	14	4	4	3	1	3	18
Stallworth	4	1	2	1	2	2	0	1	3
TOTALS	240	53	101	21	26	51	23	27	127

Baltimore	23	24	35	32	—	114
New York	28	34	26	39	—	127

Milwaukee presented a different problem. The Bucks were fundamentally Alcindor and they had crushed the 76ers in a 4–1 series.
Philadelphia won the second game in Milwaukee and that's all.

We had finished first in points differential at 9.1 off 115 scored
against 105.9 given up. The Bucks were second at 4.6 off 118.8
scored against 114.2, mainly because of Alcindor. He was their
offense and defense. We spread it out.

We played them six times and won the first four. They won the
final two but we had some players hurt, and I was also resting a few
for the playoffs with the Bullets after we clinched. This is the way
the regular season series went:

November 1—It's Alcindor's first game against us as a rookie
and we win at home, 112–108, to run our season start to 10–1.
Alcindor plays 48 minutes, scores 36 points and grabs 27 rebounds.
Reed gets into foul trouble and plays only 27 minutes. Bowman
comes up with a big game. He hits 6-for-11, nails eight rebounds,
blocks three shots and steals three passes intended for Alcindor by
fronting him.

Reed almost gets into a fight with Alcindor. "I got hit from
behind by an elbow," says Willis after turning quickly and holding

his punch in the last second. "I didn't do it on purpose," says Alcindor. "I was a little tight, but time is on my side."

November 3—Knicks win again, 109–103, in Milwaukee. "You can't have a bad night from Alcindor and expect to win," says Bucks coach Larry Costello after Lew scores 17 points and grabs 16 rebounds in 38 minutes.

"I had mental fatigue before the game. I let Willis shoot uncontested," says Alcindor as Reed gets a series-high 35 points.

"Reed outplayed him tonight but that's not going to happen again," promises Costello.

"I stunk," says Alcindor.

December 5—The Knicks destroy the Bucks in the Garden, 109–63, making their record start 16–2. It's 10–0 after a few minutes. Reed gets into early foul trouble once more and Bowman comes through again. He grabs nine rebounds and deprives Alcindor the ball by fronting him. The Bucks are demoralized and fall behind by as many as 38 points as Bradley hits a career-high 29.

Guy Rodgers of the Bucks says: "Boston had Russell back there to erase mistakes but the Knicks have more all-around team defense. It's the best overall basketball I've ever seen." Alcindor says: "They have depth and they play the game together. It's a monster team."

December 10—The Knicks make it four in a row over the Bucks, 96–95 at Milwaukee. The Bucks lead with 11 seconds to go but Bradley hits from the corner on a perfect play. Flynn Robinson, normally a Knick killer, is pressed by Riordan and misses the equalizer three seconds from the buzzer.

Bob Dandridge, who shares 23 rebounds with Greg Smith, has a big game against the Knicks for the first time. Dandridge puts his team in front by four points with 2:16 to go but the Knicks overcome that. Frazier pulls a groin muscle and has to leave with 8:24 to go and the Bucks leading 77–75. "I'm glad we've gotten most of our games with them out of our way," says DeBusschere after the Knicks beat rookie Alcindor once more.

I say, referring to Bradley's winning shot: "In all the years I've been in basketball, that's the first time I saw a play work exactly as it was practiced.''

January 2—Milwaukee finally beats the Knicks. It wins 118–105 at home as Alcindor scores 41 and grabs 18 rebounds. Dandridge is all over the place, rebounding and stealing the ball. The Knicks are as close as 106–102 but Milwaukee puts it away with eight in a row as it shoots 50-for-88 in the game. "Nobody likes to be number two and we learned a lot from number one," says Dandridge, one of six Bucks in double figures.

"The last few games we felt it inside," says Alcindor. "It was directly after losing to the Knicks by one point. That one was like a smack in the face.''

Reed scores 16 points and gets 9 rebounds in 11 minutes. He says he's not surprised by Alcindor's big game. "They go to him more against us," Willis points out. "They clear it out for him. They open it up so no one can drop off and help. They took advantage of all the shots he has and he has an abundant supply.''

Alcindor hits 18-for-29. He has 24 points by the half and the Knicks hold him to 17 for the second half. Freddie Crawford comes off the bench and helps with 5-for-9 and eight assists. "I don't think they're capable of playing all the time like they did tonight," insists Reed.

March 18—The Bucks win the final game in the Garden, 116–109, as Frazier sits with a groin injury and DeBusschere is limited to six minutes because he's sick. Alcindor shoots 10-for-20 for 26 points and grabs 16 rebounds. "I'm more fluid, I'm not worrying," says the towering center as he heads for his first playoff in his first season.

Says Reed, who plays only 27 minutes: "The future doesn't look very bright for us centers. As the season has gotten on Alcindor's offense has gotten steady. He knows what he's going to do with the ball now. He's taking advantage of his size and everything.''

Everyone was talking about Alcindor and Reed as though they were going to be the only players in our playoffs. "They tried to make a big thing about me and Wes Unseld and now it's Lew

Alcindor,'' was Willis's reminder that there'd be more to the Knicks-Bucks games.

Alcindor had dominated his statistics battle with Reed but we had won four of our six regular season meetings. Reed had outscored Alcindor 35–17 only in the second game. And Alcindor had out-rebounded Reed in every game.

Willis simply explained that the series was bigger than both of them. No one man was going to win it. Reed acknowledged that Alcindor was awful tall for him and also had matured.

"His offense has become more deliberate," said Willis. "He'll probably score a lot of points. I don't think I'll be doing anything like stopping him. We play team basketball. You just don't come out and say: 'Stop that one man.' That's not our team."

Larry Costello had his own game plan. He knew our style better than he knew the two-handed sets he used to hit as a member of the 1967–68 champion Sixers. "The key is our defense," he said. "The Knicks are gonna have to hit their outside shots. We're not going to worry about Willis Reed beating us with twenty-footers from the corner. He won't get rebounds, either, if he tries that."

He was going to anchor Alcindor in the middle and have him jump at all our shooters. He preferred to do that rather than let us drive the lanes. We were going to have to hit from outside or lose, was the way Costello planned it.

Moving Alcindor on defense too much would make him vulnerable on rebounds. Costello was concerned about that because he had seen Alcindor grab only seven in 47 minutes during one of the playoff games with the 76ers.

"We prefer him moving around," explained Costello. "If he played like Wilt did, stand around under the basket, he'd get all the rebounds. We're asking him to play defense."

Alcindor's presence was responsible for Dandridge's development as a defensive force. The Bucks had drafted Bob out of Norfolk State on the fourth round and we had to worry about him. He had quick moves and hands.

Dandridge and Alcindor were mainly responsible for turning a last-place team into a threat to our championship dreams. "I didn't know what to expect from this team,'' acknowledged Costello. ''Last year, we never came up with a loose ball. Dandridge is good at that. He's a good defensive player. He makes steals. He takes a chance once in a while. Just a fifty-fifty chance. None of us gamble.''

Dandridge just had a terrific series against the Sixers. I was planning to use DeBusschere on him but Costello wasn't sure he'd work it the other way. ''Dave is bigger and stronger than Bob, so I'm not sure Bob will be guarding him,'' said Costello.

Dandridge didn't seem to care. He figured he was quick and smart enough to play anyone with reasonable size. ''I plan to make more contact with him in the playoffs,'' said Dandridge. ''He's been getting into foul trouble lately.''

He recalled all the trouble he'd had with DeBusschere in the first two games of the season. ''At first I was afraid to challenge him,'' said the relatively frail Dandridge. ''I guess I was psyched out. He can bruise you but I'll have to do it. He has to help Reed so maybe I can sneak away and get a shot.''

The first game was April 11 at the Garden. It was the day that Navy Captain James A. Lovell, Jr., Fred W. Haise, Jr., and John L. Swigart, Jr., took off on the Apollo for a third moon landing. Peggy Lee was selling out at the Waldorf-Astoria. The movie *Patton* was at Radio City. My friend Dustin Hoffman was featured in *Midnight Cowboy*. And a full lobster dinner at the Press Box cost $6.50.

Oh, yes, Wilt Chamberlain was back playing for the Lakers, who had just tied the Phoenix Suns 3–3 in the other semifinal. That winner was to meet the Atlanta Hawks with that winner facing our winner for the championship.

We had four days to prepare for the Bucks. I only needed half that so I gave everyone two days off. Reed grumbled about the long layoff to Bradley, the Knicks' player representative.

''Four days between games is ridiculous and it's a whole week for Milwaukee,'' said Willis, who was primed to play right away.

I gave the team a light workout the first day back. We ran through a few plays just for timing. Then we went to the Garden to pick up our tickets.

Someone told me they were hot tickets. They were being scalped for $50 apiece. "To watch us play? That's ridiculous," I said. I couldn't picture anyone paying that for any game.

I spent the day before the game on defense. I had it all mapped out. I didn't have to tell the Knicks how to play defense anymore, only how I'd like them to play against Alcindor. He was the target. We couldn't let him destroy us.

So I told Willis to keep forcing Alcindor away from the basket. Then I wanted Frazier and Barnett to gamble and drop off in front of Alcindor to keep him from getting the ball.

When Alcindor got the ball, I wanted DeBusschere or Bradley, whoever was on the weak side, to help on Willis's blind side. That would keep Alcindor from getting an uncontested skyhook in the middle.

I was giving Jon McGlocklin and Flynn Robinson the outside. They were good shooters but we had to sacrifice something to help Willis with Alcindor. I was inviting the Bucks to beat us from the outside if they could. We'd match them at the shooting game.

It wasn't all serious at practice. I had some fun with Stallworth. He had been the one guy I couldn't hit with a fine all season. I kept telling him I'd nail him and he'd say: "Never."

Well on that last practice day for the Bucks, he walked in five minutes late. "I gotcha," I said to him.

"Whaddya mean?" he said. "It's not three-thirty yet."

I informed him practice started at three. Stallworth tried to worm out of it by turning to Frazier and saying: "Hey, Clyde. Didn't you hear practice was at three-thirty?"

Clyde would have said no even if practice had been scheduled for 3:30 because everyone knew I was trying to nail Stallworth. He told Stalls it was set for three o'clock.

"Pay the five dollars," I told Stallworth. He was the final Knick nailed and I felt like I'd just hit a homer in all the ballparks. Actually, I felt like this ballclub was mentally and physically ready to beat any team in the world—even one that had Lew Alcindor at center.

There was a quiet confidence in our room as the players dressed for the game. I was usually there early but some players, like Riordan, liked to get there real early and get in some shooting.

I was walking around making some small talk and resting my brain when I heard some hollering. I looked in and there was Bradley all decked out in some new clothes. Barnett was his design adviser, and there was Princeton-and-Oxford Bill with a light brown suit and wide lapels, a bright yellow tie and suede shoes.

"Looka the dude," said Bowman.

"Way to put on an arty show, Dollar," said Cazzie as he dropped to his knees and polished the tips of Bradley's suede shoes.

"Do you want me to call you Mr. Bradley now?" I inquired. It was a long way from the torn button-down oxford shirts and tired raincoat. Just another example of how the 1969–70 Knicks developed into a team of distinction.

Someone also had covered Bradley's dressing stall with adhesive tape on which was inscribed: "Caveat emptor" and "Thanks for the merger." They were kidding Bradley because he was leading the Players Association's fight against an ABA-NBA merger.

Our defense against Alcindor worked perfectly. Now that's rather ridiculous to say when he scored 35 points and pulled down 15 rebounds. But we won the opener 110–102, which was the only statistic that always mattered.

We really dominated. We got off to a 24–19 start and the Bucks spent the rest of the game trying to figure out how to beat our defense. The key matchups turned out to be DeBusschere-Dandridge and Frazier-Robinson.

Flynn had hurt us all season and once hit 40 in a preseason game. Dandridge had promised to use his speed to confuse DeBusschere. Let me give you an example of how smart our players were without any help from me.

Frazier liked to use finesse rather than hand or body contact with the man he was playing. But he'd noticed while sitting on the bench that Flynn got annoyed when Barnett played him with a hand on his hip.

Robinson would complain to the refs and lose his poise. It affected his shooting. So Frazier played him that way, shutting

Flynn out in the first half and holding him to 4-for-16. That hurt the Bucks.

DeBusschere also had picked up a Dandridge habit on his own. The last time they had played each other, Dave had noticed that Dandridge liked going to his right for his favorite fadeaway jumper. DeBusschere not only won the battle of points 18–12 but out-rebounded Dandridge 16–5. Dave grabbed 11 rebounds in the first period alone, which is when we established ourselves for the night.

They just couldn't match our firepower. The Bradley-Russell entry produced 16-for-29, good for 36 points from that one position. Cazzie hit four straight from outside in one stretch of the first half. Then Bradley got four more during a 15–6 tear after intermission that put us ahead by 19.

Frazier had only six points but he had carried out his assignment of distracting Robinson. ''What good would it have done if I had scored thirty and we lost?'' said Clyde. ''Red told me to concentrate on Robinson and to give up the ball on offense.''

We rarely tried to drive on Alcindor. We used our ballhandling to hit the open man and took advantage of our ability to hit from outside. We didn't go through Alcindor, we went over him.

Willis did his job of using his unusual strength to rough up Alcindor as much as possible. Willis went 40 exhausting minutes and still managed to get back 24 points and 12 rebounds.

Alcindor was young then and still hadn't gained the poise he needed in the pros. He was rattled by our defense at times; otherwise he might've scored 50. He did just what we expected—what most seven-foot centers have a tendency to do when they get the ball. He put it on the floor, and we attacked.

''He's got to get the ball right out when they do that,'' said Costello, referring to how one of our guys dropped off as soon as he bounced the ball. ''He's got to hit the open man right away. When you're pressured, you've got to move the ball and yourself. When they collapsed on him, everyone stood around and watched.''

Costello was right. I stood and watched and liked it. They had good outside shooters like McGlocklin and Robinson but our defense was just too good.

McGlocklin, now on Milwaukee's broadcasting team, was a smart player and was annoyed about everything and especially himself.

"I stunk. I did a terrible job on defense," he said after Bradley went 7-for-13 against him. He refused to take all the blame, so he added: "The only way to beat a defense like the Knicks is to move the ball. Lew would just stand around or put it down or hold it."

> *"Look for the open man."*
>
> *—Red Holzman*

Costello was upset about something else. "They got about five baskets on one play and we talked about it for five days," he said. He had diagrammed the play. He had told them that Bradley, Cazzie and DeBusschere's favorite play was to run the baseline around a screen and then pop from the corner or side.

He was right. It was our favorite play but you had to stop it. Vince Lombardi had the same theory in Green Bay. He'd defy anyone to stop the plays they knew were coming. Theory is one thing and execution is another.

The Knicks could execute—on offense and defense, though defense was our ace in the hole. Everyone knew that we liked to have DeBusschere set a double-pick with Reed down low for Bradley, yet he still got wide open for the shot.

Costello recognized what we were capable of, which is why he alerted his team to watch for our outside shots. "A lot of teams you want to take those shots but the Knicks can shoot those shots," he said.

Frazier put his finger on the risk we took because of Alcindor and what it meant. "We tried to put the pressure on Lew and make him pass the ball," said Clyde. "We would like him to pass, rather than shoot, because maybe we can pick it off."

15

No wonder Frazier is such a smart analyst on Knick broadcasts these days. "We had our guys dropping off to help Willis," said Clyde. "If they start hitting outside, we can't help inside and that leaves Willis alone."

We sometimes had four guys on Alcindor when he got the ball. He still got his points with that huge wingspan that made him look like a 747. Reed managed to get some but not all of it back because he was fast enough to beat Lew down to the other end.

We managed to steal the ball from the Bucks 11 times. It was another tribute to our defense and Clyde, who swiped it six times himself. We figured we had made believers out of the young Bucks.

"Believe me, we feel like we can beat them," McGlocklin assured everybody.

What Jon forgot was that we loosened up when we had a safe lead. That's how Alcindor got 16 of his points in the last 10 minutes. We were content to ease up and save our strength for the next game.

I guess that's what inspired some media people to ask if we thought Alcindor was overrated. Sure. That's why I had our team defense concentrate on stopping him but no one else.

MILWAUKEE

	min	fg	fga	ft	fta	reb	ast	pf	pts
Alcindor	47	14	24	7	11	15	5	3	35
Chappell	13	1	2	4	5	4	0	1	6
Crawford	22	3	13	6	6	2	2	3	12
Cunningham	1	1	1	0	0	1	0	0	2
Dandridge	44	6	11	0	0	5	2	4	12
McGlocklin	29	4	9	0	0	1	1	2	8
Robinson	39	4	16	11	12	1	3	2	19
Rodgers	6	0	0	0	0	0	1	1	0
D. Smith	14	1	2	0	0	3	0	1	2
G. Smith	25	3	7	0	0	11	1	4	6
TOTALS	240	37	85	28	34	43	15	21	102

NEW YORK

	min	fg	fga	ft	fta	reb	ast	pf	pts
Barnett	41	5	17	7	9	1	2	3	17
Bowman	8	1	3	0	0	3	0	1	2
Bradley	30	7	13	4	4	5	6	4	18
DeBusschere	41	8	18	2	4	16	1	1	18
Frazier	45	3	9	0	0	5	5	3	6
Reed	40	10	19	4	4	12	4	5	24
Riordan	10	1	3	3	5	1	0	1	5
Russell	18	9	16	0	0	2	0	2	18
Stallworth	7	1	2	0	0	1	1	2	2
TOTALS	240	45	100	20	26	46	19	22	110

Milwaukee	19	25	24	34	—	102
New York	24	20	28	28	—	110

Alcindor was better in the second game, if that's possible. He was more in control, looking to hit the open man or taking the shot when he clearly had it. This time he scored 38 points and had 23 rebounds and 11 assists, but we still won by one big point.

We wound up apologizing or alibiing for him after he missed two free throws that might have won the game. We were leading 110–109 with 52 seconds to go at the time. It was embarrassing.

Some Garden fans even booed Alcindor despite his being a New Yorker. It was cruel but he was wearing a Milwaukee uniform, so he was the enemy. It's that way in all sports.

"He has nothing to be ashamed of," said Reed, stepping up to defend the 23-year-old rookie. "I think he will feel bad. He will go home and say: 'If I made those two shots, we would've won.' I'd feel bad if we had lost with the game I played. But you can't ask for any more than what he did."

Reed had 36 points and 19 rebounds and also found himself in a moment of despair. We were leading 110–109 when Willis got the ball. "I took an outside shot when I should have driven on Alcindor," he said.

Needless to say, he was tired. He felt like he had just spent the night chopping down a redwood tree. "I would go to the bench and say: 'Lord, give me the strength to play the rest of the ball game,'" he explained after playing 45 minutes to Alcindor's 48.

Costello came from the Wilt Chamberlain–Bill Russell era, the greatest battle of centers in history. He was moved to say: "I never saw two centers in the same game play so well."

It's strange how things work out at times. There was Alcindor with all his flash and game stats winding up as the so-called goat when he missed two free throws. Meanwhile, Cazzie became the hero because he made two critical foul shots that put us ahead 112–111 and clinched it.

We got a break. I think the crowd helped us. With a few seconds left and us leading by a point, Costello screamed: "Foul 'em!" but his players couldn't hear him.

We were ahead 2–0 and this time Cazzie was the difference. He gave us a productive 20 minutes, hitting five of his nine shots and those two big free throws.

I almost forgot. There also was an embarrassing moment for Cazzie. We had the largest lead of eight points in the first half. The Bucks rallied to go in front by four entering the final quarter and actually led 92–86 late. We were back in the lead by a point inside the final three minutes, when DeBusschere stole a dribble from Alcindor.

Cazzie broke for the basket and Dave hit him with a perfect pass. Cazzie couldn't miss the moment. He went up to slam-dunk and he hit the bottom of the rim. The Bucks whipped the ball down to

Crawford, who drove for a sure layup, but DeBusschere was there again to get his hand on the shot.

Frazier scooped up the ball and fired once more to Cazzie. He stopped at the top of the circle and hit a jumper that put us ahead 108–105 and we nursed it. That was Cazzie. He could turn it on and off like a light switch. He never let anything distract him, not even a missed dunk.

He kidded himself after the game. "If we'd have lost by one point, you know what I would've done?" he asked. He proceeded to make like he was hanging himself.

DeBusschere said it all. "If we stay real close, someone's gonna pick us up. That's the advantage we have over a young team," he explained.

That's the advantage the Knicks had over all teams then. A winning team never feels it's going to lose, which is what makes it a winner. Cazzie's performance was just another example.

Frazier defused Robinson once more. He had Flynn complaining to the ref about being fouled every time he ran downcourt.

Clyde still managed one of his routine triple-doubles they make so much about these days. It was one of his weaker ones. He had 12 rebounds, 14 assists and 10 points mainly because I had told him to forget about scoring.

Alcindor left his dressing room in a hurry. "When you missed the foul shots, what was in your mind?" he was asked. "I missed them," he said as he left.

"How much better can you play?" said Costello, feeling sorry for Alcindor. "Look at those points. Look at those rebounds. Look at those assists. Talk to Lew. Ask him if we cleared out for him."

Costello was informed that Alcindor had left. "That's his nature," said the coach. "He's a great competitor. He doesn't like to lose. I told him he played a great game."

DeBusschere had a poor 3-for-12 for only eight points but made some critical plays while not allowing Dandridge to go wild. Barnett stepped up with 19 points. That was the story of those Knicks.

MILWAUKEE

	min	fg	fga	ft	fta	reb	ast	pf	pts
Alcindor	48	16	25	6	12	23	11	2	38
Chappell	18	5	5	2	2	4	0	5	12
Crawford	30	2	9	2	4	5	6	3	6
Dandridge	34	6	11	2	2	5	6	3	14
McGlocklin	41	6	15	2	2	2	2	3	14
Robinson	25	5	14	3	3	1	3	3	13
G. Smith	44	6	12	2	2	8	3	0	14
TOTALS	240	46	91	19	27	48	31	19	111

NEW YORK

	min	fg	fga	ft	fta	reb	ast	pf	pts
Barnett	40	8	14	3	4	1	6	2	19
Bowman	3	0	0	1	1	2	0	1	1
Bradley	27	4	8	3	3	4	3	2	11
DeBusschere	29	3	12	2	3	4	1	4	8
Reed	45	14	23	8	10	19	2	5	36
Frazier	45	5	14	0	0	12	14	1	10
Riordan	12	3	5	1	2	1	0	1	7
Russell	20	5	9	2	2	0	1	2	12
Stallworth	19	4	8	0	0	2	1	2	8
TOTALS	240	46	93	20	25	45	28	20	112

Milwaukee	33	33	24	21	—	111
New York	35	28	23	26	—	112

"Welcome to the World Champion New York Knickerbockers," announced the hostess on our flight to the third game. "This is a nonstop charter to Cleveland."

"Cleveland? We're in the Twilight Zone," I said. We were on our way to Milwaukee, where the Bucks had to win or face a sweep in the two games there.

We were flattered by the stewardess's first announcement but puzzled by the second. It didn't really matter. We were nice and loose and confident.

We'd had three days off and had worked out lightly. The players had some fun with Cazzie, imitating how he'd missed his slam-dunk. I also nailed Whelan for reporting late and made him the last member of the team to be fined.

We all watched the Apollo 13 astronauts splash down in the Pacific for a sea rescue. James Lovell, Fred Haise and John Swigart had experienced an explosion in the module's power system four days into their flight to the moon. They landed safely and I bet the whole country cheered.

We arrived in Milwaukee with one casualty. Bill Hosket had twisted an ankle in practice. "No kidding," said Larry Costello when he heard the news. "And how's Nate Bowman and Donnie May?" Everybody's a comedian.

Costello's one-year-old daughter, Michelle, had just fallen down the stairs while he was babysitting, so why get excited about Hosket's ankle? "She's just starting to walk. She's tough like her old man," said Larry.

He reported that Alcindor had forgotten about the two missed foul shots. "He's not the kind to worry about it," said Costello, adding he expected the Knicks to cool off. "They're good shooters and I don't mind fifteen footers . . . but twenty and twenty-five footers?"

I was a little concerned because the Bucks had come so close to winning the second game and now were on their court. I was happy, though, that the pilot of our plane had ignored the stewardess and deposited us in Milwaukee and not Cleveland.

On second thought, I wasn't so happy when the Bucks did what I suspected. They beat us 101–96. We had waited five days to play the third day to satisfy TV, which was a weekend thing in those days. We were flat, as they say when they lose, whoever they is.

Alcindor made his customary contribution only slightly better. This time he had 33 points, 31 rebounds and 5 assists. Reed responded with 10 baskets but got to the foul line only three times and had only 10 rebounds.

Need I say more? The Bucks buried us off the boards 64–42. Guess who gave us a rough time? It was Freddie Crawford, the same Freddie Crawford who had played for the Knicks and whom I had released to make room for Bradley.

Ironically, Bradley had one of his worst games. He shot only 2-for-8 in 29 minutes and we chased all the way. Meanwhile,

Crawford played 38 minutes, shot 6-for-13, grabbed 7 rebounds and had 6 assists.

"I can't ever recall playing that much," said Freddie, who overcame tuberculosis in college to make the pros. "I was surprised I started. I take six fouls in six minutes sometimes. If it's two minutes or thirty-eight, I do my best and take my six fouls and get out of the game."

He had a career game against us before fouling out. "Professional pride," said Alcindor after the Bucks all but wrapped it up by outscoring us 29–16 in the opening period. "If we played our best, we'd have something to cry about," said Reed, who knew better.

Our bench offered its vocal support this time. "We play extremely poor and we lose by only five," said Stallworth, who shared 13 of our baskets with Cazzie. "They play real good and win by only five."

Bradley, DeBusschere and Frazier had only 13 baskets among them. It was no surprise to me that we lost with that kind of shooting from our big guns. The only surprise came when Costello finally decided to take Dandridge off Frazier and let him play DeBusschere at both ends.

He shuffled his lineup by benching Robinson for Crawford. So Dandridge broke loose for 22 points, 10 rebounds and 8 assists without having to worry about playing defense against Clyde. He was able to provide the outside shooting the Bucks needed when we collapsed on Alcindor.

It was a smart move by Costello. Contrary to what some people might think, coaching does help. "I couldn't give Alcindor any help in the first two games because I was playing Frazier," explained Dandridge.

We made one big move at them in the final period. I ordered the press and we almost wiped out a 16-point Milwaukee lead. But Dandridge pumped a long one to cut us off.

Otherwise, there wasn't too much noteworthy about the way we played. Except that for the second straight game, Cazzie blew a wide open slam-dunk and took another ribbing. Some of our guys claimed an NBA record for him.

"Ah, don't ask me about that shot," said Cazzie. "Good Lord, but it was unbelievable. I can make tough shots but I can't make a layup."

"Hey, Caz," yelled Reed. "Give up that dunk shot, will you?" Cazzie promised: "From now on, I'm gonna drive in and put the ball on the backboard and lay it up."

I knew it was just one of our bad games. We were due. Besides, DeBusschere played like he had something on his mind. If he did, he was entitled because he had done so much to get us where we were—two wins away from the championship final.

MILWAUKEE

	min	fg	fga	ft	fta	reb	ast	pf	pts
Alcindor	47	14	28	5	7	31	5	3	33
Chappell	24	4	11	1	3	6	1	0	9
Crawford	38	6	13	1	1	7	6	6	13
Cunningham	1	0	0	0	0	0	0	0	0
Dandridge	47	10	15	2	3	10	8	3	22
McGlocklin	44	3	16	1	2	4	0	1	7
Robinson	19	1	6	3	3	4	0	3	5
Rodgers	2	0	0	1	1	0	0	0	1
G. Smith	18	5	6	1	1	2	0	6	11
TOTALS	240	43	95	15	21	64	20	22	101

NEW YORK

	min	fg	fga	ft	fta	reb	ast	reb	pts
Barnett	35	3	10	1	2	1	2	2	7
Bowman	7	1	3	2	2	2	0	2	4
Bradley	29	2	8	2	2	3	3	1	6
DeBusschere	31	4	14	0	4	10	3	3	8
Frazier	46	4	7	5	6	4	7	1	13
Reed	41	10	20	1	3	10	2	3	21
Riordan	15	3	7	3	5	3	3	2	9
Russell	20	6	13	2	3	5	1	2	14
Stallworth	16	7	13	0	0	4	1	2	14
TOTALS	240	40	95	16	27	42	22	18	96

Milwaukee	29	29	23	20	—	101
New York	16	31	21	28	—	96

This tells the story of the fourth game against the Bucks: "We'd like to win but I don't know if we will," said Alcindor.

We had just made it 3–1 and were going back to the Garden for the clincher, we hoped. We already knew we would be facing the Lakers if we closed out the Bucks.

There was this headline in a New York paper: "LA: Hurry Up, N.Y." They had swept the Atlanta Hawks in a hurry, 4–0, and the plan was for the Lakers to fly to New York for a series opener at the Garden. That would give them two days of practice and time to adjust to the difference in time zones.

The jet lag from long plane trips always had an effect on me and some players. I did everything on New York time, though. I changed my watch when I was in Los Angeles. On the opposite side, Pat Riley's watch was on LA time long after he took the Knick job.

Don't ask me why. Coaches can be creatures of habit, I guess. It was one of my quirks. I'm surprised that none of my players ever got wise and insisted I was fining them on the wrong time.

Anyway, the Lakers were in the finals again, as though they had a patent on them. It was the seventh time in 10 years that they made it. Unfortunately, the LA Lakers lost to the Celtics six times and still were looking for their first title.

Chamberlain was back and strong enough to pull down 21 rebounds in the last game with the Hawks. Jerry West had 39 points and Elgin Baylor 31. Murderers' Row.

"I don't want a long layoff," said West. "A long one would hurt this team." He was concerned about the Lakers getting rusty. I'll bet he can still hit his jumper—with his eyes closed.

West had to be rooting for us to end it quickly because a Milwaukee win would only extend our series. Baylor figured he'd be playing the Knicks and said: "New York's big asset is depth. They just keep sending players at you."

Amazing. Costello said just about the same thing after we won the fourth game 117–105. Cazzie buried the Bucks with six baskets when they cut a 20-point deficit down to two points.

"They have a lot of talent," Larry said of us. "They went the whole second half without Bradley and he's their first-string forward. They get fantastic shooting from Cazzie Russell and Dave Stallworth. Let's face it, after a while I can't match up with their personnel.''

That was the beauty of the 1969–70 Knicks. They were a team in every respect. Those critical minutes that Costello spoke of, when our bench took charge, told the story of that team better than I can.

We were leading by 20 at the half and the Bucks were within 69–67 about six minutes later. That's pro basketball. Nothing's ever safe until it's over. I even reminded the players that 20 points at the half were nice but there was another half to go.

I didn't want to waste all the strategy and hard work of the first 24 minutes. It had been an outstanding team effort from the time we discussed what we would do in the dressing room before the game.

I asked for suggestions and DeBusschere the coach recommended we go to Reed more. Barnett agreed and advised Willis to be patient, we would be cutting off him. If no one got open for a pass, then he could drive to the hoop or step out and pop.

It was our motion offense, except we wanted Willis planted in the pivot or high to put more pressure on Alcindor from the start. I also wanted to fire up Willis, who I already knew was smoldering because of his poor third game.

I even reminded him that he had to move to the ball more and demand it better than he had in the last game. ''I realize that,'' he said. We were all thinking and acting together.

We were in command from the start. We got ahead by six at the quarter and I put Cazzie and Stallworth in for DeBusschere and Bradley. They opened it to 20 at the half. Stallworth even heaved one in from around 45 feet before the buzzer.

We knew the Bucks were in real trouble after that. So did the fans. They started blaming everything on the refs. Who else was beating their team?

A combination of things happened. From the Bucks' viewpoint, Alcindor, Robinson, Crawford, Dandridge and the others showed their guts and charged back. From my viewpoint, we got too complacent with the huge lead and began going one-on-one.

I sent Cazzie and Stallworth to the rescue again as our lead dropped to two points. I didn't realize that people from Milwaukee could make such noise. They had finally found their voices and were all over us. By then, they had forgiven the refs.

We were in serious trouble. In fact, the Bucks had three cracks at tying. Reed had four personals at the time and I assumed they'd go to Alcindor then but they surprised me.

I don't know what Costello told them. But in emotional situations like that, players have a tendency to keep doing the things that got them there. If it works, why stop? If it ain't broken, why fix it?

Crawford and Robinson, who had contributed three baskets to the Bucks' comeback, missed three times in a row. We were still staggering ourselves. We didn't answer back until Cazzie provided us with his instant offense.

He hit from the corner to make it 71–67. He hit from the corner once more to make it 73–67. And he held off the Bucks with three more bombs that made it 86–79, 90–83 and 92–83.

I played the hot hand down the stretch. Cazzie, Stallworth, Riordan and Bowman put the final touches on it by sharing the closing 17 points as the lead soared back to 20 at one time.

It was a painful loss for the Bucks, who had come so close to tying the series with a 22–4 burst. I felt sorry for Crawford particularly. His professional pride had been hurt. Besides, he was a former Knick.

"Maybe we should have gone to Alcindor," said Freddie when he had time to think about it after the game. He was so caught up in the emotion of the moment he actually thought he had missed all three tying shots.

Freddie was reminded that Robinson had blown one, not that it made him feel any better. "I tried to work a pick and roll with Alcindor once," said Crawford. We wouldn't let him—which was one small credit to our account that seemed bankrupt at the time.

At least, I thought so from my seat on the bench. I seemed to be the only one concerned. I was in charge of the buttons and I think I pushed every one but the one that had "panic" on it.

"I was never really scared," said DeBusschere. "It was just a matter of settling down,'' said Reed. ''We've got too much poise on this ballclub.''

That was easy for them to say. They still had their hair. They weren't getting paid to coach 12 different Knicks to a championship. They didn't even have to keep telling the press: ''I can't worry about things I can't control.''

We had done a fine job of shutting down Milwaukee's main outside shooters. In four games, Robinson was 14-for-54 and McGlocklin 17-for-50. ''They can't stay cold forever,'' said Costello, who didn't have much time left under the circumstances. ''We can't get three or four guys hot at once. We just haven't gotten the scoring from our guards that we got during the season.''

He thought of that and also of what Cazzie had just done to his team. Costello didn't have the luxury that I did. I had an assortment of players who came off the bench and helped. ''The turning point came when we got within two points,'' said Larry. ''Cazzie came in and hit three straight. That gave him a big boost.''

Gave Cazzie a big boost? What about us? Cazzie just about lifted us into the championship playoff with that one big contribution. He made Robinson, for example, recognize the futility of it all.

''It puts a helluva lot of pressure on our team,'' said Flynn as he compared what he was doing with our success. ''Lew and Dandridge are the only ones doing their jobs every game. I'm letting them down. Without Jon and me hitting like we've been hitting all season, it becomes an altogether different team.''

We were a happy team in our dressing room. ''The Minutemen certainly earned their money tonight,'' Stallworth said to Cazzie.

''When it got down to two points, I said to myself: 'We need some baskets.' I told myself not to rush my shots,'' said Cazzie.

I didn't realize at the time that he was talking to himself but it worked out fine. ''I knew the guys were a little tight and I have to open them up a little when I go in,'' he said. ''When I made it seventy-one to sixty-seven, I told myself that's what you're supposed to do. They were big shots. They were like penicillin. It gave them a lift.''

I always respected Cazzie. He wasn't in the happiest situation playing behind Bradley but he never lost his confidence. He had the ego of an outstanding player, yet there was another side to him.

He used to shine shoes as a kid, so one day he decided to return to the LC Shoe Rebuilders in Chicago. "The people had seen me play basketball in college and they had seen me in the pros," he explained. "I went back to see what type of reaction there would be."

They remembered the kid who had shined shoes there. "They snubbed the boss," continued Cazzie. "They said: 'I want to find out what it's like to have Cazzie Russell shining my shoes. It was a shine for a quarter and I'd keep fifteen cents and give the boss ten cents. That's where I started making some money in 1958 and it gave me a pretty good attitude. I wanted to keep my sense of balance. My humanity. Going back there kept me in touch with reality."

His sense of reality with the Knicks was simple. He explained it this way: "I get a pick. I get open for one or two seconds I got to hit."

Frazier put it this way: "Cazzie shot their brains out. We needed all he gave us today. He's a streak shooter. When he hits three or four in a row he kind of thinks he can't miss. He pulled us out. But how do you blow a twenty-point lead is what gets me."

Me too. Thank goodness I was too busy trying to do something about it. I had no time to bleed to death or even to think about the Dewar's I'd need to calm my nerves.

It made an instant expert out of Cazzie. He started to tell everyone how to play against Alcindor because he had once scored on a drive past Lew's goaltending presence. "That's the way to do it. You go right at him," he informed all of us.

They reminded Cazzie that he had finally made a layup just to needle him. Barnett had stolen the ball and fed it to Cazzie. He laid it against the backboard instead of jamming it, which was fortunate because Barnett threatened to shoot him if he had missed.

Bradley had another tough game—two in a row. He had only six points again, and I had to sit him longer than I intended. But the game had turned so sharply and we needed shooters, which is why I went to Cazzie and stayed with him.

I knew Bradley was feeling bad for himself and about me, probably. I could always see it on his face. The smile of satisfaction was gone and he was scowling.

I wasn't worried, though. He was too much of a competitor. He was always there when we had to win the big ones. He was our Tommy Henrich—Old Reliable.

I had done everything imaginable when the Bucks suddenly got hot. I called time-out once and reminded our guys they had to see the ball. That was the first thing my creative mind came up with because it always worked.

Milwaukee had other ideas. The Bucks decided to finally make their shots. They scored 16 in a row at one time before Cazzie broke the streak and their hearts.

That's what they call panic time. Only the coach can't afford to do that. My job was to think of something to change the momentum when the Bucks were on their 22–4 streak.

I called time and put Warren in for just a minute. I wanted to give Robinson someone different to look at because he was hot. Barnett was on the bench with four personals.

"That's what we're paying him for—to come off the bench and be ready," Frazier said of Cazzie. The same for Warren or May or Hosket.

I wanted to see what happened. It got down to 69–65 so I called another time. I had to send Barnett back in. I couldn't delay or else the Bucks would roll right past us.

Alcindor was annoyed at the refs. He shot 13 fouls, more than anyone, yet he felt he should have had more. Reed always had to rough him up.

"When we got four personals on Willis, we tried to get the fifth but we didn't," said Alcindor. "I should've gotten some free throws. They didn't give me any."

Frazier actually got two more rebounds than Alcindor. I attributed that to our team rebounding. Reed and DeBusschere boxed out and Clyde grabbed a game-high 11.

Once Robinson tackled Frazier on a breakaway and Clyde demanded two shots. Referee Richie Powers explained intentional fouls called for only one, so Clyde said: "It reminded me of my football days in Atlanta. I should have stiff-armed him."

One more thing happened in the dressing room after it was over. Barnett suggested the Bucks should phone in the next game. They should save themselves time and money by wiring their moves through Western Union. It was the mail-order-chess man in him coming out.

MILWAUKEE

	min	fg	fga	ft	fta	reb	ast	pf	pts
Alcindor	48	14	26	10	13	11	1	1	38
Chappell	8	1	2	0	0	1	0	1	2
Crawford	30	5	12	0	0	6	3	3	10
Dandridge	43	8	12	2	4	5	4	4	18
McGlocklin	27	4	10	2	2	1	0	1	10
Robinson	33	4	18	3	3	7	7	3	11
Rodgers	6	0	2	2	2	0	3	1	2
G. Smith	45	7	8	0	0	9	6	3	14
TOTALS	240	43	90	19	24	40	24	17	105

NEW YORK

	min	fg	fga	ft	fta	reb	ast	pf	pts
Barnett	37	8	15	2	2	5	8	5	18
Bowman	4	1	1	0	0	1	0	2	2
Bradley	22	2	4	2	2	5	3	1	6
DeBusschere	25	5	12	1	1	10	3	3	11
Frazier	39	4	10	9	11	11	6	2	17
Reed	44	13	29	0	0	10	3	4	26
Riordan	19	3	7	2	2	3	1	0	8
Russell	26	9	17	0	0	6	1	2	18
Stallworth	23	5	10	1	1	4	3	2	11
Warren	1	0	0	0	0	0	0	0	0
TOTALS	240	50	105	17	19	55	28	21	117

Milwaukee	22	23	34	26	—	105
New York	29	36	17	35	—	117

Barnett turned out to be right. He hit five straight shots and scored 11 points in the first five minutes of the fifth game back in the Garden.

That was it. The game was over right there. We won 132–96 and the 19,500 fans had a party. They wound up singing: "Goodbye Lewie, we hate to see you go."

We had beaten the young Bucks 4–1 but we knew they would be back next season a little tougher. In fact, word came that day that Oscar Robertson had signed with Milwaukee. That meant the Big O had finally gotten a center he could enjoy. Together they would win the championship the next season.

16

They cheered us and booed Alcindor all night. "They had to sing an ode to him," said Crawford. "He's a legend right before their eyes."

Alcindor was the villain. He was tall, talented and a threat to the Knicks' security. The fans embellished their song with rhythmic applause. Alcindor didn't give them the pleasure of acknowledging a thing.

"I can't feel anything about it," was his reaction. "That's their problem if they want to act like that. Ever since I played in college and the pros they've cheered against me here."

They even tore down Power Memorial High since he abandoned New York. It was his last monument in the city where he was born. It became a victim of economics.

The fans didn't like Alcindor from the first time he faced the Knicks. They seemed to resent him more when he slam-jammed on Reed near the end of the opening quarter in the final game.

That made it 27–15 and the fans felt it was meant to embarrass Willis. "The captain was beautiful tonight," said Frazier after Reed scored 32 points in 34 minutes. "I think he got a little mad when Alcindor stuffed that one."

Alcindor closed out his first playoffs against the Knicks with 27 points and 11 rebounds. He only played 32 minutes. Costello knew the game was over so he removed the 7'2" rookie who was destined for the Hall of Fame—and destined for a change of name, to Kareem Abdul-Jabbar.

We played an excellent defensive game. Frazier and Barnett wouldn't let the Milwaukee guards bring the ball upcourt. We were up by 16 at the end of the opening quarter and it was just a matter of how much we'd win by.

We were up by 40 at one point. I took out the starters one at a time. They deserved a curtain call the way they had performed against the Bucks. First it was Reed, who had outscored Alcindor for the first time. Then Barnett, who had scored 27 points. Then DeBusschere, Bradley and Frazier.

I sent in everyone but Hosket. He had the bad ankle. The people didn't care or didn't know. They screamed: "We want Hosket!" I had to tell our announcer, John Condon, to explain why Hosket couldn't play. He was cheered anyway.

"That's the first time anyone ever got a standing ovation for a sprained ankle," DeBusschere told him. I called time and Hosket flipped the crowd by acknowledging its cheers with an arm wave.

I then yelled: "For gosh sakes, Hosket, limp a little. Take a little heat off me. Those people want to see you and you're walking too good."

It was a festive night for a festive crowd. "The fans in New York do appreciate good basketball," said Cazzie. "It was a professional exhibition of basketball and it makes you sheepish to even have the audacity to follow anything like that."

The last thing we heard when we left the floor that night was organist Eddie Layton playing "California Here We Come," if you'll pardon my changing the I to we. Layton, who also played the organ at Yankee Stadium, had as good a season as we did.

We were 94 games into our unforgettable season. Nothing had disturbed the team effort everyone had displayed. From the first day of training camp to the time we were to play the Lakers the mission was there.

"There was a day in training camp that Willis came in to the locker room after all the final cuts had been made," recalled Hosket. "He kinda made a short talk. He said it was to his knowledge that

MILWAUKEE

	min	fg	fga	ft	fta	reb	ast	pf	pts
Alcindor	32	11	22	5	5	11	2	1	27
Chappell	13	1	3	0	0	6	0	1	2
Crawford	23	5	14	2	2	3	2	2	12
Cunningham	16	4	8	0	0	4	1	2	8
Dandridge	25	1	10	0	1	7	3	4	2
McGlocklin	27	8	16	0	1	7	4	3	16
Robinson	16	1	6	6	7	2	1	0	8
Rodgers	17	2	3	2	4	1	6	3	6
D. Smith	26	2	5	3	3	12	0	1	7
G. Smith	38	2	9	0	0	2	2	2	4
Williams	7	2	2	0	2	2	0	2	4
TOTALS	240	39	98	18	25	57	21	21	96

NEW YORK

	min	fg	fga	ft	fta	reb	ast	pf	pts
Barnett	32	11	15	5	7	3	1	3	27
Bowman	14	1	4	1	1	4	3	4	3
Bradley	34	12	20	1	2	8	4	2	25
DeBusschere	32	6	17	4	5	11	5	2	16
Frazier	36	1	8	0	0	4	6	3	2
May	5	2	3	0	0	0	0	2	4
Reed	34	14	22	4	6	10	4	3	32
Riordan	21	5	10	1	2	5	2	1	11
Russell	14	1	4	0	0	0	0	0	2
Stallworth	11	3	8	2	2	2	1	1	8
Warren	7	1	2	0	0	2	1	1	2
TOTALS	240	57	113	18	25	49	27	22	132

Milwaukee	19	26	27	24	—	96
New York	35	34	32	31	—	132

everyone in the room had signed a contract or was under contract for the year.

"He said to all of us: 'If you've decided what you're going to play for and agreed to it, then I think that's the last time we'll discuss money all year. I don't know what you're making and don't care. Everyone has signed a contract, so let's not discuss money. Let's play ball.'"

That's why Willis was captain. He had an unbelievable sense of balance. He liked money but never was obsessed by it. He was one guy who would kill to win. He set the tone and everyone followed.

I can't imagine that Willis would be any different today. He was a responsible individual who would honor a contract. I would safely say he would be worth $5 million a year by today's standards. And he would deserve it.

"Take it all, Willis," Alcindor advised him after we had eliminated the Bucks. It was a nice gesture by a young man who had just been treated so rudely in his hometown. "It's a great pleasure to play with Willis," said Bradley.

I was pleased to hear that Oscar Robertson liked the way the Knicks played and thought we could beat the Lakers. There's nothing like peer praise. The Big O knew good basketball when he saw it.

"All they have to do against the Lakers is to play like they just did and they can win," he said. "The Lakers have West outside and Wilt inside. It won't be that easy to sag on Wilt because Jerry can murder you outside. Fall off Jerry and you get shot out of the game. Play him tight and they can go to Wilt, who can go to Baylor or Counts or Jerry or drive."

We knew all of that. I also was a little puzzled at first by the way Oscar had presented our case. It was more like what the Lakers were capable of doing to us instead of vice versa. He finally said: "Of course, if the Knicks do everything right, they'll be hard to stop."

That was more like it. Our team was designed to play our game, no one else's. Everything we did on defense was intended to keep the other team from doing what it wanted. We knew that West and Baylor would be tougher with Wilt back.

"I don't think I have it all back. But I don't want to use the knee as a crutch," said Wilt.

"I think what helped was the seven-game series with Phoenix," said Laker team doctor Robert Kerlan. "It helped his rehabilitation. There is no swelling and the tissue has hardened. He's really amazing."

We already knew that. We also knew that even a less than 100 percent Chamberlain could rebound, block shots and intimidate our shooters enough to be a force.

"I don't think he can jump as high but he's still strong," said Joe Mullaney, who had done a fine job of winning Wilt back after the previous season's finish with van Breda Kolff.

Mullaney was a New Yorker who had migrated to Providence as coach of the Friars. He grew up around Madison Square Garden and was familiar with the Knicks—also with Riordan, who had played for him at Providence.

Riordan had been an effective 6'4" college forward and was considering the pros. He discussed it with his coach. "He told me to be realistic," recalled Mike. "He said I'd have a tough time adjusting to the backcourt, where I'd have to play in the pros. He thought I should take a fellowship and go to graduate school."

Riordan fooled a lot of people—Mullaney, me and all those who overlooked his determination and let him become the 128th player picked. That couldn't happen today because there are only two rounds. Everyone after that is a free agent.

Riordan needled his former coach by reminding him about two other protégés interested in the pros. "He told Lenny Wilkens he couldn't shoot well enough and told Johnny Egan he was too small," said Mike. "He pokes fun at himself for not being a very good judge of talent. He says he's stopped making predictions."

Riordan thanked Mullaney for what he'd done for him before going out and trying to beat him. "It's more personal for me," he said of the championship games coming up. "He gave me a chance to play first-class college ball. I wasn't too highly sought after as a high school player. He was kind of a spear carrier, himself, for Bob Cousy at Holy Cross."

Chamberlain was among the experts who analyzed us. "If the Knicks have any weakness it figures to be rebounding," he said from his towering view. "Phoenix was the greatest rebounding team we played against. The Knicks don't have any rebounding outside of DeBusschere and Reed. If we're gonna beat them, we are gonna have to outrebound them."

He was putting himself on a spot but Wilt was always candid as well as confident. He conceded this much to us: "They shoot much better than anyone and also cause turnovers. They get the ball back and possession is important."

It's funny how he brought up the 1967–68 season at that time. It was his last season in Philadelphia before moving on to Los Angeles. The Knicks and Sixers met in the opening round of the playoffs and we lost 4–2. I had taken over the team by then.

"We put the Knicks out and, actually, they put us out," he recalled. "I thought they would have beaten us if Frazier hadn't hurt his foot. But we lost [Billy] Cunningham with a broken wrist and that hurt us against Boston."

Chamberlain then said something that turned out to be prophetic, in a sense. He acknowledged that Reed was always tough on him and added: "So what if he gets thirty or forty and we win? If he gets 'em inside, then I haven't done my job. If he's shooting twenty-five- or thirty-footers, and if we get beat by them, I'll let him have them."

Wilt believed that in spite of it all the Lakers could still beat the Knicks. Most people outside of New York agreed because of LA's awesome firepower. Baylor, West and Chamberlain were hard to pick against.

They had taken the Celtics and Russell down to the last shot of the seventh game the season before. Wilt didn't have Russell to contend with anymore. He was still annoyed, though, by the way everyone blamed him for the Russell team's winning so many against him.

He shrugged off talk that it was going to be a Reed-Chamberlain battle. "I've been through that with Russell," he said. "If they're gonna talk individual duels, then I won all of them. But they then talk about the value to a team."

It was always Wilt's contention that the Russell teams beat his teams because they had better support players. He still will argue with you about that. All I know is hurt or not, Wilt was a distinct threat to our winning our first championship.

DeBusschere wanted to know why all the fuss about Chamberlain and not Baylor, his man. "I've been playing Elgin for eight years now and it hasn't been a pleasant experience,'' said Dave. ''He keeps amazing me. He keeps coming up with a shot I've never seen before.''

Baylor was the first I ever saw risk a 24-second violation by hanging in the air so long. He had tremendous hand and body control, much like what Michael Jordan introduced 20 years later. He was the toughest guy to play one-on-one.

DeBusschere did it best, which was no surprise. He kept Baylor moving, hoping Elgin's legs would tire. He'd also play him close so he couldn't drive and forced him left, away from his strength.

We couldn't count on DeBusschere too much to help us on team defense. The Laker attack was too powerful to cheat against. Up to that point, Chamberlain had 27,426 career points, Baylor 23,023 and West 20,139. That was over 70,000 for regular season and playoffs.

''Maybe we can hold West to forty-three instead of thirty-three,'' rationalized DeBusschere. ''It will be decided on how we contain them. We can score and, even though Wilt is in there, we can shoot over him. It depends on what our defense does to them.''

It looked like an impossible assignment for us. The Lakers had maybe the greatest forward until then in Baylor, one of the greatest guards in West and the great Chamberlain at center.

The Lakers with Chamberlain had dominated the Knicks 5–1 in 1968–69. We took the 1969–70 season 4–2. Wilt played only the first game and we won it. Here's the way the regular season went:

October 18—Chamberlain's only game and the Knicks win 99–96 in the Garden. West plays 41 minutes and scores 42 points on 16-for-23. ''Tonight I tried to guard him as best I could,'' says Frazier. ''I sacrificed offense because Barnett was on. I concentrated on stopping West because that's best for the team. I tried to run him to his left and hang on. That seems to be the best way.''

Barnett hits 8-for-8 in the second half and gets 19 of his total 20 points in one 19-minute stretch. Stallworth comes off the bench with 7 straight points that put the Knicks ahead 39–38 and we never fall behind.

''They don't lose their poise, they don't panic when they're behind,'' says West. ''I didn't think they played that well, though.''

November 9—Cazzie misses his third straight game because of a bad back. Wilt is out with knee surgery and the Knicks win 112–102 in LA. It runs our hot start to 14–1. The Lakers are cold. They get no baskets in seven minutes during the first half and hit another dry spell of six minutes after intermission.

DeBusschere gets his nose broken and accuses Counts, who points the finger at Roberson. "Yes, I hit him but it was an accident," says the rookie center, who has taken over for Wilt. We put it away with a 13–0 streak that creates a 93–81 lead. West gets 28 points, practically a shutout for him.

November 25—Joe Mullaney has only seven players in uniform: West, Counts, Dick Garrett, Willie McCarter, Mike Lynn, Johnny Egan and Bill Hewitt. The Lakers lose 103–96 in the Garden for our 13th straight victory and the second time LA has contributed to the streak.

The Knicks shoot in front by 13 right away but have to sweat it out because of West and Mullaney. The coach dreams up the idea of isolating West on Barnett on one side of the floor by anchoring the other four Lakers on the opposite side where four Knicks have to play them.

"They're playing a zone!" screams Mullaney at the Knicks' defensive reaction. Ref Mendy Rudolph agrees and hits the Knicks with two technicals within 30 seconds.

An 11-point streak, seven by West, puts the Lakers in front 82–78. But the Knicks come on and win it anyway.

December 26—No Baylor this time, yet the Lakers beat the Knicks 114–106 at the Forum. West gets 40 points and 10 assists. The Knicks lead by 20 (44–24) but Jerry shoots 12-for-18 and 29 points after intermission, though the Knicks double on him. "He was fantastic. It was a one-man show tonight," says Frazier admiringly.

"The way I feel, let West get fifty, sixty or eighty—just don't let the other guys score," says DeBusschere, peeved at the bad defense. "We left Roberson, Hairston and Erickson wide open." The Lakers go ahead to stay 86–85 as West hits 13 of 18 Laker third-quarter points.

February 17—Mullaney brings a healthier team to New York. This time he has eight men in uniform—no Wilt, Erickson, McCarter or Hairston. The Knicks win 114–93.

DeBusschere hauls in 12 rebounds in the first quarter and 29 for the game. Reed gets into foul trouble and leaves with his fourth a few minutes into the third period. He never gets back.

Bowman plays the rest of the way and nails a career-high 13 rebounds. Cazzie helps by going 4-for-5 in the third quarter on his way to 18 points.

March 15—The Knicks clinch the Eastern Division title in San Diego the night before and lose 106–101 in LA. Frazier plays only three minutes because of a slight groin pull but the Knicks still put out. They trail by 17 but go ahead 91–90 before yielding.

West had a lot more to say about us before the championship series started—all of it good. He respected us and, I assumed, so did all the other Lakers.

"We played well but the Knicks played better," he said. "We're conscious of their defense, which makes them more effective. We must be careful passing the ball and only take good shots.

"When the Celtics had their good teams, they didn't just have one great defensive man. They had Bill Russell, of course, and Tom Sanders and K. C. Jones, the best at their positions. People think this is an offensive game but the Knicks' defense, like the Celtics', is their offense. Reed, DeBusschere and Frazier made All-League at their positions. The Knicks are one of the best teams I've ever seen."

West also gave us an update on Wilt. "He's been better every game," said Jerry. "On offense, he's not shooting as much. But on defense and rebounding, he's done the job."

We had three days to prepare for the Lakers. The first was an off day and the other two were light workouts. The day before the first game was really a strategy session. We sat around and exchanged ideas.

It was like a board meeting. This was a team effort and that's the way I always treated it. I was the Chairman of the Board but wasn't about to ignore any suggestions that I felt would help the corporation.

It was decided that Frazier and DeBusschere had to play West and Baylor honestly. No cheating on them. That meant Bradley, playing Keith Erickson, and Barnett, playing Dick Garrett, would have to gamble and give Willis some help with Wilt.

Tickets were scarce and scarcer. Mindful of the Garden sellouts, management arranged for fans to watch the games for $5 on cable TV in Felt Forum. The Knicks were the city's hottest ticket.

Mayor Lindsay dropped into our dressing room to wish us luck the night of the opening game. The Mets had just lost a 1–0 game to the Dodgers on Tom Haller's single off Ron Taylor in the 15th inning.

Also, Jane Alpert, a 22-year-old anti-Vietnam Weatherman, was facing a Chicago rap when 56 bombs were found in an apartment. And clocks had to be set back because of Daylight Saving Time.

We played on New York Winning Time in the series opener. We won 124–112 but, as they say, the score didn't represent the kind of game it was.

We led by 20 points at one time but still had to fight from behind a 5-point deficit in the final quarter. Reed was the difference. He played 45 minutes, scored 37 points and pulled down 16 rebounds.

He did it all despite hurting his left shoulder while jamming the ball over Happy Hairston in the first half. "I don't know how it's going to be on Monday," said Willis, referring to the second game. "I'm gonna get some heat treatment."

Wilt did exactly what he said he would do. He gave Willis the outside shots and Willis hit them—precisely, 8-for-10, and we led by 10 at the quarter. The decibels reached a new high with each basket.

Willis didn't even slow down when he hurt his shoulder. His basket then put us in front 47–30. "There was contact on the play. I knew it would stiffen up," he explained.

He still managed 25 points by the time we reached the half with an 11-point lead. Wilt was giving Willis the outside but was sticking around inside for the rebounds. He wound up with 24 and Baylor got 20. Together they got only four less than we did.

That's what kept the Lakers in the game when it appeared to be on the way to a rout. We were lucky West wasn't hitting. He made only 2-for-8 in the first half. He wound up with 7-for-15 in the second half but he was murder at the foul line as usual with 15-for-17.

I didn't exactly feel comfortable with our lead of only 11 at the half. We had played the better basketball but the Lakers were still too close. I talked mostly about keeping up our defensive pressure at halftime because I suspected something was going to happen.

It did. We went from hot to cold soon after we opened a gap of 19 points. Wilt and Elgin swept everything but the court. We'd miss, they'd rebound and West would score. We actually went into the final quarter trailing by three.

Wilt never blocked a shot in the game but we were losing. The momentum had shifted. Riordan had come off the bench to play West when Frazier got into foul trouble and was about to waste a 19-point contribution to our cause.

I tried everything. Even Cazzie didn't work at first. He had an awful seven minutes in the opening half, which wasn't damaging because we were on our way to a 20-point lead. But when I called on him at crunch time, he delivered.

I sent him in for Bradley with LA leading 95–91. We needed pressure shooting, so who else but Cazzie? He gunned a jumper that put us ahead 99–98 and beat Wilt on a challenging layup. We won the game by outscoring the Lakers 35–20 in the final period and 31–12 after falling behind 94–89.

Our offense woke up just in time to support the defense. "Maybe I was trying too hard," was the way Cazzie explained his inexplicable start. "This was my first championship. Willis and Stallworth told me I was hesitating, holding back on my jump shot."

I see a lot of players do that. They don't take their shots when they've got them. They're indecisive, and by the time they decide to shoot, the defense has recovered. Cazzie and Bradley were the perfect examples of players shooting within the flow of the offense without hesitating.

Cazzie surprised himself by not firing as soon as he had the shot. I remember some fan somewhere shouting to him: ''Shoot, Cazzie, shoot!'' and he said: ''Someone has to tell me?''

The Lakers let the big first game slip away. From my viewpoint, we earned it, they didn't give it to us. Reed was the main man for us with 19 in the first half on 9-for-14 and 18 in the second on 7-for-16.

Wilt played all 48 minutes and complimented Willis with: ''The man's a great basketball player.'' But he issued this warning to Riordan, Cazzie and Willis: ''I'd like them to keep on driving. They caught me flatfooted this time.''

The Lakers had some advice for Wilt. ''He's got to go to the basket more,'' said Baylor after seeing only 14 shots to 30 for Willis.

The coach agreed, Mullaney saying: ''We've got to use Wilt at the other end. I think he can get as much as Willis.''

We figured it was Wilt's knee. He just hadn't fully recovered from surgery despite his miracle appearance when everyone figured he'd never make the playoffs. No one was in a better position to know than Willis.

''I think he's still hampered by the knee,'' said Willis. ''I don't know how much less mobile he is but he can't move as fast on a drive. I don't think he reacts as quickly and I don't think he can go up as high.''

Frazier also insisted: ''He's lost a lot of his movement. I saw a couple of times when his knee gave out and once they called him for traveling when he had to take an extra step.''

It was Frazier who came out of an ordered defensive game to score when we most needed it. He shot only 3-for-5 in 30 minutes but he made the play that actually saved the game.

We were leading by 99–98 with five minutes left when he stole the ball and scored. He missed a foul shot awarded on the play. Reed tapped the rebound back to DeBusschere and he hit a jumper for a four-point play. That was it.

"What's the use of talking about my mobility? That would only be an excuse," said Wilt.

So Mullaney did. "It's hard for me to say how much he's lost but there is a loss," he said. "I told Wilt that Reed would go outside and I'd like to have him play Willis up to fifteen feet. I'd like to see him go out further the next time than he did tonight."

Dr. Kerlan still marveled over what he was seeing. "I was against him playing when he did," admitted the surgeon, who had performed the operation for torn knee ligaments. "I would have preferred him to wait until next year. Frankly, whatever he does has got to be considered remarkable."

I know I always felt Wilt was remarkable, especially the way he came back to play in that championship series. He could have taken the easy way out and waited until next year.

I gave Riordan 25 minutes because West got Barnett and then Frazier into foul trouble. West buried 16 points in the third period alone. Riordan got some of them back as he shot 7-for-12 good for 19 points.

Riordan's strength was driving to the basket. He weighed 200, was quick and could power himself high to the backboard. He loved challenging Wilt or anyone to stop him once he was in drive.

He and Bradley stayed after practice for 30 minutes the day before the first game for a little one-on-one. They were two gym rats going head to head.

Bradley shot long jumpers and Riordan drove the hoop. They kept score and Bradley said: "He beat me." Wilt said just about the same thing after Riordan beat him on two crucial drives.

Riordan and Cazzie gave us four baskets down the stretch. "We got beat by other things," said Wilt, referring to our bench, Mike and Cazzie. "There's always one guy on fire to keep things sustained," said Riordan.

That was the Knicks. We had eight or nine men who could beat you. No team in those days could match that.

One more thing. Wilt introduced a new foul shooting technique with the same results. He went to the line 10 times and made one.

He stood a little more than a foot back of the line and kept hitting the back of the rim.

"I'd like him to shoot from two feet back," suggested Mullaney. "I've told him to take his spot, then, without looking down, move back a couple of inches. He keeps hitting the back rim because the shot is too short for him." I figured he was so strong, he should've shot them from midcourt.

"No one's going to bury anybody," predicted Willis. "Both teams have a lot of poise and are capable of coming back at any time."

LOS ANGELES

	min	fg	fga	ft	fta	reb	ast	pf	pts
Baylor	39	10	17	1	2	20	3	4	21
Chamberlain	48	8	14	1	10	24	5	2	17
Counts	7	3	5	0	0	2	1	1	6
Egan	18	2	6	2	2	0	1	3	6
Erickson	37	4	11	4	4	3	1	2	12
Garrett	30	4	9	2	2	1	0	2	10
Hairston	13	3	7	1	1	4	1	2	7
West	48	9	23	15	17	3	4	4	33
TOTALS	240	43	92	26	38	57	16	20	112

NEW YORK

	min	fg	fga	ft	fta	reb	ast	pf	pts
Barnett	41	5	11	7	8	5	9	5	17
Bowman	3	1	2	0	0	1	0	1	2
Bradley	30	7	16	2	2	2	2	3	16
DeBusschere	39	8	20	3	3	16	5	3	19
Frazier	30	3	5	0	1	5	6	4	6
Reed	45	16	30	5	7	16	5	2	37
Riordan	25	7	12	5	5	2	2	3	19
Russell	18	4	12	0	0	1	1	3	8
Stallworth	9	0	0	0	0	0	0	2	0
TOTALS	240	51	108	22	26	48	30	26	124

Los Angeles	25	29	38	20	—	112
New York	35	30	24	35	—	124

Riordan and Cazzie were great coming off the bench. They knew their roles and I had absolute faith in them whenever I felt they were needed. They had one thing in mind—win the game.

Danny Whelan was an expert on Cazzie. As our trainer, he was the mother hen of the dressing room and most familiar with everyone's quirks. Cazzie was one of his favorite subjects.

"He was a nutritional expert with a teapot," explained Danny. "He always got a new writer in the dressing room. From Podunk or whatever. Cazzie would give him an interview but always would say: 'after practice' or 'after the game.'"

The writer assumed he was going to get an inside story so he'd come back in great anticipation. "Cazzie would say: 'Wait a minute,' and he'd get his teapot out and plug it in and make his tea," continued Whelan. "Cazzie would pour the tea into a cup and say to the guy: 'Whaddya want to know?' He would have the guy hypnotized by then."

Cazzie would start talking about herbal teas, vitamins and special foods. "The writer figured Caz knows all about diets and stuff, so he starts talking nutrition," said Danny. "It wasn't basketball. It was all nutrition. Cazzie says he really watches what he eats. The first thing he does when he gets up is to have his tea and before he goes to bed he has his tea."

Whelan switched to recollections of our bus trips from games in Philadelphia. "We used to call in for the sandwiches before we left,'' he said. ''They'd load them on the bus. So I always asked the players what they wanted. Cazzie's was baloney and cheese. After all those speeches. Baloney and cheese on white bread.''

That reminded DeBusschere of the time the Players Association held its convention at the El Conquistador in San Juan. It involved a golf foursome among him, Bradley, Riordan and Cazzie.

''If there was an opposite of Cazzie it would be Riordan,'' said Dave. ''One day we decide to play golf. Cazzie played the day before and shot seventy-one, par or under par. He told us that, anyway.''

Cazzie was ready to challenge anyone. Riordan decided he was going to play. ''Mike said he'd played about three or four times in his life,'' said DeBusschere. ''So Cazzie comes out with red bag, red shoes, red pants and red hat. He was impeccable.''

Now they were waiting for Riordan. They were waiting to tee off and no Mike. Suddenly he showed up. ''Here comes Riordan,'' DeBusschere went on. ''He's got on his low-cut sneakers with no socks. He's got Bermuda shorts all ripped and an old T-shirt. And he proceeds to beat Cazzie.''

Cazzie gave Riordan some shots, of course, but it didn't work. Mike really needled him. '' 'Hey, Caz. What did you shoot yesterday?' '' recalled DeBusschere. ''Caz was trying to hit 'em so hard and so far. And here was Riordan slipping and sliding in his sneakers and hitting 'em down the middle.''

That was Riordan: a self-made individual, tough as nails, who wanted it badly and was willing to sacrifice for it. ''His role, which he took great pride in, was to give the foul,'' said Bradley. ''And it's got to be the first time in the history of sports the crowd erupts when the guy who is put in—when all he does is give a foul.''

Game two in our series with the Lakers took place on April 28 in the Garden. There had been reports in the papers that Reed might not play. Foolish people. They didn't know Willis like we did.

''Maybe I won't,'' said Willis with that disarming smile of his. We worked on some special situation involving West. We wanted to be ready for the final seconds and the final shot he was sure to take.

We discussed what we'd all do, who was to go where and when.

That's what I mean when I say your homework has to be done before a game, not during it. We were preparing for a situation that was sure to come so we would know how to react.

Willis laughed when people talked about his shoulder as though it was a serious consideration. He pointed at Wilt and said: "It takes a man with a lot of guts to come back and do what he's doing. The guy just played forty-eight minutes with a bad knee. Nobody knows how bad it is and he never alibis."

Willis meant it. He wasn't stroking Wilt so that he might go a little easy on him. "I've taken cortisone pills for all my aches and pains . . . the knee and shoulder," said Willis, preparing himself for the physical battle to come.

He expected a little more heat from Wilt, especially since Mullaney wanted Chamberlain to drive the hoop more. "If he goes to the basket, it'll put a lot of pressure on me," said Willis. "You may stop him for one play but he's likely to score the next twenty."

Reed was a Chamberlain supporter. He appreciated what Russell had done but wasn't about to dump on Wilt as many did. "There's no center who could do more things than Wilt," said Willis, echoing my words. "He proved he can do whatever a team wanted him to do—score, rebound, block shots and get assists. He never had a chance to play with a group of players as Russell did. Only once and he proved he could do it in Philadelphia."

Our concern was that Wilt would prove he could do it, again, in Los Angeles against us. We had to rely on our defense because almost everyone outrebounded us.

West reminded everyone about one other oversight involving us. "Picking up loose balls and passes, that's defense," he explained. "How many times do you really go head to head with one man these days? The game's not played that way anymore."

Not by the better teams—at any time, even today when the game has developed into more one-on-ones because of the athletic skills of the players. I was reminded that West, despite his speech about our team defense, had scored 33 points against Frazier, Barnett and Riordan in the first game.

The Lakers had an answer to our pressure defense against West.

They had Dick Garrett bring the ball down most of the time. Garrett, who was a rookie, had played a season at Southern Illinois with Frazier and they had a bet going on the series.

Well, not exactly a bet, because that would have been against the rules. "The one who loses has to pay for a party back at school," said Garrett, another expert on the Knicks.

"The Knicks play good defense and they have five guys who can all shoot fifteen-footers," he explained. "Against Atlanta and Phoenix, we just forced the guys into Wilt and he was knocking a lot of shots under the basket. That never happened here."

Meanwhile, Frazier was thinking about West and how impossible it was to play him. Clyde was known for his fast hands. He told this story about being in a bar as a full glass fell off. "I reached out and grabbed the glass without a drop spilling," he claimed. "It scared me that I was so fast."

He couldn't use his speed to grab West, though it worked that way in the first game. Jerry had drawn three of Clyde's four personals, four of Barnett's five and two of Riordan's three.

Frazier had a better game plan for West this time. "I felt I let the team down the last time," he pointed out. "I felt I had to get back and stabilize the defense and he kept moving. I was swiping at the ball. With him you can't get careless trying to steal the ball. He shoots too fast. I was putting too much pressure on him. I'm going to play him straight up this time."

Wilt had warned us about driving and trying to take advantage of his rehabilitating knee. We wouldn't or couldn't listen. Basketball is a game of instinctive reaction and Wilt hadn't blocked a shot in the opener, so who was afraid of the big, bad man?

With the Lakers leading 103–101, Riordan drove the lane on him. Mike was thinking of going all the way or dumping off to Willis if Chamberlain came at him. "I couldn't see Willis so I tried to jump and lay it over Wilt's shoulder," explained Mike after Chamberlain intimidated him into missing.

Reed powered in from the opposite side for the rebound. He got it and shot but Wilt recovered in time to deflect it. "It came off

Chamberlain real quick and hit my hands,'' said Willis as the Lakers got the ball out of bounds.

There were the usual postmortems. "Riordan came in on me tonight,'' said Wilt, feeling a lot better. "He did something with the ball—I don't think he knows what he did with it.''

Riordan did but it didn't matter. Wilt's presence had distracted him so that he actually flipped a floater after changing his mind in midair. Mike also recalled a preceding play where he was stuck in the air and laid it off to Bradley but West stole the pass.

It was excellent defense by the Lakers with the game on the line. "Sometimes it's even better when you don't knock a shot,'' said Wilt, meaning that intimidating the shooter is a message that's sometimes better to deliver.

We still had a slim chance to win. With 46 seconds to go, LA led by only two. Plenty of time for a tie. Willis gave Wilt some of his better moves and thought he had a step on him. As Willis drove for the hoop, Chamberlain smothered his shot.

Frazier recovered the loose ball with five ticks left on the 24-second clock. "I was going to the hoop for a rebound when someone threw me the ball,'' said DeBusschere. "I had to get the ball up fast to beat the clock so we could get the rebound.''

The action was so wild and fast, DeBusschere didn't realize that it was Clyde who had passed the ball to him out of the scramble. When Dave missed, there was another scramble between Reed and Chamberlain and this time Stallworth came up with the ball.

Stalls struggled to get free of the crowd around him. He didn't realize he was in the three-second lane until it was too late. There were only 18 seconds left but we still got the ball back for another crack at it.

It took another strange bounce. Frazier and DeBusschere double-teamed Garrett at midcourt and he made a rookie mistake. He leaped above the backcourt line trying to hit West with a lob pass and Reed stole it.

Garrett had fired a clutch shot from the corner to put the Lakers ahead 103–101 but this time he felt miserable. "I should've called time. I should've held the ball but Jerry was open,'' he explained.

I couldn't believe we were getting so many chances but winding up with nothing. We were a cool bunch and we were not panicking, but how many cracks can you get and waste?

We only had one more. There were five seconds left when Willis hit Barnett with a release pass off the steal. Garrett and Erickson had dashed back for the Lakers. And Stallworth had somehow gotten into position for a rebound.

Barnett took a couple of dribbles, pulled up at the head of the key and popped a 20-footer. The ball bounced off the side of the rim and Erickson grabbed the rebound by boxing out Stallworth. We lost and the Series was tied.

"I didn't really know how much time there was left," said Barnett. "He should've dribbled a few more times," said West.

My job was to not let the tough defeat get the players down. I only kept the dressing-room door closed for a minute or two, which was normal procedure. It was a hard loss but I told the players to forget it—that the Lakers could've beaten us worse the way the game had developed.

Some reporter came into our dressing room and said that Rick Roberson had claimed: "The Knicks just lost the series tonight." Good luck to him.

Wilt felt good about having added 24 rebounds and 19 points to his 44 minutes of definitive action. "I don't know if I looked like the Wilt of old," he said, "You forget, I'm thirty-four. And it's not just one injury. You can't do at thirty-four what you did at twenty-four. It seems some people want me to do a miracle job every night."

One night like the one we'd just had was enough for me. Wilt and the Lakers still didn't convince Riordan. "In the forty-eighth minute they were better," was all Mike conceded. "That was the only difference."

There were other bits of aggravation, the kind you think of after losing. I didn't call time when Reed stole Garrett's pass. I usually did in cases like that but didn't want to spoil a breakaway.

I thought of Reed jumping into the lane too fast and wiping out a Frazier foul shot that would have given us a 91–84 lead—also, the time Clyde stole the ball after the Lakers had rebounded a miss and was fouled going to the hoop. One ref signaled two shots, the other said no.

I was upset until I found out why. The 24-second buzzer had sounded before the Lakers' shot, so that cost us a possible two points. In the final analysis, LA made the more significant defensive plays.

"Our team is better geared to a defensive game," was West's reminder in the LA dressing room. "We didn't allow a hundred twenty points tonight. We were more ready to play. If you had been in here before the game, you would have seen how quiet it was."

The Lakers knew they had to win. They couldn't afford to spot us the first two games, though they were going home. "They were double-teaming us and we didn't make them pay," said Frazier. "All we needed was one more pass. They forced us into bad shots down the stretch."

Frazier forgot to mention that he picked up his fifth personal with nine minutes to go and I had to sit him until the final three minutes. He still got a triple-double with 12 rebounds, 11 assists and 11 points.

Losers can always figure out why they didn't win. Winners don't have to.

LOS ANGELES

	min	fg	fga	ft	fta	reb	ast	pf	pts
Baylor	36	6	9	1	2	5	5	3	13
Chamberlain	44	9	20	1	3	24	2	3	19
Counts	8	2	5	1	2	2	0	4	5
Egan	6	1	1	0	0	0	0	0	2
Erickson	37	4	7	1	2	2	6	4	9
Garrett	40	5	13	7	8	4	6	2	17
Hairston	19	2	5	0	1	8	1	1	4
Roberson	4	1	2	0	0	0	0	2	2
West	46	12	28	10	15	1	1	3	34
TOTALS	240	42	90	21	33	46	21	22	105

NEW YORK

	min	fg	fga	ft	fta	reb	ast	pf	pts
Barnett	41	7	15	5	6	4	1	5	19
Bowman	3	0	1	0	0	1	0	1	0
Bradley	39	7	16	2	3	3	0	3	16
DeBusschere	42	7	17	4	6	14	2	3	18
Frazier	39	5	9	1	3	12	11	5	11
Reed	45	12	29	5	10	15	5	3	29
Riordan	15	1	5	0	0	4	3	2	2
Russell	7	1	3	0	0	2	0	1	2
Stallworth	8	3	5	0	0	4	1	0	6
Warren	1	0	0	0	0	0	0	1	0
TOTALS	240	43	100	17	27	59	23	24	103

Los Angeles	28	24	29	24	—	105
New York	24	28	29	22	—	103

All the excitement of the championship season transferred to the chartered plane we took to Los Angeles. Normally we flew commercial because we had a small complement of players and media. This time we had so many people it was almost as tough as getting a seat to the games.

Very few games are indelibly etched in your mind when you have been involved in as many as I have. That goes for about everyone who ever played the game at the professional level.

Those where I can remember specific details after nearly a quarter of a century are exceptional. That was game three against the Lakers. By now there must be millions of people who say they were in the Forum and saw West hit the 55-footer that sent it into overtime that night.

It was the shot heard around the basketball world and put us on the verge of falling behind 2–1.

We intended to kill enough of the clock to give the Lakers little or no time to respond. Bradley was to get a pass behind a pick and hit one of his clutch jumpers but he was covered.

That's where options and smart players come in. Barnett didn't force a shot. He flipped the ball to DeBusschere near the circle and

Dave hit a jumper. I figured we'd won. The Lakers had no more time-outs and they had two or three seconds to get the ball 92 feet downcourt and through the hoop for a tie.

What happened then is confusion to this day—at least as far as I'm concerned. Chamberlain took the ball and slipped it to West. And Jerry took a few steps and hit the tying basket with what was finally estimated to be a 55-footer.

Everyone agrees on that. The rest, nobody agrees on. I looked at films the next day and it appeared as though Wilt was in bounds when he passed the ball. I had to wait 22 years for confirmation.

There are arguments about it to this day. "Let me explain that," said Wilt. "There should be no argument. I never got out of bounds. The game was over as far as I was concerned and I just kinda took the ball, took one step backwards and gave it to Jerry and he put it in the basket."

Now he tells me. We had to go through all the anguish of the West shot and almost lost the game and the championship. "The game was over and that's why, I do remember, I ran off the court," continued Wilt. "Everyone thinks that I ran off the court because I thought the game was won by Jerry West's shot. What they didn't know was that I got off the court and I didn't step out of bounds before I passed the ball."

Wilt was surprised that it had taken so long for someone to ask about the incident that really involved an illegal basket. It happened so fast amid all the confusion that no one really noticed it.

He ran into the dressing room and they had to get him back for overtime. "I went into the dressing room because I thought the game was over and they had really won," he explained not long ago. "I didn't have enough time to give the ball to West. I thought the time had run out and I just flipped him the ball and left. I never even saw his shot."

He confessed he didn't mind rewriting dramatic history. "It was dramatic but not to me," he said. "What I also remember—and Jerry West is a good friend—is that Jerry went oh-for-ten, I think, in overtime. Everyone talks about the shots he made and I didn't see but I do remember him going oh-for-ten in overtime."

I don't think Wilt's version will spoil West's historic moment or what he put us through. Drama is drama when it happens and I'm sure West will settle for that.

West took Wilt's pass, legal or not, and dribbled up the middle and around Barnett. He fired a running one-hander and it went through the basket like it had eyes.

"I was just trying to get the ball in the middle of the court," explained Jerry. "Willis picked me up and forced me that way. When I let it go, it looked good and straight enough. My body was behind it and I was up in the air. I was just about at the top of the foul circle. I took off and figured I covered about six or eight feet more."

DeBusschere collapsed under the Laker basket, where he had rushed back to protect against anyone or anything. He never expected what he saw. "I just couldn't believe it. My heart sank," he said. "It's the longest clutch shot I've ever seen. I was directly under the basket and my heart dropped into my stomach."

No one was more stunned than Reed. He was the closest to West when he shot and followed the flight of the ball from 55 feet or so away. He can still see it.

"The funny thing about it was, I'm back there because Wilt throws the ball," recalled Willis. "I'm gonna harass Jerry but make sure I don't get close enough for them to call a foul. I was under the basket because the ball had just gone through on Dave's shot."

He remembered that we had run the same play two or three times and Bradley hit jump shots from the corner. "It was a double screen," explained Willis. "I used to set a screen on the baseline. DeBusschere would come across the line and set a screen for Bradley. And I would turn and reset a screen for Bill and DeBusschere would pop out to the free-throw line."

How about that? Willis still remembers that play. It was one of our favorites and we won plenty of games with it. "This particular time two Lakers went with Bill and DeBusschere gets the ball wide open," said Willis. "If you see the film, nobody's on Dave and he makes the shot."

Willis explained that DeBusschere now knew there was going to be a long pass and got back to protect our basket. "By this time Wilt's thrown the ball," resumed Willis. "So I run and try to distract Jerry. He shoots. I'm watching it from one end and DeBusschere is watching it from the other."

Stereo vision. Reed considers it funny now. He even laughed when he recalled DeBusschere falling flat on his back after the shot. He also remembered Barnett's reminder that we still had a game to play.

"You know what he said?" asked Willis, promptly answering: "I'm going to tell you his exact words. I'll never forget it because this is one of Richard's lines. He said: 'What's wrong with you guys? This game's not over. It's just started.' And he was right. It was just like playing a five-minute game."

All of us were stunned. Erickson had hit a desperate 25-footer at the halftime buzzer to put us behind by 14, and now this. Clyde stood frozen on the floor staring into space and I had to call him over to our huddle. We had to regroup fast. We were in the Forum and that was enough to make things appear more impossible.

"It was depressing, a shot like that at a time like that in a game like that," explained Frazier. "I was looking at Jerry and then I watched the shot and I said to myself: 'That damned ball is going to go in.' I'm like a bird dog pointing to the dressing room. It was a nightmare."

Barnett brought us all out of it. Both teams were tired and we outscored the Lakers 9–6 with Barnett hitting a final 10-foot jumper to make it 111–108.

We were leading 108–105 at one time but the Lakers wouldn't quit. DeBusschere had blocked a shot by Baylor and taken a pass from Riordan to put us up by one, then hit a long jumper to make it three.

LA came right back to tie with two minutes to go. They never scored again. Willis grabbed the game ball and said: "Ain't nobody going to get it from me." I wonder if he still has it.

He deserved the game ball. He had another huge game with 38 points and 17 rebounds in 49 minutes. West played the entire 53 minutes, despite hurting his left thumb in the first half, and scored

34 points. Wilt also worked the entire game and contributed 26 rebounds in addition to 21 points.

I used four of our starters over 40 minutes and Mullaney used all five of his. It was an exhausting game for the players, the coach and the fans.

"Yeah, we outplayed them all the way," said Chamberlain. All the way, maybe, but not at the end.

LOS ANGELES

	min	fg	fga	ft	fta	reb	ast	pf	pts
Baylor	45	4	13	5	6	12	11	6	13
Chamberlain	53	7	10	7	13	26	4	4	21
Egan	5	1	1	0	0	1	0	0	2
Erickson	46	9	17	1	2	4	3	2	19
Garrett	44	6	14	1	1	4	1	5	13
Hairston	19	3	3	0	0	3	0	5	6
West	53	11	28	12	16	1	9	2	34
TOTALS	265	41	86	26	38	51	28	24	108

NEW YORK

	min	fg	fga	ft	fta	reb	ast	pf	pts
Barnett	46	7	18	4	5	2	4	5	18
Bowman	4	0	1	2	2	2	0	2	2
Bradley	37	3	13	1	1	8	4	4	7
DeBusschere	44	10	20	1	1	15	3	2	21
Frazier	49	8	17	3	4	11	7	2	19
Reed	49	17	30	4	8	17	3	2	38
Riordan	10	0	2	0	0	3	1	2	0
Russell	16	1	5	0	0	3	1	3	2
Stallworth	9	1	3	2	2	2	1	0	4
Warren	1	0	0	0	0	0	0	1	0
TOTALS	265	47	109	17	23	68	24	23	111

Los Angeles	26	30	17	29	6	—	108
New York	20	22	26	34	9	—	111

LA was concerned about West and I was worried about Reed. His knee was killing him. He had been taking cortisone but only his will to win kept him going.

The papers were full of stories that West might not play the fourth game. I believed that like I believed Willis wouldn't play. They were the indispensable men of both teams and they knew it was their responsibility to play.

West had one advantage with his injury. It was his left thumb, not his shooting hand. He might be unable to catch the ball without pain but he could sure still shoot it with the other hand. X rays had shown no break so I was certain we would have to focus our defense on him as usual.

Willis was a different story. He had been kicked above the left knee, the troublesome one. Why is it when you have an injury you always seem to get hit there?

We felt we had the advantage now, especially after the Lakers' third-game disaster. That had to hurt. I'm sure a lot of our players felt that way. In fact, Barnett, always the optimist, said: "These chumps are ready to be taken. They must be way down after that last game. If we can pressure them right off, they'll probably fall right over."

I didn't subscribe to that. Coaches can't afford to assume anything. Every game is a new situation and the best you can do is try to control things, with no guarantee you can or will.

I took nothing for granted. That went from the Laker players down to their fans, who were rather complacent compared to ours in New York. The LA crowd came late and left early.

"They leave with three minutes to go with LA behind by ten or ahead by ten," said Bradley. "They are not as sophisticated as the fans in New York. They are there for entertainment."

I always felt that helped us and the visiting teams. They were quiet spectators in LA but in New York they shook the building and the other teams with their support of their game—the city game.

"The people don't sit as close to the floor in LA," explained Bradley. "The floor is elevated almost like a stage. It's a very nice place. No tension, no pressure. Even the visiting dressing room is better than the one we have in New York."

There was a special feeling whenever we walked into the Forum. It was so neat and relaxing. It was like playing basketball on vacation. The weather was always warm and comfortable. We wore leisure clothes and even the Hollywood Park racetrack was a furlong from the Forum.

It was a much more casual atmosphere than in New York and many other places. That could be dangerous, of course. It could lull players into a sense of security and it did many times. Bradley was right in everything he said about it, which was not unusual.

LA was a pleasure to visit as long as we won. There were a lot of other places the players and I preferred not to go to. Bradley explained why.

"Part of going into enemy territory is what they've got prepared for you," he said. "Going into smelly dressing rooms with hot showers that steam up the place, everyone stepping on each other because the dressing rooms are small, like in Chicago. You already have a disadvantage with things like that."

Expansion and modern buildings have just about eliminated all that. Only Chicago and Boston still have the same old buildings with the antiquated, small dressing rooms. And that will be taken care of in time, as everything else is.

LA fans were casual and blasé compared to New Yorkers and others around the league. They never beat you. We believed that West had to keep having exceptional games to beat us and even then the Lakers weren't guaranteed to win.

We played better team defense. We had a smarter team game. And DeBusschere was doing a fine job of minimizing Baylor off the boards. That put an extra load on Chamberlain, who was super even in his condition but not superman.

We had lost a little of our poise in the second game when the Lakers pressed us. I also thought there wasn't any real reason to drive into Wilt's traps when we had the shooting to go over him.

All of which made sense to me except we lost the fourth game and the series was tied again, going back to New York. The news wasn't too good as we faced each other on May 1. Our GIs had rolled into Cambodia in an extension of the Vietnam War and what was a basketball game compared to that?

There was one other bit of interesting but not balancing news. Diane Crump was about to become the first woman rider in the

Kentucky Derby. She was going to break down forbidden walls with a horse named Fathom.

I was thinking I might be better off going to Hollywood Park when I walked into the nearby Forum that night. How come I was never so right when I went to the track? We lost 121–115 in the second straight overtime game.

West and his bad thumb produced 37 points and 18 assists. He only played 52 minutes. Willis also played 52 minutes but his aching knee limited his mobility enough for him to have a subpar 12 rebounds and 23 points. Meanwhile, Chamberlain was getting 25 rebounds and 18 points.

Our guys were a little bitter—partly at themselves for blowing the chance to go up 3–1 and partly over the West stories. Frazier came into our huddle when I called our first time-out and said West had just changed hands and banged his left thumb hard with the ball and nothing happened.

I had no time for such things. When they asked me about West's thumb I informed them I wasn't a doctor. I told them I was too busy to worry about him. If he showed up in a suit and not in uniform then I'd believe he wouldn't play.

I told them I was too concerned with making my own monumental decisions on strategy to worry about West. I considered the whole media splash so much trivia. Our players didn't, apparently.

I knew Willis was hurting and I could only guess about West. "It was pretty evident that Willis could not move tonight," said DeBusschere. "He still played a gallant game. His knee wasn't publicized as much as the other guy's injury."

DeBusschere got upset when reminded that West had said he couldn't have played if the game had been a day earlier. "Bull. He could've played with a broken left wrist," said Dave. "I thought it was a joke that he might not be able to play. I played with a broken right thumb in the playoffs once."

The Lakers were persistent in defending West. I also would've been if I were on the other side. "His thumb really ballooned after the game the other night. He couldn't get a grip on the ball because he couldn't close his hand," said Mullaney.

Then there was general manager Freddie Schaus, who coached West at West Virginia and played 67 games for the Knicks in 1953–54. "I saw that thumb yesterday," he said after the series became 2–2. "I didn't see any way that even West could play. It was bad."

Reed put this cap on it: "The papers blew it out of proportion. As far as I'm concerned, there was nothing wrong with him."

Reed had plenty of support from West's 13-for-26 field goals, 11-for-12 from the foul line and all those assists. Jerry had performed just about how we all figured he would despite the blitz of stories that he might not play.

"They'll have to shoot him in the leg to keep him out," volunteered Phil Jackson, who was out with back surgery but on a special picture-taking assignment.

Frazier's reaction to the scare stories that West wouldn't play was: "Why, because of a broken heart? If he had a broken leg he would've played. This means a lot to him. He's a pro. He has a lot of pride. I think it helped psych them up. That team without West would be through. They'd be hurting."

Reed was a real problem. A reporter walked over after the game and pointed at Willis's badly swollen knee. "Don't touch it," Willis all but screamed. On the other hand, or thumb, West's 37 points and 18 assists meant he had contributed to only 73 points.

"West had his best game tonight. I don't know if he ever had a line like that," said Reed.

We were actually hurt by John Tresvant, a 6'7" active forward picked up from Seattle by the Lakers. He showed up for the first time in the series in the final 56 seconds of regulation with LA leading by a point and did some damage.

In six minutes, he had three rebounds, two assists, 3-for-4 from the foul line and two big steals in overtime. We couldn't respond because Willis just couldn't carry his normal load. I had to go with him as far as I could because he was the one player who didn't have a major backup.

> *"There's no point in being made beautiful now if I'm just going to run into Willis Reed again. He's broken my nose twice. Once more and he gets permanent possession of me."*
>
> *—Jerry West*

Tresvant made probably his biggest plays after West's jumper just beat the buzzer and put LA ahead 105–103 in overtime. He stole a pass intended for Willis and drew two free throws. He made them both, hit West with a long scoring pass and then stole the ball from Barnett.

It was an interesting LA dressing room after the game. Mullaney had to explain why Tresvant hadn't been playing. "I wanted to play a smaller man on Bradley," he explained. "I didn't think Tres was quick enough."

Tres had this reaction: "He didn't think I could handle Bradley? In my opinion, Connie Hawkins is the quickest forward in the league. How can I play him and not Bradley?"

Just then someone walked over, stuck out his hand and said to Tresvant: "I'd like to introduce myself. My name is Jack Kent Cooke. I'm sure we'll be seeing a lot of each other."

Johnny Egan also came off the bench and contributed three baskets on six shots in 11 minutes. Egan played for the Knicks from 1963–65 and was part of the deal that sent Johnny Green and Bad News Barnes to the Bullets for Walt Bellamy.

Mullaney, his old college coach, had put him in after we got off to a hot start by hitting 9 of our first 11 shots. LA went from there to go ahead by seven at the half.

"Our bench gets the momentum going," said Egan, who had the biggest hands for a small guy I've ever seen. "I think we should give Wilt and West a few minutes rest. I think Mullaney will from now on."

Nate Bowman was 6'10" and 245 but no physical matchup for

Wilt. We really lost our chance to win in regulation in the second quarter. They outscored us then by 10 points and held on until we caught them in the final quarter.

We were behind 54–47 at the half and I don't know how we survived the third period. We actually had the ball 12 times in one stretch without scoring. We had eight turnovers and only four shots. What a way to try to win a championship.

It was the worst basketball I had seen the Knicks play under the circumstances. The Lakers could have put us away right there but we still outscored them by three in the period and stayed alive.

At our worst, we managed to slice the LA lead to four points entering the final quarter. DeBusschere was in foul trouble with four personals so I gave Stallworth a lot of time on Baylor.

Stalls was normally a smart, quick defensive player. He had all the physical skills to play Baylor but not this time. Elgin played like he'd just gotten out of prison with no DeBusschere to keep him locked up.

Dave sat on the bench yelling instructions to Stallworth about guarding Baylor but that didn't help. Elgin broke out for the first time with 30 points. We caught the Lakers anyway because of a late wake-up call to Frazier.

Clyde accepted the scoring burden, which he was capable of doing when the situation called for it. He was way off in the first half but contributed 13 of 16 points in the second half.

That's when we were trying to catch up under the handicaps created by Reed and DeBusschere. Besides, Bradley was having another off night with 3-for-11. Clyde actually gave us a chance to win it in regulation when we had the ball with the score 98–98.

There were 18 seconds to go and I let 9 run off the clock before I called time. I suggested the same play on which DeBusschere had hit the shot he thought had won the third game in regulation. It worked then, why not now?

Simple strategy. Dave also told Willis he was going to drive this time and he'd drop it off if Wilt jumped out at him. Reed was to move to the open spot and take the pass for what would be the winning basket.

Only DeBusschere never got the ball. The Lakers tightened and Clyde got stuck with it. He couldn't pass it so he shot it. He hit the front rim and it was overtime for the second straight time—with a drastically different result. DeBusschere fouled out, Reed was limping and Bradley was still absent on offense before fouling out. I don't know how we scored 16 points in overtime and still lost. Yes, I do. The Lakers got 22 and it was back to New York for a fifth game.

LOS ANGELES

	min	fg	fga	ft	fta	reb	ast	pf	pts
Baylor	45	12	24	6	7	13	3	2	30
Chamberlain	49	7	13	4	7	25	7	3	18
Egan	11	3	6	0	0	0	2	3	6
Erickson	43	6	13	2	2	9	4	4	14
Garrett	38	3	9	1	1	2	1	5	7
Hairston	17	1	5	1	2	5	1	0	3
Roberson	4	1	3	1	2	4	0	2	3
Tresvant	6	0	1	3	4	3	2	1	3
West	52	13	26	11	12	5	18	4	37
TOTALS	265	46	100	29	37	66	38	24	121

NEW YORK

	min	fg	fga	ft	fta	reb	ast	pf	pts
Barnett	41	14	25	1	1	3	3	5	29
Bowman	1	0	1	0	0	0	1	0	0
Bradley	32	3	11	1	1	3	3	6	7
DeBusschere	33	9	14	2	3	11	2	6	20
Frazier	51	3	11	10	13	6	11	2	16
Reed	52	10	23	3	6	12	2	4	23
Riordan	14	0	4	0	0	0	1	3	0
Russell	20	4	7	0	0	3	1	1	8
Stallworth	21	5	9	2	2	13	4	1	12
TOTALS	265	48	105	19	26	51	28	28	115

Los Angeles	24	30	17	28	22	—	121
New York	27	20	20	32	16	—	115

19

I was very concerned about Reed. He had made it through the fourth game despite great pain but how much longer could he go on? I still don't know how he pushed himself for 52 minutes.

We were still confident we would win as we flew out of LA the next morning. A head count indicated we were all together except Bradley, who had left earlier for a reserves commitment. The flight included whiz photographer Phil Jackson. He was an expert by now.

Jackson could discuss lighting, lenses and camera angles with the best of them. His pet project was to catch West in shooting action. Jerry's jump shot was artistry in motion.

"He goes up before you know it and he lets go of the ball so fast," explained Phil, who conceded: "I'm still not an excellent photographer but I'm getting better. I come up with a good shot one out of ten times. That's not too hot in basketball but it's not bad in photography."

I had Jackson along for two reasons. He belonged as a member of the team, and I wanted him to sort of scout and tell me if there was something about the Laker defenses I should know. Phil had an incisive mind so why waste it?

He was our philosophy professor. He had definite ideas about the sociological problems of man and never hesitated to express them. He was very sensitive about human values and relationships. It has helped him deal with the different personalities of the Chicago Bulls.

Riordan remembers having an early experience about those things with Phil. "When he first came in he was considered a cowboy from Montana," said Mike. "When we were walking around the streets of New York, he would stop and look at some of the people that were lying on the sidewalks."

Phil, obviously, had never seen anything like it in Deer Lodge, where he grew up. He considered the sight of the sidewalk people weird and disgraceful. "He'd say: 'What about these people?' and I would say: 'What about them?' " continued Riordan.

Jackson wondered why no one was bothering to offer them a hand. Mike's response was typical of New Yorkers who had gotten used to it. "I said: 'Phil. They don't need a hand. They're bums. If they needed a hand it would be entirely different. Keep on walking.' "

It was still hard for Phil to understand. Jackson told Riordan that it was an example of how heartless and inconsiderate New Yorkers were. "I told him if he lived in this environment for a period of time he'd be just like the rest of the people. It's a process of conditioned reflex," said Mike.

Riordan explained to Phil that it was easy for him to be so critical coming in from another town. Mike went away to the service and played the Eastern League before he saw Jackson again. By then Phil had played a season with us and had been exposed more to New York's routine complexities.

"I see him, again, in the springtime after he's been here a year and I'm driving down the street with him and he's like Jekyll and Hyde," said Riordan. "He was screaming from the window. Giving the people the bird. Hollering. I said: 'Hey, Phil, look at yourself. You're just like the rest of us,' and he said: 'You know, I guess I have changed over the last six months.'

"I reminded him of the time I talked about conditioned reflexes. I said to him: 'You don't even give those bums the time of day anymore, do you?' He realized you can become a product of your environment."

Jackson's basketball insightfulness wasn't going to help us much this time. His pictures might be useful for the eight books that were in the works. Most, I assumed, were dependent on our winning the championship.

We got home too late on New York time to practice. We worked the day before the fifth game but Reed and DeBusschere didn't. I had Dave just walk through the plays to give his tired legs a rest. Covering Baylor didn't exactly give him a chance to relax and he also had a tendency to get leg cramps.

Baylor wasn't exactly a gazelle himself. It was the stomach pull that had benched him for almost 25 games during the season, not his older legs. "I tried to run but couldn't," said Elgin after he just shot around at the Lakers' workout.

Cazzie also missed practice because of military duty. We sent Willis to the doctor and were informed that both knees were bothering him. The right one was more tender than the left. It had a knot below the kneecap.

Whelan called it "a schoolyard knee," the kind you get from playing on cement surfaces. They still gave Willis's left knee more attention because that's the one that had restricted him in the fourth game.

They prescribed ultrasound, whirlpool and a day off. Whelan also was prepared to provide the same treatment Willis had undergone throughout the last game. Danny would massage the inflamed muscle above Willis's left knee and apply salve during time-outs. "I couldn't touch it in the second half, it got so tender," explained Danny.

Whelan also applied ice to the knee and treatment would continue to game time. If Willis needed cortisone he'd get it. "It feels better. I'm all right," Willis kept insisting.

I remembered him saying the same thing before the fourth game and then watching him hobble through all those minutes against Chamberlain. We needed Willis's mobility at both ends against Wilt and there was no way we could be sure. Little did we realize what was about to happen.

We also weren't getting enough out of our offense. I had told Clyde to concentrate on playing defense against West but he was carrying it too far. He was passing up good shots. He was only taking about 10 a game and I wanted him to shoot more.

He was being too unselfish at a time when we needed a little better shooting. I couldn't fault him because that was the nature of our team. We hit the man who had the best open shot, period. I don't think anyone on the team would have tolerated anything else. That's why those Knicks remain to this day an unforgettable team.

They ate, slept and bled together. I remember Riordan, of all people, consoling Bradley after we lost the fourth game in LA. "Dammit, I blew a few big ones," said Bradley in the dressing room.

"You? You've got nothing to blame yourself for," said Mike. "I'm the one. I blew a bundle. I missed five shots in the first quarter alone. Everybody else was hitting. If I'd made mine, we could have blown them off the court right then."

No one ever pointed the finger at another player. Each was ready to take the blame when we lost. "You've got nothing to reproach yourself for. You made the big one. You sunk the one that put us ahead," Riordan reminded Bill.

That was before Bradley fouled out in the overtime. We were trailing 96–95 with 56 seconds in regulation when Egan fed Wilt in the lane and he went over Reed to jam it in. We received a break when Chamberlain was called for a three-second violation, so we were still down one instead of three.

That's when Bradley hit from the corner to put us ahead 97–96 and helped get us into overtime. I understood how he felt after we lost. He was the kind who would blame himself because he had just had 3-for-13 and 3-for-11 games.

There wasn't much I could tell the players. I knew they were tired and hurting. I knew that words couldn't motivate them at this stage of the game. I simply said they had to push themselves harder and harder. This was no time to crack. We had come too far to do that.

The whole season was wrapped up in the next three games or less. We had to win this one at home or we would be in serious trouble. I didn't realize what serious trouble was until we got into the fifth game.

20

More accurately, I didn't realize what trouble was until eight minutes into the game. By then, the Lakers had hit 12 of their first 15 shots and were in front 25–15. Willis couldn't run or jump. He didn't even have a rebound and I was thinking about taking him out for a while.

I decided not to because it was still early and I knew Willis. He could shake off all the pain and rise above it when things looked the worst. And things sure looked bad.

I watched Barnett hit Willis with a pass at the foul circle and he sliced past Wilt. "You know what happened," recalled Willis. "I was having a problem with my left knee. I had a lot of pain. Right before the game, there was a discussion as to whether they were going to give me a cortisone shot."

Willis preferred not to take it. He said the knee felt fairly good. "I favored the knee a lot, though," he explained. "So when I drove on Wilt, I guess I put so much stress on my right leg, I pulled a ligament in my hip and I went down."

Willis had cushioned his fall with his arms and had rolled over on his right side. He sat up and put his hand over his face to hide the pain as the game went on without him.

LA picked up the loose ball as DeBusschere rushed back to cover Wilt. The ball went to Wilt and Dave somehow tied him up and managed a jump ball. I called time and rushed out onto the floor with Whelan.

"When I fell, I thought I was hurt badly," said Willis. "I lay there for a while. I hardly could get up. Danny runs out after I'm standing for a while and asks how I feel. I say I'm feeling a little better."

Willis finally walked to the bench but realized he was too badly hurt to continue. When I remembered it later, I thought I sent in Nate Bowman to replace Willis.

Hosket says he remembers it better. "I'm sitting on the bench and all of a sudden there's like four empty seats," he recalled. "I'm saying how in the world is Bowman going to handle Wilt? There's no way. I get an elbow to my ribs. I think it was Riordan. He says: 'Hey, Hos. Red wants you.' I say it's about time."

Hosket wasn't thinking about not getting much playing time in the playoffs. He, like everyone, knew his role was to be ready to play when I needed him. You just couldn't satisfy all 12 players.

"I figure Red understands I know the game so he's going to say: 'Hos, what do you think we oughta do?' I thought he was just looking for some advice," resumed Hosket. "So I go over and sit down next to Red. I'll never forget this part because he actually put his arm up on my shoulder."

Someone has to remain cool in a crisis. I still am not sure of his version but Hosket insists: "Red says this to me, 'Now you're going in and take Wilt,' and he said something else but I don't remember a word. My mind went absolutely blank when he said I was going in and take Wilt."

Hos recalls going to the scorer's table to check in. "In the fifth game, I was the guy who went in for Willis and you could feel the air come out of Madison Square Garden. Like people were saying: 'How much did we pay for these tickets and look who they're putting in now.'"

He said he made a stop on his way into the game. "As I got out on the floor, Willis is at the end of the bench sitting sideways and putting ice on his hip," he explained. "He used to call me Wilmer. He yells: 'Wilmer! Wilmer!' I go over and he says: 'Lean on him.' Here's a guy two sixty-five who's played against Wilt all the time and he says I should lean on him."

It is hard to dispute a detailed recollection such as that but I always thought I used Bowman first. The boxscore says Hosket played 4 minutes. I know Bowman got 7 minutes against Wilt, which means Stallworth and DeBusschere split the other 29 minutes of emergency duty at center.

We swarmed all over Wilt and West, forcing 30 turnovers, 10 in the final period when we outscored the Lakers by 14 points. This is hard to believe even now: Wilt and West, two of the greatest scorers of all time, got only three and two shots, respectively, in the second half.

Stallworth and DeBusschere did the job. "I didn't think Wilt could stay with me, not with my speed," said Stalls. "I wanted to keep him from making contact with me. I'd play him on one side and then the other. Sometimes I'd front him. Sometimes from behind. I'm pretty quick."

DeBusschere was strong but not so quick. He also played Wilt smartly. "I got behind him and I couldn't see over his head," explained Dave. "I'd never played him before. I just had to keep him from the ball and taking shots. If he went to the hoop, I'd have had to let him go over me. I stayed on the side and tried to force him a bit."

We were losing by 13 when we went to the dressing room at the half. Willis was laid out on the training table. He had just been given some shots to help kill the pain but he couldn't move. Dr. James Parkes told me Willis could play if not for the pain. He couldn't aggravate the injury more than it was already bothering him.

I decided to forget it. I didn't want to jeopardize Reed's health in any way. I didn't even know if he would be able to play anymore in the series. I told the team that and gave it my best Gipper treatment. I suggested we go out and win this one for Willis.

In the meantime, we discussed the emergency and what we should do under the circumstances. It was then that Bradley came up with his one-three-one idea of offense. "The first thought after Willis was injured was there it goes," recalled Bill. "The second thought was let's regroup. This was a night of collective achievement."

It was a daring concept under the conditions. As Bill pointed out, the Lakers were using a zone defense with Wilt in the middle, so why not a zone offense? "It is used to clear a zone," explained Bradley, who refused to take credit for the suggestion or publicize it.

In fact, after we had won, Frazier informed the media: "Bradley thought of the idea." And Bill informed the press: "Say Clyde told you about it, not I."

I agreed to use Bradley's zone offense because we were only down by 13 points and it was worth looking at. We needed a surprise move because of Reed's loss. We had to open the Lakers' defense and put some pressure on it. They figured to jam the middle even more with no Willis to worry about.

This is the way we worked it: Frazier played the point, Bradley was the middleman at the top of the key with Barnett and Cazzie on the wings at either end of the free-throw line, and DeBusschere or Stallworth was the deep man.

It was a team effort all the way down to our noisy fans. "You had the feeling that the whole crowd was in the game and not vicariously," said Bradley. "I was in the game. They were in the game. We all were in the game."

Only the Lakers weren't. Neither was Willis, who sat in the dressing room and listened to the game by unique hookup. John Condon, the Voice of the Knicks for so many years, gave Willis his own play-by-play over a special phone while also performing his public-address duties.

"I wanted to get back but I couldn't lift my leg," explained Willis. It was easy to see the way he dragged it as he left the game to go to the dressing room.

I talked to Dr. James Parkes once more about Willis. All the players went into the training room to see Willis before we went back onto the floor. They pledged to win for him. They knew how he felt about their going on without him.

Frazier tried easing Reed's pain by saying: "You big sissy you. We ain't gonna let you be captain anymore. But when you come back, you'll be captain, won't you?'' Willis grinned and then he was all alone by the telephone.

Cazzie triggered our remarkable response when he first came off the bench with three straight baskets in the second period. Stallworth put the finishing touch to it with five field goals in the final quarter. That was our bench.

That final quarter was something to see. We were alive and so was the crowd but the Lakers just stopped dead. Stallworth was fronting Wilt and then darting around him on offense. DeBusschere, Barnett, Frazier and Cazzie were pressuring everyone in sight. And I sat and marveled at what that Knick team did under such a great handicap.

So did John Havlicek, who had dropped in on the game after returning from his premature vacation. ''It will be a miracle if the Knicks come on to win this one,'' he first said as we stayed close. ''It's the greatest thing to watch the way they've come back. This team has a lot of heart.''

It was baffling, yet it wasn't. LA seemed mesmerized. I guess it figured Wilt was too much for DeBusschere, Bowman and Stallworth so everything went to him. They forgot about West, who had gotten them there, and our defense took Wilt out of the game.

He hardly got the ball because we wouldn't permit it. We were normally small with Willis but a lot more so without him. We were still active and smart and we simply outscrambled them.

We neutralized the Wilt mismatch by stealing those passes that weren't too tough for him to handle. It was a pressing defense at its best. Barnett, who was playing West, forced him into the corners where Frazier would double up and steal the ball.

I guess the master coaching move came when DeBusschere got into foul trouble early in the final period. I had to get Stallworth back on Wilt and you know the rest. Stalls didn't lean on Chamberlain, he just flitted around him. Wilt wound up with only four points in the second half and West never got a basket.

We gambled on defense but the Lakers didn't take advantage of it. Another pass or two and they might've exploited our double-teaming but, I guess, we made them lose their poise.

We got it down to three points when DeBusschere picked up his fifth personal. The first thing Stalls did was hit a jumper from the side over Wilt. Then after LA added a foul shot, Barnett cut it to one.

The Lakers called time and our huddle was really hopped up. I had a difficult time calming them down. I just told them to keep pressing and don't let West get started. Stallworth was doing a terrific job on Wilt, so what could I tell him?

Bradley tied the score at 87 and then untied it with a shot over Mel Counts. It was all over from then on but for the shouting of our fans. They cheered us and booed Wilt every time he missed a foul shot. We just ran away and hid in the closing moments.

It was remarkable. We were outrebounded as Cazzie was our high with 8 but we got 37 more shots. They had only 66 and we had 103. We pressed them into 19 turnovers in the second half alone when they should have been destroying us. We put them on the foul line for 40 shots to our 19 and they made 30.

Frazier was a demon at both ends. He not only scored 21 points and had seven rebounds, he led the attack on the ball as we picked up all over the court. Clyde forced five turnovers in the second half. Bradley had three, Cazzie and Stalls two each and Barnett one.

We had won it for Willis. He had chewed his fingers almost to his elbows listening to Condon's reports. He got awfully nervous when DeBusschere missed a shot when we were leading 105–98. It was a safe lead because there were only 30 seconds left but Willis was still worried.

Frazier, however, stole the ball after the Lakers rebounded. "That's it! That's it!" Willis shouted to an empty dressing room. "It's gonna be all over!" Condon screamed over the hookup. "Frazier steals again! Frazier's shot is good!"

How we won that game is now a part of basketball history. We came from 16 points behind to win 107–100 after the Lakers had hit 11 of their first 13 shots. It was a comeback that rates with all comebacks under the circumstances.

"The fifth game," Bradley said, "was really the turning point but also where most was at stake. It had the greatest degree of uncertainty, and clarity had gone. Guys came off the bench and made contributions that were enormous.''

> *"They were a strong team, but there was no question who would win until Willis hurt his leg in the fifth game. The Knicks' club was one of the greatest teams ever assembled.''*
>
> *—Phil Jackson*

It's surprising what sticks in your mind. Of all the plays that night, Bradley and DeBusschere remembered one—other than Reed's misfortune, of course. "The Stallworth move is the one I won't let go of,'' recalled Bradley. "His drive on Chamberlain along the baseline. That was the shot of the second half.''

We were leading 101–96 by then and there was 1:52 to go. Stalls gave Wilt a head fake and then drove the baseline on him. He went under and over the basket with a reverse short hook.

Willis braced himself for the tidal wave of teammates he had to face when it was over. "I wouldn't have believed it if I hadn't seen it. A super effort,'' said Havlicek. "They had five big leaders out there all working together without Willis. It's the greatest comeback I've ever seen.''

Everyone rushed into our room and hammered Willis, who had a grin from here to his hometown of Bernice, Louisiana. Cazzie hugged and kissed him, saying "We did it for you, big fella.''

They really let loose, especially the guys who had filled in for Willis. "Hey, Stalls. You did pretty good for a fifth-string center,'' said DeBusschere. "You didn't do so bad for a fourth-stringer,'' replied Stallworth. "I told Wilt I didn't want to embarrass him, so I sent in my backup centers,'' ad-libbed Hosket.

DeBusschere told Willis that Wilt was too big for him, and Willis said Wilt was too big for him too. As far as I was concerned, Willis was the biggest of them all and we needed him back.

Someone asked if we'd be taking him to LA for the sixth game. "We'll take him and I'd like to take him with me all summer,'' was my response. I had discovered that life would be awfully boring without him.

LOS ANGELES

	min	fg	fga	ft	fta	reb	ast	pf	pts
Baylor	43	8	15	5	6	11	5	2	21
Chamberlain	45	9	12	4	9	19	3	2	22
Counts	12	0	4	1	1	4	0	2	1
Egan	13	2	2	2	2	0	3	3	6
Erickson	40	3	6	1	2	4	6	4	7
Garrett	33	7	12	4	4	5	0	4	18
Tresvant	8	0	1	5	7	0	0	2	5
West	46	6	14	8	9	2	4	2	20
TOTALS	240	35	66	30	40	45	21	21	100

NEW YORK

	min	fg	fga	ft	fta	reb	ast	pf	pts
Barnett	44	6	17	4	5	0	3	3	16
Bowman	7	0	2	1	1	4	0	2	1
Bradley	38	7	15	2	3	7	2	4	16
DeBusschere	36	6	21	0	0	6	2	5	12
Frazier	46	9	14	3	3	7	12	3	21
Hosket	4	0	2	0	0	0	0	0	0
Reed	8	2	5	3	3	0	1	0	7
Riordan	15	1	1	0	0	0	0	0	2
Russell	32	8	14	4	4	8	5	4	20
Stallworth	19	6	12	0	0	6	3	3	12
Warren	1	0	0	0	0	0	0	1	0
TOTALS	240	45	103	17	19	38	28	25	107

Los Angeles	30	23	29	18	—	100
New York	20	20	35	32	—	107

West's final words after we won the fifth game and moved within one of the championship were: "Maybe we'd have been better off with Willis in there. Losing Reed was the worst thing that happened to us. It turned into a strange game without him."

For the Lakers, not us. We were fine. We were now leading 3–2 and LA appeared disjointed. West couldn't get over the idea of his and Wilt's taking only five shots in the second half between them.

I'm sure West also couldn't figure out if it had been them or our defense. "It seems like we never got a shot," he said after Baylor had gotten the Lakers' only three baskets in the final quarter. "It's hard to explain. It seemed like I never got into the flow of our offense. They collapsed so much on Wilt and maybe we were passing up some shots trying to get the ball to him."

West was reminded that the Lakers had only 22 shots after intermission. "I know teams with a couple of good goers that can take more shots at a bar," he responded. "They made the shots when they counted and we didn't do anything right. It was like a nightmare. It wasn't a nice feeling out there."

There was more Laker remorse. "They came out running like hell," said Erickson, who had only six shots in 40 minutes. "Either we're going to take advantage of their not having a center or they're going to take advantage of Wilt not coming out after them."

Mullaney analyzed it, as all coaches should. "They played a different kind of defense," was his tribute to the Knicks. "They gambled a lot and it paid off. They didn't let us set the pace. They speeded it up like a fast movie. All these playoff games have been the same and suddenly it switches around one hundred percent."

Mullaney complained at halftime that one of the baskets was tilted. That's the one we had shot at first and the Lakers were to have it for the second half.

I didn't care because we had won. Besides, from where I was standing or sitting or looking, the whole world appeared to be tilted—our way, I hoped.

We had a light workout in New York the day after the fifth game. Willis went to the doctor and joined us at the airport. Dr. Parkes also flew out to Los Angeles so he could supervise the special treatment he was to give Willis before the sixth game the following day.

All the players asked how Willis was and we didn't find out until we saw him dragging his leg. We should have sent him to Lourdes, not Los Angeles. He needed a miracle to play.

He didn't get it. He didn't appear in the sixth game because the treatment didn't work. We had come a long way together since I first saw him at Grambling.

Reed remembers that first encounter. "My biggest memory of

Red was, we used to play games on Saturday and Monday nights,''
he said. "Basically, coach Fred Hobdy never had a chance to
prepare, so we had to slip in the gym on Sunday afternoon without
the lights on and go through a walk-through to get ready for our
game. We had classes all day until it was time to play the game."

Willis says that's when he met me. I was scouting then. "At this
particular practice, he comes in," he recalled. "He had like a nice
trench coat—I assume it was a London Fog—a gray pin-striped suit
and was smoking a cigar. A real New York businessman. You
couldn't tell me he wasn't a rich guy.''

Little did he realize that he was going to make me a rich man.
Now we were on the brink together. The title was only a game away
but he wasn't going to be there. In body, yes, but not in uniform.

Dr. Parkes took Willis to a health center near our hotel at the
airport for massages and heat treatment. They were there early the
day of the game. It didn't work.

Willis, never one to give up, suggested he still had a day to make
the game after we got to our hotel. I said we wouldn't gamble. We
had a seventh game back at the Garden if we lost. I preferred to wait.

That's the way it worked. Dr. Parkes told me before the game: "I
doubt if Willis will be able to start." I decided not to use him at all.
He sat on the bench and watched us get murdered 135–113 in the
Forum.

Truthfully, Wilt killed us. Our miracle performance against him
in the fifth game had had an impact on him. I had suspected as
much, though I tried to hide it in the dressing room. I told the players
the Lakers were ready to be taken.

I was hoping I could somehow trigger some of the adrenaline that
had flowed when the players saw Willis could no longer play the
fifth game. Nobody could stop Wilt. I opened with Bowman and
went through everyone I could think of short of sending in Danny
Whelan.

All Wilt did in 46 minutes was to score 45 points on 20-for-27
shooting, grab 27 rebounds and shove our faces in it. "It's a shame
to have the whole season depend on one game. It's a shame one

team is gonna have to be sad after Friday night," said Wilt after the series went to 3–3.

Sure. If he sincerely thought it was a shame that the season had dwindled down to one game, then why did he do so much to win the sixth game? I'm only kidding—particularly since he had some nice things to say about us.

"Whoever wins, the Knicks should be complimented to be where they are," he volunteered. "By all rights we should be celebrating as world champions right now. When Willis got hurt, I was terribly sorry for him. He's played the greatest basketball against me of any center I've ever faced."

He sort of apologized for picking on our little guys. "Stallworth comes in and maybe I have a hundred-pound advantage and he has to play me. That's a difficult assignment," he said, forgetting about what Stalls had done in the fifth game.

I guess he meant it was a difficult regular assignment. Once you might get away with it. This time we didn't. They outrebounded us 61–40 and we were out of our misery when they outscored us 36–16 in the first quarter.

Garrett finally went wild on Frazier. He hit for 16 points in the first half and shot 9-for-11 overall. "He got only two points in the second half," was Clyde's reminder. "I was dropping off to help out on West but nobody was picking him up in the first half." West, of course, had a routine 33 points against us this time.

Frazier was conscious of another important thing, with only one game to go and possibly without Willis again. "The party is falling on my shoulders," said Clyde, who had a distaste for picking up big checks.

That sounded like a warning to the Lakers, which was okay with me. Garrett hit seven straight in the first period and ran it to 8-for-8 before missing. He and Wilt were 24-for-32 at the end of three quarters and 29-for-38 in the game.

We held our own in the middle periods, when we actually outscored the Lakers by one. Cazzie and DeBusschere wouldn't let us quit. And Bowman scored 18 points and grabbed eight rebounds against Wilt but we never were in it after the opening period.

It was an entirely different script from the fifth game in New York. "We stuck with our regular offense instead of going specifically to Wilt," explained Mullaney after the Lakers had once led by as many as 25 points. "We got locked in the other game when Wilt had an obvious advantage. Tonight we tried to take it as it came. We played a natural offense."

I was glad they had thought of that a game late. "He looked like the Wilt of old," suggested Willis.

"Definitely old," said Wilt after a sharp display of fadeaways and slam-dunks. Wilt just bowled everyone out of his way.

> *"Let's end the season right. Let's be the last team to go home."*
>
> *—Red Holzman*

Willis was last seen limping past the Lakers' dressing room on his way to the airport. I sent him home with Danny Whelan so he could rush back and get a full day's treatment in New York before the seventh and final game.

We went out the next morning. So did the Lakers. West and Baylor were close to their first championship and so were the Knicks. Someone was going to break the tie. Our question was: Will Willis play? And if so, how much?

LOS ANGELES

	min	fg	fga	ft	fta	reb	ast	pf	pts
Baylor	36	3	12	2	2	13	5	3	8
Chamberlain	46	20	27	5	14	27	3	3	45
Egan	8	1	1	1	1	0	0	1	3
Erickson	32	3	7	0	0	3	7	2	6
Garrett	38	9	11	0	0	1	6	2	18
Hairston	22	5	9	3	5	4	6	3	13
Lynn	1	0	0	0	0	0	0	0	0
McCarter	2	0	1	0	0	1	1	0	0
Roberson	2	1	1	0	0	0	0	0	2
Tresvant	11	3	3	1	1	6	3	4	7
West	42	12	22	9	9	6	13	2	33
TOTALS	240	57	94	21	32	61	44	20	135

NEW YORK

	min	fg	fga	ft	fta	reb	ast	pf	pts
Barnett	29	4	10	2	2	2	8	4	10
Bowman	29	9	15	0	1	8	1	5	18
Bradley	31	3	9	0	1	1	3	2	6
DeBusschere	36	12	25	1	3	9	3	4	25
Frazier	43	6	12	2	4	6	7	2	14
Hosket	5	1	2	0	0	1	1	2	2
Riordan	12	1	4	0	0	2	2	2	2
Russell	31	10	14	3	3	5	2	2	23
Stallworth	21	5	13	1	1	6	1	4	11
Warren	3	1	1	0	0	0	1	0	2
TOTALS	240	52	105	9	15	40	29	27	113

Los Angeles	36	35	28	36	—	135
New York	16	35	29	33	—	113

21

It seemed like the whole world was waiting to hear if Willis was going to play the seventh and final game. That was the question. Everyone knows the answer now. Then, the city of New York held its collective breath as Willis went until almost game time before providing the decision.

"I just knew one thing, as I sit here twenty-plus years later," he said. "Having grown up in a little town, a country boy in Louisiana dreaming about playing in a championship, I was going to try. They'd never say that this guy didn't have enough nerve to go out there and try."

Everything he did hurt. "I didn't want them to win the championship without me," he said. He had the off day and the time before the game to get as ready as he was going to be.

Willis's plane had landed at JFK around 6:45 in the morning and he went right to the Garden with Whelan. They got there at 7:30 just about when we were leaving, Los Angeles time.

"It was so early, the pigeons were on the sidewalk having their breakfast," said Whelan. "When they saw Willis, they got frightened and scattered."

Whelan treated Willis with massages, hot packs, whirlpool and ultrasound for around three hours. He then sent Willis back to his apartment in Rego Park to rest until the day of the game, which was May 8, 1970.

"I'm much improved but I still feel some pain," he said. "If they said right now: 'C'mon Willis, play,' I couldn't do it. I'm just hoping when I wake up tomorrow the soreness will not be there.''

He woke up and the soreness was there. He saw Dr. Parkes so we could get a progress report, then went to the Garden for another hour of hot packs from Whelan. ''By five o'clock or so we should know if we'll shoot the moon,'' was Whelan's bulletin.

There was doubt but not on the part of any of the players or me. ''I still think he'll play,'' said DeBusschere. Then Cazzie expounded on the situation that was so meaningful to all of us.

''If I know Willis, he'll be in there,'' he said. ''I know how he thinks. If he can kill himself and rest over the summer it's worth it. He goes to training camp the seventeenth of September, he goes all the way and then injures his hip. Do you think he wants to wait until training camp again?''

Someone wondered what Cazzie would do if Willis couldn't make it. Our chief health-food addict smiled and said: ''I think I'll take a little extra carrot juice and wheat germ.''

Willis spared him that. This championship meant too much to him. He also recognized what it meant to West and Baylor. ''They have everything,'' said Willis through his discomfort. ''They've done everything. They have been the best but they've never won a championship.''

Neither had we, which is why I was a bit surprised to see how the players acted in our dressing room that night. Except for the anxiety over Willis, there was no tension. It was like we were going out to play the Lakers a regular season game. One of 82.

Willis was sitting on the training table as everyone walked by. It had been decided to give him cortisone shots but not until the last minute. ''I'm gonna play. It still hurts but I'm gonna play,'' he reassured me and all the players.

It was the most emotional moment of the season but I couldn't afford to be nervous. I told the players how proud I was that they had done everything that was asked of them. I mentioned that Willis would start at center if he could, but we didn't know how long he'd be able to play.

Willis wasn't there to hear it. He was in the trainer's room to get his shots—a combination of cortisone and carbocaine. The players went out, leaving Willis, Dr. Parkes, Whelan, me and Phil Jackson, snapping his pictures.

"Basically, all the guys come by and I remember DeBusschere saying: 'Hey, big fellow. If you give us twenty minutes tonight we're gonna win this thing,'" recalled Willis. "I had gone onto the floor to shoot a little. I took a few shots and made them. I realized I could still shoot but I couldn't move."

He went out with Donnie May as his retriever. He had an audience of Dr. Parkes, some ushers, a horde of newspapermen, Laker coach Mullaney and Chamberlain standing in the runway. He hit his first two shots of about a dozen and quit.

When he also made his first two warmup shots a few minutes before the game, which was about an hour later, the Garden shook. So did the Lakers, apparently. That was a vivid sight none of us will ever forget.

Willis couldn't run or move laterally during his early shoot-around. "I couldn't pick the leg up. I just had to drag it," he explained. "It was real horrible pain. I knew I had to take the shots in my leg if I wanted to play."

What then? He went back to the dressing room for his date with the needle. "The most important thing was that I went back in and had to call my daughter because she was five years old that day," he recalled. "She was in Louisiana. I'll never forget May eighth because that also was her birthday."

A lot of things were happening at that time. Willie Mays had just turned 39. Unemployment rates had just risen to 4.8 percent. And Frank Sinatra was in London greeting Princess Margaret at a charity concert he was staging.

Of course, Willis was on the phone talking to his daughter Veronica in Mansura, Louisiana from our dressing room. This was the conversation, as Willis recalled later:

"Isn't it somebody's birthday?"

"It's mine."

"Did you get my card?"

"It's a pretty card. Does your leg still hurt?"

"Yes."

"Are you gonna play tonight?"

"I'm gonna try to. I think I'm gonna play."

Veronica must have been the first one in the country to know. There was no newspaperman around to whom she could give her scoop. Willis also recalled calling his mother down in Bernice.

"I needed to call home," said Willis. "I called her around five o'clock while I was resting. I told her I was hurt. I told her I was going to play. I told her what the doctor might have to do. She told me she'd pray for me and the team."

How could the Lakers beat that? Victory was inevitable with that kind of support. Willis, meanwhile, had to sweat out all those hours before game time. He remembers his teammates walking over to him and trying to make conversation.

He told Cazzie: "It's not so good." He told Stallworth: "I've got to be careful." And, as he recalled: "Barnett came in and said: 'Get the hell off that table. We've got a game to play.' The only thing I didn't hear was Red reminding me to get back on defense."

I didn't have to remind him because he had heard that and "See the ball" and "Never turn your head on defense" until he and everyone else were sick of it. It was a situation that had Willis talking to himself, apparently.

"I kept telling myself," he recalled, "that they're all thinking Willis is here and everything's okay and I got to do something not to disappoint them." Funny thing. He did just that, as it turned out. He couldn't disappoint us and himself.

The Lakers also were thinking and talking about Willis. "If there's any way he can play, he'll play," predicted West after the Lakers had beaten us without Willis to tie the series 3–3. "He might hurt them if he's not at his best but he might help them, too. I think they have to take the chance. You don't like to see a team lose when it's not at its best. It's like stealing something. Seeing him on the bench took something out of it."

Wilt concurred. "This may sound corny," was his approach, "but I know this means a lot to Willis and us. We don't want to come in the back door."

We promised not to let that happen. In fact, after we lost the sixth game, Frazier informed everyone in Los Angeles that "All we were doing tonight was getting them overconfident." He had a way with words even then, long before he ever thought of going into broadcasting.

I went to Willis and told him he didn't have to play. I meant it. I never forced a player to play against his will. I always relied on the doctors first and then the players' judgment. If they didn't think they were ready to play then I didn't play them.

"I told Red I'm gonna try. I gotta try," Willis remembered. "The season meant too much for everybody. I knew all along I was going to give it a shot. Especially when Dr. Parkes told me I couldn't do any permanent damage to myself."

The only thing that remained was to inject him. That was Dr. Parkes's decision. "He said he'd like to wait as long as he could before he started," explained Willis. "He said it would take a certain amount of time to do it. But when he actually did, it took him more time than he thought it would."

I had allowed Willis to miss my pregame talk but I wanted him to go out with the team. "Red comes in and Dr. Parkes has this big needle," said Willis, still cringing at the memory of it.

It was much larger than the ordinary ones. Dr. Parkes explained: "It was a spinal needle. Willis had such big, strong muscles, you had to use a spinal needle to get deep into them. That's why the needle looked so big to him."

Whelan's description of that scene is memorable. "You know how Dr. Parkes was," said Danny, refreshing my memory. "Like he was taking care of a little kid. He had a long gosh-darned needle. It looked like it was going to go through Willis's hip."

There were only three of them—Willis, Danny and Dr. Parkes. They were in the trainer's room. I was wandering around the locker room. Whelan recalled: "I said to Willis: 'Is it gonna be worth it to do all of this for one game?'" Willis was to undergo a series of injections. "And Willis said: 'I told you all year, if we ever got to the point that we were in a championship game, I would crawl on the floor if I was hurt.'

"So Dr. Parkes started to put the needle in," Danny's description continued. "And he said: 'Am I hurting you, Willis? Am I hurting you?' That's how Dr. Parkes was. It was hurting but Willis said: 'Would you put it in, Doctor, please?' "

Willis was interested in getting out onto the court. So was I. He wanted to get in some practice shots. When I saw him dragging his leg, I wondered.

Yet I knew Willis had a great tolerance for pain. As I said, I don't know how many times he broke his nose but he'd go over to the bench and tell Danny: "Pinch this back in." Danny would pinch the nose back into place and Willis would go right back in.

I was getting antsy as Dr. Parkes kept working. "Dr. Parkes has got this big needle," said Willis, recalling that I had alerted them that we had to go. "Dr. Parkes has already given me some injections. He must've stuck me five or six times in different places."

Dr. Parkes had to puncture Willis's big muscles and inject an area. That's why it took so long. I asked how much longer and Dr. Parkes said a little longer and I said I couldn't wait. I had to go out on the floor.

There was a game to be played. There was a full house of fans on the verge of hysteria. The Knicks had captured a city that had been waiting 24 years for an NBA championship and we were one step away.

Bill Goldman, who won a writer's Academy Award for *Butch Cassidy and the Sundance Kid*, was a perfect example. He was a Knick fan, not just a celebrity. He was sitting there where the teams come out of the dressing room. Today he sits under a basket at our end of the floor at almost every game.

He's an authentic Knick follower and, typically, enthusiastic and emotional, though you would never suspect it the way he controls himself. He was at that seventh game in 1970 and he confessed:

"I'm hysterical. But I hear all sorts of stories about people getting into condition for the game. One guy is taking a sleeping pill so he gets a good night's sleep. Others are wearing the shirts and sweaters that worked in the last game. Everyone is doing what he has to do to help the Knicks win.''

They were all wound up and waiting for the game to start. I decided to leave the dressing room. I wouldn't wait any longer. Willis laughs hysterically when he recalls what happened next.

''Dr. Parkes says to me: 'Oh, Willis. I know those needles are hurting you. If it makes you feel any better, when it's all over you can stick me with some needles.' He had a good line of B.S.''

No one was aware of the drama in our dressing room with Willis and the needles as the Lakers and Knicks shot around. ''I'm sitting there and grimacing in pain and I'm saying to myself: 'Are you crazy for doing this? Just get it over with so I can get on with this thing,' '' said Willis.

They finally got it done. Willis put on his uniform and warmups and headed for the floor. Dr. Parkes reassured him that he would be all right in a couple of minutes. The injections would work on him.

I was just leaving the runway and about to enter the arena when I heard a roar. I knew it couldn't be for me. I turned around and discovered it was for Willis. He had just come out of the darkness of the runway and the people had seen him.

Bill Goldman was sitting not far from the players' entrance to the floor and had been the victim of a false alarm. ''Suddenly I hear this guy sitting near me say: 'There's Willis,' '' recalled Goldman. ''I turn around and it's Cazzie.''

That was the emotional frenzy in the Garden when Willis finally made his appearance. It was one of the most dramatic moments in NBA history, as far as I am concerned. It will live forever with those who saw it—not because it happened in New York but because of the entire set of circumstances.

Marty Glickman, the first Voice of the Knicks back in 1946–47, was well aware that the 1969–70 team had captured New York. He was working with HBO, which owned Manhattan Cable, which was using Knick games to attract customers.

There was no MSG network at the time and Manhattan Cable was in its pioneer days. ''We started the season with five thousand customers,'' explained Glickman. ''By the playoffs, we had forty thousand because of the interest in the Knicks. People who didn't have cable and couldn't get tickets were going to bars on Ninth and Tenth Avenue and paying to see the playoff games.''

That's why Willis wanted to play. That's why he endured so much agony to make it. That's why, when Willis walked into sight and got one of the loudest standing ovations I ever heard, he recalls thinking:

"This is a helluva predicament to be in. Everybody in Madison Square Garden is saying everything's all right. The captain's here. And I have to go out and play the best big man who's ever been around. Not with two legs but one leg.''

It was a very moving moment even for tough professionals. ''The way I remember his entrance was the anticipation of the crowd and everyone standing with all eyes on that entrance,'' said DeBusschere. ''They somehow knew he was coming out. We were just warming up but you knew by the crowd noise that something was happening.''

DeBusschere remembered that some people saw Willis coming and started screaming. It built up to an explosion when everyone in the Garden saw him walk out. They didn't even notice him dragging his leg at first.

The moment is captured in the special videotape ''New York's Game: The History of the Knicks.'' It shows Willis coming onto the floor, and Marv Albert describes every moment.

Some of our players focused their attention on the Lakers as soon as Willis walked out. ''Basically, I was looking at Wilt and looking at West,'' recalled DeBusschere. ''They were absolutely staring at that entranceway. I always felt a lot was taken out of them right then. Then, of course, he hits a couple of shots.''

Willis not only hit his first two flatfooted jumpers in the warmup, he did the same thing in the game. ''I still get chills just watching the way those moments are captured on the videotape,'' said Bradley. ''You looked at their faces and there was Chamberlain, who has just scored forty-five in the sixth game against Nate Bowman. Now he thinks that Willis is going to be leaning on him a little.''

Then Willis hits his first two shots. That memory prompted Bradley to say: "If you can get any higher? You're playing seventh-game world championship, right? You're in the Garden and people are going to be loud, anyway. This took it to another level."

Bradley said he didn't see Willis come out of the exit but that scene after he appeared is indelible in his mind. "The funny thing," he added, "those moments define Willis's personality to more people than anything else. It's consistent with his personality. He's going to put out one hundred ten percent no matter what. That moment is what really etched it in people's minds forever."

DeBusschere pointed out that Willis really gambled for the team and we all won. "He was willing to give it a shot when he was really hurting," said Dave. "He could've been a flop. He also could've said: 'It's too hard for me to do this and I can't help you guys.' He could've come out and fallen down and thrown up airballs and all that. But when a guy is hurt and he's willing to take those two shots and hits them he's got guts."

Willis's first two warmup shots will stick in my mind. I was anxious to see what he could do in the game and I have to say I was concerned. He was doing things in slow motion because of his hip.

I found out much later he was being deliberate because he didn't want to tip off the Lakers as to how badly damaged he was. "If I was quick enough and had my health I could neutralize Wilt," said Willis. "When I go out and take the two warmup shots, everything I did I wanted to do real slowly, real smooth so nobody could detect that I was really scared."

Scared? That's impossible. Not Willis. If I couldn't scare him no one could. I believe he meant scared in terms of being apprehensive about how much he could push himself in his condition. All of us had put the world on his shoulders and expected him to carry the Knicks to the championship.

I guess the Lakers felt the same way. As soon as Willis showed up on the floor, they turned and watched his every move. He made a distinct effort not to drag the leg by walking slowly with no perceptible limp. They handed him the ball and he shot flatfooted instead of his usual jumper.

Our guys were watching the Lakers for their reaction. So was Willis, who kept peeking at them. "Every time I turned and looked down the other way, after coming out—I wouldn't stare, I'd just glance—it seemed Jerry and the Lakers had stopped," he said. "They were looking at me. Then I shot my free throws. The pain was still there but I wasn't going to show them."

I don't remember too much about Willis's entrance or what happened before the game. I had already indicated to the scorer's desk that Bowman would be starting at center. The procedure was they'd come into the dressing room while the players were still there and you gave them the starters.

Willis was taking shots at the time and his availability was uncertain. That's why I kept reminding him and Dr. Parkes about the time. I had to give out our lineup so I told them Bowman would be starting at center.

That was on my mind when Willis walked out behind me. Then I had to inform Mendy Rudolph that I intended to make the change. He had to tell the scorers as well as John Condon, who was in charge of announcing the starting lineups, that Bowman was out and Reed was in.

"The biggest part of all this—if you can write a script, this is a movie script," said Willis later. "Me coming out after everybody else and I hit my warmup shots. The first two shots in the game we get I get 'em and I make 'em. We're geniuses. We make up this great script. People actually think this was all a plan. It was a great happening."

People don't realize that the pain was still there when Willis lined up with Wilt for the opening tap. While we were playing the Lakers before 19,500 at the Garden, the Mets were losing 7–1 to the Giants at Shea before 43,845 fans and blasting radios.

"Well, at least we got a split," said one fan in the crowd. "The interest in the Knicks' game is crazy," said another fan. "Everybody sees me with a radio and they ask if Willis is playing. They ask how many Frazier's got."

Rain held up the Mets game so those with radios went under the stands. When the Knicks won, the people at Shea chanted: "We're number one.'' Same thing at the Garden. I guess it was the same all around the city.

Willis did his job, the Knicks did their job. ''The pain's still there when we start,'' he recalled. ''I had twenty-seven minutes in the game. Maybe it was better but I had to drag the leg. I couldn't pick it up.''

The big mystery was what happened to the Lakers, and especially Wilt, under the circumstances. ''Let me say this. I watched the game again this summer. I've got a tape of it,'' said Willis. ''Wilt had just scored forty-five against us. I don't understand why they didn't come to him the whole night.''

Wilt dealt with that fate later, first expressing his reaction to Willis's dramatic entrance and his hitting his first two warmup shots. ''I wasn't in shock,'' he insisted. ''I was used to theatrics. I played with the Harlem Globetrotters, the greatest theatrical organization in the world.''

He didn't really think Willis was that badly hurt. ''I felt if he was well enough to come out on the floor, he was well enough to play,'' Wilt went on. ''Yeah, he was hobbling but there are lots of things that hobble. I had a dog that used to hobble because he was hit by a car. When he started to hobble I'd say: 'Nice dog,' so every time he did something wrong he used to hobble. There was nothing wrong with him but he used to hobble.''

Don't misunderstand. Wilt wasn't comparing Willis to a dog or even suggesting that he might be faking. Wilt had too much respect for Willis and I have too much respect for Wilt to believe that.

He was only suggesting, I assume, that he couldn't feel Willis's pain so the hobbling had no real effect on him. Another thing: Willis might have done a good job at faking out Wilt, at least, with his contrived slow movements during his brief warmup.

Wilt's point was: ''I wasn't there when he took the needles. I was not the doctor nor did I see that needle. All I saw was a big, black basketball player come out there and he was very, very good and he inspired them. Not only that, he hit his first two shots against *me*.''

From our viewpoint, that had to be surprising to Wilt, if not shocking. It certainly didn't seem to convince him that Willis was too crippled to play or even be effective. It was part of a movie script, remember?

"I backed off him and said to myself: 'Let me see what you got,' and he showed me," continued Wilt. "He hit the two and then left. Smart guy. He hit two and got out of there."

That was a coach's decision, not Willis's. I had to nurse him because of his injury so I replaced him with Bowman as soon as I could after Willis got us off to a great start.

He hit the first basket of the game. Chamberlain then powered past him for a dunk and I thought: "Here we go." The Lakers were going to take advantage of Willis at every opportunity and use Wilt's strength to drive to the basket all the time.

Bradley came back with a free throw and Willis hit again. They were to be his only points in the game. He missed all three of his remaining shots and managed only three rebounds. Yet he leaned on Chamberlain enough to give DeBusschere and the rest of us the time and help we needed for a 113–99 runaway.

We harassed Wilt and fouled him enough for him to blow 10 of 11 free throws. He wound up with 21 points on 10-for-16 and 24 rebounds. But the Lakers were never really in it after we broke to a 15–6 lead inside the first five minutes.

Willis was voted the MVP and Wilt doesn't understand that to this day. "He wins the MVP, which may be deserving," he explained. "But there's a guy named Clyde who only had about 36 points, 12 rebounds and 14 assists and they give the MVP to Willis Reed."

Wilt's memory wasn't bad. He had the 36 points right but the rebounds were 7 and the assists 19. That wasn't his point. "I say: 'Wait a minute.' Does that say Wilt screwed up, again? I say: 'C'mon.' And they're telling me how great Willis Reed was," he explained.

Wilt never questioned the size of Willis's heart, though. He still respects that Knick team and measures all our players then in terms of today's players. He laughs when they suggest Reed, DeBusschere, Bradley, Frazier and Barnett wouldn't be quick or big enough now.

"All those guys could play today. I'm tried of hearing about guys who are so much bigger now," he said. "It's brains and the size of your heart. If you calculate the height of the teams in the 1960s and those today there's about an inch difference in average. If you throw out the Manute Bols, the Mark Eatons and a few other seven-five guys, you know, the great basketball players, then maybe the inch is gone. It's a crock."

DeBusschere had asked Willis for 20 minutes and I played him for 21 in the first half. We walked off leading by 17 at intermission. Willis limped off to another shot in the dressing room. I had to use him only six more minutes in the second half.

His strong body and strong psychological lift were not needed more than that. Willis had kept Wilt, the world's strongest athlete as far I was concerned, from pulverizing him.

Willis's mere presence was like a needle to us. Everyone picked it up. Frazier poured in 7 of the 11 points that opened a gap of 13 quickly. At one time Clyde, Bradley and DeBusschere hit 15 of 21 shots.

We were on fire and there was nothing the Lakers could do about it. We pressed and trapped and never let them get into any game rhythm. We short-circuited most attempts to get the ball into Wilt so he could take advantage of Willis.

We had come out for the second half without Willis. He was late because Dr. Parkes was giving him another shot. Mendy Rudolph was about to toss up the ball. There was a center jump at halftime then. I replaced Bowman with Willis once more.

I finally removed him after he picked up his fourth personal in the first six minutes of the second half. The crowd gave him a standing ovation for his courageous performance against such overwhelming odds, represented by Wilt and the Lakers.

They had come to New York figuring they had the physical edge because of Willis but he wouldn't give up. "We always trapped them," he recalled, explaining how our team defense kept the ball from Wilt. "I could lean on him but couldn't make any quick moves. I could box him out but I couldn't jump."

It was an excellent team effort which the fans supported with shattering noise, which also had its effect on the Lakers. We worked hard to keep the ball away from Wilt and forced LA to take outside shots. "They had a bad shooting game," said Willis. "When they got the ball into Wilt, he had this habit of putting the ball on the floor and we'd steal it or knock it away."

Frazier was the catalyst that night. I had had him concentrate on defense since the playoffs started but this was the final game and he erupted. He did some job on Garrett and still found time for slightly phenomenal shooting and passing.

Clyde had 23 points by the half and just about sent a message to Garrett to be prepared to pay for the party at SIU. It was one of the finest games Frazier ever played for the Knicks, but who remembers?

"People don't even know I was in the game because of Willis," said Frazier later with reverence, not malice. We unleashed him at the perfect time and he responded.

I believed with Willis handcuffed, we needed more offense from someone. Clyde had sacrificed himself for the good of the team but now we needed his scoring. His job was to hit the open man but as he pointed out: "I was the open man."

He took charge just as we had seen in the NIT final a few years back in the performance that convinced the Knicks to make him their No. 1 draft pick. "I actively looked for my shots," he said.

We had one thing in mind when we left the dressing room for the second half. No letting up. Keep pouring it on. The only way we could lose now was by giving it back.

A funny thing happened. I don't know why but we were on the court 10 minutes before the Lakers came out. I think we were so anxious to get going, we left too early. We were absolutely flying high.

There was only one anxious moment after that. Willis went up to beat Wilt to a rebound and got hit by DeBusschere. It didn't bother Willis at all. He shook it off until I sat him near me when we were leading by 79–54 in the first six minutes of the third period.

Clyde had done it with two brilliant steals that he converted into baskets while running off six straight points. The Lakers managed to get within 113–99 but the countdown was on. Our crowd counted them out in the final seconds and all of New York erupted.

I remember Barnett hitting the final jump shot and then we all ran to the dressing room—world champions for the first time and the taste of victory champagne, in which we all showered. Vintage 1970, of course.

We created a lifetime of memories that night. "The only thing I remember about that game is the early part," said Bradley. "I remember the late part," said DeBusschere. "I remember how we put the game out of reach."

22

We allowed TV cameras in our room for the first time. Ordinarily we kept them out, but championship champagne celebrations are traditional in all sports so we complied. That's why Howard Cosell was seen nationally on ABC-TV being showered by May, our wine steward.

May then moved on with DeBusschere to do me a favor. They sneaked into my small office while I was masterminding for the media and double-drenched me. They got me, my nice Brooks Brothers suit and beautiful hair soaking wet by pouring the contents of a bottle on my head.

There was delirium in our dressing room. DeBusschere was safeguarding the basketball he had confiscated at the final buzzer. It belonged to him because he was the last to have it and had run off with it when the game ended.

We were the champs. I couldn't help thinking of the other dressing room. In fact, after things had calmed down, Chamberlain dropped by to shake hands and congratulate us. "You guys deserved to win. You outplayed us," he said, and then he was gone.

The Lakers had pushed us to seven games with a Chamberlain who most people figured would never make it back from his serious knee surgery. West and Baylor had tried again and failed to win their first championship.

They were the unhappy losers who always became the forgotten or the also-rans. It was depressing for them and overwhelming for us just down the corridor in the Garden. Only 100 feet or so and one game separated each team from celebrating or going home empty. That's what they mean by the thrill of victory and the agony of defeat.

West was in an agonizing mood and suggesting he might quit. "I don't have anything to look forward to next year," he said. "I'm going to spend the next few days thinking about the future. Basketball has been very good to me but there's more things than basketball."

He didn't really mean it, as things turned out. He stuck around until he and Wilt put together their fabulous 1971–72 season. That's when they won a record 33 in a row and topped it by getting even with the Knicks by beating us 4–1 for the championship.

That was West's first and only title as a player but I seem to recall he has won a few as the Lakers' general manager. But that night of May 8, 1970, was a terribly frustrating, personal blow to him. Chamberlain plus West plus Baylor seemed to add up to the championship but it wasn't the winning equation.

"I've been here a lot of times," West reminded everyone who took the time to listen. "Maybe we just haven't had the best team. But I've made it a lot of times. That's more than some people can say."

It was absolutely true except it was no consolation to one of the top competitors of all time. He was so upset by failing to win the title once more, he couldn't see himself walking down the same dead-end street again.

Baylor, on the other hand, was older and had a different reaction to his latest frustration. "I haven't given up completely. There's always hope," said the Hall-of-Famer, who retired because of his knees the season that the Lakers won without him. "Someone's got to lose. It's unfortunate that it's always me. Last year [1968-69] I thought we had the team to go all the way. This year I wasn't sure until Wilt came back."

All the Lakers agreed that our fast start had taken them out in the final game. "We let them get the momentum," said Baylor. "It was silly to let them dictate things," said Wilt. "It's difficult to play when you are so far behind," said West.

I think Joe Mullaney described it best. "The Knicks have a team that fits together nicely," he said. "We have different types of players and, if you are building from the bottom up, you wouldn't have them together. I think their team lends itself to a better team situation."

Baylor agreed. "The Knicks play so well as a unit," he pointed out. "They keep the ball moving and hit the open man. Everyone gives up the ball."

Elgin had to give up without winning a championship as a player. He's now chasing again, as general manager of the Los Angeles Clippers. I would guess everyone's rooting for him to get a ring someday. That's the Holy Grail in the NBA.

Willis has his own perspective as to what happened to the Lakers the night of the seventh game. Why didn't the Lakers and Wilt destroy him? He was a one-legged player and they allowed him to have an impact.

He insists it was a matter of circumstances and not really the Laker game plan. "I've played in games during my career, from the beginning to the end of a game, where the team was hyper and out of control," he explained. "That's the way the Lakers were that night. Even with a good game plan."

Is it safe to say that to this day he wonders why the Lakers didn't take advantage of him? "I think they really got caught up in the moment," he said. "I think they got caught up in the emotions of Madison Square Garden. Take the same game, put it in LA, we lose the game. The emotions of being at Madison Square Garden, our home court, the fans and us playing at the level we did. And them on the road as the visiting team. I think those were the factors."

That's Willis. Always honest, candid and fair. Never anything slanted just to make himself or his team look better. That's why I always roomed the rookies with him. He was a father figure with the leadership qualities that contributed so much to the success of the Knicks.

He still thinks the fifth game of our final series with the Lakers was the big one. "The flow of our team in the seventh game was going to be the same as long as I was out there only to set picks and pass the ball," he said. "The continuity of our offense would be better even if I was just moving the ball. I had to also block Wilt out."

I wish all players would study the way Willis blocked out. The way he did it and explains it is so simple. "Wilt was so tall, wherever the rebound was, he'd just reach right over me," he recalled. "Wherever I was standing, if I had him eight feet from the ball, that's where he'd be when they shot it. I'd just step into him as soon as the shot was taken."

That's an example of why the Knicks won the championship that night. Yes, we had emotion going for us but you still must know how to play basketball. We were simply a better team that night and that season than anyone.

We deserved all the benefits and satisfaction from the celebration in our dressing room—also all the recognition the team has maintained through the years.

None of us wanted to leave that night. We were happy but emotionally exhausted. Yes, even the coach, the trainer and those writers who had waited since 1946–47 for this to happen.

"The greatest pleasure was to play on this team," said Bradley, who feels the same way today. "I don't have to give the party now," said Frazier. "We're the world champions," said DeBusschere.

Then there was Hosket, who had contributed in his own little way. And May and Warren, who sat on the bench and still worked as hard as anyone to make this a championship team while Cazzie, Stallworth, Riordan and Bowman got the playing time.

Hosket expressed it for all the Minutemen. "The only place to be is on a winner," said the part-time Knick, who had been on championship teams in high school, college and the Olympics. "I'm glad I was here. But I don't know where I'll be on Monday. That's when the expansion draft takes place."

Two days later we lost Hosket and May to Buffalo and Warren to Cleveland. They are still in the 1969–70 team picture and, along with the memories, as brief as they were, they can't take that away from them.

Hosket remembers leaving the Knicks and then receiving a package from us. "It was from Danny Whelan," he said. "There was a playoff check in it for nine thousand dollars and a note that asked me to send my warmup outfit back. I never did."

Management threw a private victory party at the posh Four Seasons the night after the game. It gave me and the players 24 hours to recover. All the players had to say a few words. So did I. No one was bright or clever. We were too washed out.

Mayor Lindsay also lived up to his word. He had the Knicks over to Gracie Mansion for a day. I guess if it were today, there'd be a ticker-tape parade through the city. Times do change.

The party was held on the lawn of the mayor's mansion and I can still see it now. There was a microphone at the head of the steps to the house and Mayor Lindsay stepped to it to address the Knicks and the invited guests. He said, and I am paraphrasing because it was so long ago: "I want to wish good luck to the three Knicks who have just been drafted into military service."

Some aide had advised him that three of our players had been drafted—May, Hosket and Warren—and he misunderstood. The remark was well-intentioned, anyway.

Besides, the mayor had more important New York business on his mind than the Knicks at that moment. We were a footnote on his agenda, though an important part of New York and NBA history, as it has since developed.

Some of our players had celebrated their own way the night we won the championship. Willis, for example, was hurting all over, so he went right to his apartment to relax and be alone.

"There was a knock at my door. It was one of my neighbors," he recalled. "I had to get up and attend a party. I was pretty well smashed when I got back."

Willis Reed felt no pain, finally. Neither did the Knicks, world champions of 1969–70.

LOS ANGELES

	min	fg	fga	ft	fta	reb	ast	pf	pts
Baylor	36	9	17	1	2	5	1	2	19
Chamberlain	48	10	16	1	11	24	4	1	21
Egan	11	0	2	0	0	0	2	2	0
Erickson	36	5	10	4	6	6	6	3	14
Garrett	34	3	10	2	2	1	1	4	8
Hairston	15	2	5	2	2	2	0	1	6
Tresvant	12	0	4	3	3	2	0	2	3
West	48	9	19	10	12	6	5	4	28
TOTALS	240	38	83	23	38	49	17	19	99

NEW YORK

	min	fg	fga	ft	fta	reb	ast	pf	pts
Barnett	42	9	20	3	3	0	2	4	21
Bowman	21	3	5	0	1	5	0	5	6
Bradley	42	8	18	1	1	4	5	3	17
DeBusschere	37	8	15	2	2	17	1	1	18
Frazier	44	12	17	12	12	7	19	3	36
Reed	27	2	5	0	0	3	1	4	4
Riordan	10	2	3	1	2	2	1	2	5
Russell	6	1	4	0	0	3	0	0	2
Stallworth	11	1	5	2	2	2	1	3	4
TOTALS	240	46	92	21	23	43	30	25	113

```
Los Angeles   24   18   27   30   —    99
New York      38   31   25   19   —   113
```

23

We have taken care of old business up to this point. There is only one order of new business that seems to remain. That's convincing people the 1969–70 championship Knicks could play and succeed in today's game.

I know it's 23 years later. I also know that most fans think the game is a lot quicker and the players are taller and more agile these days. Yet it is a viable question in many minds.

It is a question that the players and I are still being asked by many people. We have decided to play a fantasy game for whatever it means. It wouldn't resolve anything but one game for the championship of then and now might be a little fun.

It would be between the 1969–70 New York Knicks and the 1991–92 Chicago Bulls. One game would take it all and, I hope, offer some insight as to how yesterday's players would perform in today's game.

Remember it's only a fantasy, which is explained this way in the dictionary: ''imagination esp. when unrestrained, the formation of grotesque mental images, a daydream, etc.'' I guess insanity might also fit those meanings.

I set one ground rule. Phil Jackson would coach the Bulls. He's one of them because his bad back kept him off the 1969–70 team all season. I wonder where his loyalty would rest?

I'll tell you our matchups. Bradley would play Scottie Pippen, DeBusschere would be on Horace Grant, Barnett probably would be playing Michael Jordan, Clyde would take Jim Paxson and Willis, of course, would play Bill Cartwright.

Frazier saw it a little differently. He agreed with every matchup except he assumed he would be playing Jordan until he was informed otherwise.

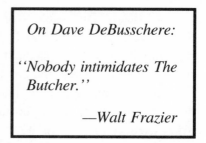

On Dave DeBusschere:

"Nobody intimidates The Butcher."

—Walt Frazier

"Then I'd be helping out on him," was Clyde's quick adjustment. "The scenario would be the one when we played West or we played Robertson or Earl the Pearl. Barnett would hound him and then I would come over and trap him."

We would also have Cazzie, Stallworth, Riordan and Bowman coming off the bench. They would have B. J. Armstrong, Will Perdue, Scott Williams and Stacey King.

"I wouldn't worry about Grant other than I wouldn't let him get on the break and I'd keep him off the boards," said DeBusschere. "The guy we'd have to worry about is Pippen."

Other than Jordan, of course. DeBusschere was discussing Pippen first because he's a forward and that was in Dave's domain. "He would be Bradley's problem because Pippen's quicker and Bill's a little quicker than I am. He'd be able to stay with Pippen better than I could," said DeBusschere.

There's another dimension to that matchup. DeBusschere was an exceptional rebounder against anyone and I'd want him on Grant, who is a very active 6'10" and a dangerous rebounder. I believe Dave still would keep him off the boards a lot better than the guys Grant faces today.

"Bill would be able to stay with Pippen a lot better than I could," continued DeBusschere. "But the main thing he'd have to do is not let Pippen get out on the break. I think they're very effective when they run. When they don't it's Jordan's ballgame. He'll work a two-on-two and try to push it off to Pippen or whoever's there."

The problem with Pippen is that he's not a one-dimensional player. He's an excellent player. Good passer, good outside shot and a good three-point shooter, too. A real test for Bradley, who assessed the assignment this way when asked what he'd do: ''I would just say help.''

Realistically, Bill would love the challenge. He preferred to play Rick Barry, John Havlicek, Bob Love, Jack Marin and anyone I gave him because that was the thrill of the game to him. The greater the physical mismatch, the greater the challenge and motivation.

It must be said right here that the game has changed since 1970. There are the three-point shot and other rule changes besides the acknowledged increase in the size and speed of the players. We tried to deal with all those things within the context of our game.

> ''I think on offense, the '70 Knicks would find it pretty easy to score today.''
>
> —Walt Frazier

Bradley did just that when he mentioned Pippen. ''He's fast in open court and he's also six-eight,'' said Bill, who had a slow 6′5″ body but a brain as quick as anyone's. ''Take the Chicago player that I had to play—six-eight Love. Compare Love to Pippen and you'll see how the game has changed.''

Love didn't handle the ball well. He didn't have range farther out than about 15 feet. He would stand in the corner and pop. On the other hand, Pippen could be a big guard if Jackson needed him that way.

Pippen would be very tough for Bradley. We'd handle it by adjusting as we always did. ''We'd deny him the ball and not let him run on the break,'' said DeBusschere. ''Bill's gonna get help from Willis and myself. I don't have the problem with Grant that I had with a shooter like Chet Walker. I don't have to worry about Grant other than to keep him off the boards.''

Grant is an excellent rebounder but we wouldn't be too concerned about his shooting. He can't put the ball on the floor like a Pippen and drive past you. There are other shooters. Grant likes to crash the boards and I'm sure DeBusschere would handle that.

The Bulls would have to contend with our overall defense, which would minimize their one-on-one skills. For example, as Bradley said: "They'd have a difficult time. I'd have to overplay Pippen and we'd leave ourselves a little bit vulnerable on the back door with the expectation that Willis or DeBusschere would be there. I'd also try to force him a little out of his range."

Bradley was not underrating Pippen. "I think he's potentially an incredible player," he said. "He's stronger than Dr. J. and a little more agile. A better shooter. He'd be a big, big problem."

Big but not impossible because of our team defense. That was our strength. The way I see the game being played today, they'd still have trouble doing what they want to do against our defense. Other than the individual efforts of Bill Russell on the Celtics, I still think we played the smartest team defense ever.

That's what must be considered and understood as we continue this fantasy game. We believe our team defense could stop or handle anybody, including Michael Jordan, Scottie Pippen and the championship Bulls.

Jordan may be the most gifted player we've ever seen—on the ground and in the air. He is capable of destroying all the well-laid defensive game plans but we'd have to play him.

I'd open with Barnett on him because Dick would challenge him and bump him and play him as smart as anyone. We'd try to make him give up the ball. That's all you can really do. He's too dangerous with it.

Barnett might not be playing him all the time. I might be switching him and Clyde just to give Jordan a different look—confuse him, if that's possible.

"I'd like to see the ball in Grant's hands a lot," said DeBusschere. "That's where I'd be sliding back a lot. Make him take the ball."

That's where the rules are a little different today. You have to be more careful of a zone. There's a line you can't cross or they'll call an illegal defense. That would be a minor adjustment our players could handle.

Basically, we'd try to make the Bulls play our game. "We'd force them into a halfcourt game," said Frazier. "We'd keep them from running. That would enhance our chances. We'd slow down the tempo. Which is what we'd have to do with any team today. We'd run when we had the opportunity but we'd look to slow it down.''

I think we'd be capable of doing that. We were a smart defensive team that seldom was vulnerable to fast breaks. Our rotations always had guys in position to get back.

> *''I've always believed that the 1970 Knicks, even though they'd be much smaller than most of the teams today, could play with any of them because we played defense.''*
>
> *—Walt Frazier*

It would then develop into their half-court game against our team defense, which would be to our advantage. At the other end, our half-court offense would be superior because we had so many good shooters. The Bulls couldn't match us that way. They hit the open man very well but can't match our overall firepower from outside.

''They'd have height on us,'' said Frazier. ''Mainly the Pippen-Bradley matchup. Their edge would be athletic skills and running and they'd try to isolate Bradley. Pippen handles the ball eighty percent of the time and he'd also be looking to post Bill. That's why we'd have to get back all the time to keep Pippen from driving.''

Frazier hasn't forgotten Jordan and how he destroys a team all by himself. Clyde sees him more than all of us these days and knows what makes him tick. He sits and sometimes thinks how he might play him.

''First you give him the perimeter shot and hope he's not making it,'' he said. ''If he makes it, you're in trouble because you have to come up on him and that opens it up. We'd have to double-team Jordan. I would have to cheat on Paxson, who can be dangerous but is the weak link.''

It's percentage basketball. Paxson can hit the outside shot but we'd rather see him with the ball than Jordan or Pippen. So our defense would check him and take its chances until he did something to make us change. He might hurt us but he wouldn't beat us like Jordan and Pippen.

"They'd be more difficult when they're running and starting all their shenanigans and moving the ball around," said Frazier. "By making them come down slower, our defense is positioned better. We have a much better chance of denying them."

We believe we could do that because we did it against the best. Jordan and Pippen may be exceptional but we also had some exceptional players in our time. Many of them are in the Hall of Fame. None of today's players is—yet.

That doesn't make yesterday's players better. I only mention it to create the proper perspective. In my opinion, it's how you play the game that counts and the 1969–70 Knicks knew how to play basketball. There may have been teams that had better players but no players had a better team.

We came close to winning four championships in a row. Injuries prevented it. But that's a story for another time.

24

By the way, whose rules will we be playing? "Can we have the three-point play? We'd like it," said Bradley, who would benefit from it today. So would DeBusschere, Barnett, Cazzie, Stallworth and Riordan.

If we give them their rules, then they've got to give us the home court. It's only fair. Why couldn't I talk to Jackson about that? I wouldn't talk to him. I'd order him.

It was agreed then that the game would be played under today's rules but in the Garden. "Is Jackson the coach for them or the point man on the press for us?" asked Bradley, recalling how Phil's windmill action helped us win the 1972–73 title.

I reminded Bill that I had designated Jackson as the coach. The funny thing about Phil that people don't realize is that he could play defense at five positions. At center, both forwards and he could play both guards.

"I'd like to see Phil dribbling that ball," said DeBusschere, remembering what an adventure that was. I reminded Dave that I was talking about Jackson's defense and nothing else. "Oh, defense. Okay," was his response.

What about us scoring on them? "Well, Bill would keep Pippen very active," said DeBusschere. "We'd open them up and Willis would have an absolute field day. They'd have to guard us on the outside because we could hit the shots so well."

We'd be setting screens and picking all over the place. We'd also be moving the ball so that the Bulls couldn't dig in on defense. We would test their halfcourt ability to handle our offense, which was distributed among five of the smartest players I've ever seen in one group.

"Both starting forwards plus Barnett are all three-pointers," was Bradley's reminder of how devastating our long-range shooting would be against whatever defense the Bulls played.

What I've seen is that Jackson has put in the Knicks' defense. He uses the same traps and double-teams as we did, with one difference. Willis anchored our defense. Jordan seems to be Phil's key man. He's the one you worry about most when you have the ball.

Jackson's done an outstanding job in that respect. The Bulls have an excellent defense. People shouldn't forget how much Phil has improved that since he took over the job. He's got them all finely tuned to it. That's coaching.

"What happened last year," said Bradley, referring to the 1991–92 championship season, "was that they played team ball and Jordan also realized he didn't need to hold the ball more than a few seconds to make his plays. You don't hold it and let everybody watch you."

Bradley sounded as though he was talking about the second coming of our team. Frazier saw the similarities but wasn't as flattering when it came to comparing the two teams.

He couldn't see the Bulls overcoming the advantage Reed would have over Cartwright, whom I drafted for the Knicks in 1979 and respect very much. "No contest. Willis would eat him up inside and outside," said Clyde. "It would be similar to what Willis did to Jabbar."

Frazier meant Willis would draw Cartwright outside as he did on offense against Kareem. If Cartwright gave him room, Willis would hit the jumper. If Bill moved out on him, Willis would drive—all of which would put that much more pressure on the Bulls' defense.

"They would catch hell trying to deny Willis alone," Clyde's thesis continued. What about Jordan? How about the damage he does on defense?

Clyde had an answer. "We'd make Jordan pay," he said. "See,

Jordan creates havoc because he never plays his man. He's all over the place like I used to be early in my career.''

I remember. I never tried to put the handcuffs on Clyde because I recognized he was a natural on defense. He had the instinct for it that no coach could teach. He also had the quick hands and mind, so I let him do the things that made him a constant pick on the NBA's all-defensive team.

He still had to learn to play within himself—not out of control. He had to understand that, if he was too wild and risky, he'd be putting too much pressure on the team defense. That came with experience and knowledge of what Reed, DeBusschere, Bradley, Barnett and the others were capable of doing.

Frazier knows that Jordan is such a unique athlete, he constantly drops off his man because he can recover so quickly. ''When Jordan floats, how is he gonna float off of me or Barnett?'' said Clyde. ''We'd make him pay. He'd have to play us straight.''

We'd run Jordan and all the Bulls into picks. We wouldn't let them disrupt our offense and we'd have Willis, DeBusschere and Bradley setting picks and screens in our five-man motion game.

In that respect, the Bulls would have to worry more about us. Our defense would be in a better position to concentrate on Jordan and Pippen. As great as they are, they would have to worry about all of our players.

Frazier kept coming back to Willis and what he'd do to the Bulls at both ends of the court. ''I thought I was a good defensive player until I watched the films of the Baltimore series one year, how Earl kept eluding me,'' he said, looking back at the 1968–69 playoffs. ''Willis kept bailing me out. I found out that part of my defensive prowess I owed to Willis.''

We wanted teams to penetrate because we knew Willis was back there. If he had to jump out at someone, DeBusschere or Bradley would roll over and cover for him. As good a job as Jackson has done on the Bulls, I just don't believe their team defense is as good as ours, mainly because of Willis.

''Also DeBusschere. He was a solid defensive player,'' said Clyde. ''We were intelligent. That's part of the intangibles that would make us very effective against the Bulls. Today's teams don't play with the savvy that we played. They never make Jordan pay for the way he plays defense. We'd go into the game knowing what he wants to do.''

Frazier mentioned a specific. ''We'd throw the ball into Willis and see what Jordan does,'' he explained. ''We'd rotate the ball around the perimeter, which is what the Bullets did to me. They'd finally sucker me in and end up getting the ball to Earl for a fifteen-foot shot.''

That's when I reminded Clyde he had to play it straight and not chase the ball. We would try to exploit Jordan's defense the same way, although I don't think that would be as easy as it seems from this distance.

Frazier also realizes he was talking theory but it was interesting theory the way he put it. ''Now if Jordan is taken out of his game defensively, he has to guard his man exclusively,'' he continued. ''He can't be giving help inside. That's why he's so good. He creates the havoc and that's how they get their transition game.''

That's how we also did it. Frazier or Barnett would steal the ball and off we'd go on our fast break. Jordan is a master at it but there's always a risk playing the ball as Jordan does.

''He's not the only one. Pippen's another guy we'd burn back-door,'' said Clyde. ''He's always sticking his nose in. He follows the ball. Bradley and I can always get the back door on him. We had the ESP. When you made a mistake, we burned you. It's not like next time. When we were reversing the ball, if you're making a mistake, you're gonna pay for it right there.''

Frazier credits his old roomie for making the Bulls a team but not good enough to beat us. ''They were not a team, they were Jordan,'' was Clyde's reaction to Jackson's contributions. ''He talked Jordan into sacrificing his game. Their savvy has all improved.''

I am not overlooking the Bulls' ability to hit from outside. When that happens, you have to move out and that opens the middle. Jordan, Pippen, Paxson and B. J. Armstrong are not exactly amateurs from long range.

They also have learned very well how to get into position for a pass from Jordan when he's doubled. "I'd like to be Paxson on that team," said Bradley, who has watched Jordan fatten him up. "He just waits and waits."

Frazier wouldn't leave it there. He had other ideas—for example, that Jackson would be advising the Bulls on what he knew about our habits or tendencies.

"He's gonna tell them 'Watch Clyde. He's just like Jordan. He'll be roaming around so watch the ball,'" said Frazier. "He's gonna say: 'We gotta run these guys. We have the team speed. We have one big advantage and that's Pippen against Bradley. We have to exploit that matchup somehow.'"

Frazier obviously has made a study of Jordan's game. Who hasn't? He sees technical flaws that can be exploited, but who is capable of doing it? Clyde retired long ago.

Yet he doesn't mind sharing his Jordan scouting report with today's players or victims. "You can burn Jordan at times because he's going to the offensive glass," he pointed out. "Our guys would be boxing them all out and Barnett would be releasing as soon as Jordan went to the board."

It sounds so easy and reasonable the way Clyde describes it. That's the good thing about playing a game on paper. The bad thing is there's no way of proving it.

It would take a lot of hard work, no doubt about it. We just couldn't do what we wanted to do that easily. We'd want to make Jordan give the ball up and overplay Pippen. They have so much talent and energy, I would have to keep an eye on our guys and make sure they didn't get too tired.

Of course, I think our bench would be better than theirs. I wouldn't hesitate using Stallworth, Cazzie and Riordan against them. The only thing that might suffer would be rebounding. We would need DeBusschere and Reed out there as much as possible.

DeBusschere explained why. "You can run on the Bulls because they go in and try and penetrate," he said. "They all try and crash. You get the rebound and get out. Particularly Willis can run on Cartwright."

The Bulls would be vulnerable because they have Jordan, Pippen and Grant crashing the boards all the time—also Perdue when he's in there. The important thing is to catch them following up their shots by nailing the rebound and flinging it out fast.

We also might be able to take advantage of their double-teaming the ball. Jackson is using the Knicks' defense but I think we were more adept at it. We were more decisive in our moves. They're a little slower reacting because they have had less experience.

"When there's a double-team, the guy that left his man to double-team does so aggressively because he knows that a third guy is going to cover his man," explained Bradley. "If you don't believe that, you're never going to do it. The guy leaves to cover because he knows someone else is going to cover his man down low."

If the Bulls don't get rid of the ball quickly against the man doubling they're dead. Once they see us coming on a double-team, if they don't move the ball right away, they're in trouble.

Our guys perfected that defense and I believe the Bulls still are learning to do it instinctively. It's a matter of thinking and timing. Jordan and Pippen are exceptional at that, which is why their team defense is the best in the NBA right now.

Jordan looks like the perfect player to me. Not to Frazier, though. Clyde seems to have picked up a few things. "He's got a weakness. He's not a good dribbler," said Clyde. "He dribbles the ball too high. He doesn't have the right tempo. He's not a natural. That's his weakness."

I don't agree. It doesn't matter. Jordan has such big hands, he handles the basketball like it's a baseball. Besides, they don't call palming the ball these days. He can cup it and change direction so sharply, there's no way anyone can play him one-on-one.

We'd have to steer him into a trap or double on him outside and hope he'd pass the ball. "I know when Michael is trying to score or just trying to create and pass off," said Clyde. "He has a bad habit when he passes. He leaps in the air. So what our team would do when he jumps in the air, there's no need in going to him now. You go to the men—the passing lanes. That's how you get him to throw the ball away."

Clyde insists that the guys playing Jordan make the fundamental mistake of going at him once he's in the air instead of dropping off—on the outside, naturally, not close to the basket.

"The guys go right to him instead of where he has to throw the ball once he's committed himself," said Clyde. "When he's in the air like that, he's not looking to shoot. He'd looking to kick it out."

Clyde supported his analysis by asking what happens at the other end when you have the ball. "If you do that, commit yourself, he's going to steal the ball everytime," he explained. "He's waiting for you to go up in the air and he's going where the pass is supposed to go. He'd never be able to do that on me because I'd be doing the same thing that he does on defense."

I told you we had a very smart team. Clyde figured out that once Jordan is in the air, he's no longer a threat. It made me wonder why they call Michael "Air Jordan."

Clyde's point seems to be that it's better to let Jordan hang than leave a man he can hit with a pass. He's right. That's why coaches go crazy when they see anyone with the ball commit himself by going into the air. It took a long time to get that message across.

It's Clyde's contention that not many players these days are thinking men's players. He concedes they are quicker, more agile and can jump higher. They have exceptional physical skills.

"These guys are terrific athletes impersonating basketball players," he said. "Take a guy like Dennis Rodman. He's not a basketball player. He's a specialist. And that's what the game is today. It's a specialist's game. People are obsessed with speed and slam-dunking."

He excludes the Chicago Bulls because they play a team game much the way we did. Which is why we have just played the fantasy game.

Who would win? I gather you know the answer to that by now. "We'd win easy," said Clyde. "We'd win by seven," said Bradley before altering it with: "I'd say we'd win on a last-second shot by DeBusschere."

DeBusschere, of course, believes that the Knicks would win

mainly because of Willis. I also think we'd win against a tough team with a tough coach.

Someday, maybe another quarter of a century from now, Jordan and Pippen may sit down and play their own fantasy game against the 1970 world champion Knicks. They can win that game.

But not today.

Today I won't let anything spoil my Unforgettable Year.

Index